Stonewall Jackson

Southern Classics Series

Southern Classics Series

M. E. Bradford, Founding Series Editor

Donald Davidson	The Tennessee, Volume I
Donald Davidson	The Tennessee, Volume II
Caroline Gordon	Green Centuries
Caroline Gordon	None Shall Look Back
Caroline Gordon	Penhally
Caroline Gordon	The Women On the Porch
Johnson Jones Hooper	Adventures of Captain Simon Suggs
Madison Jones	The Innocent
Augustus Baldwin Longstreet	Georgia Scenes
Andrew Nelson Lytle	Bedford Forrest and His Critter Company
Andrew Nelson Lytle	A Wake for the Living
John S. Mosby	The Memoirs of Colonel John S. Mosby
Thomas Nelson Page	In Ole Virginia
William Pratt, Editor	The Fugitive Poets
Elizabeth Madox Roberts	The Great Meadow
Allen Tate	Jefferson Davis
Allen Tate	Stonewall Jackson
Richard Taylor	Destruction and Reconstruction
Robert Penn Warren	John Brown: The Making of a Martyr
Robert Penn Warren	Night Rider
Owen Wister	Lady Baltimore
Stark Young	So Red the Rose

Stonewall Jackson

The Good Soldier

ALLEN TATE

with a preface by Thomas Landess

J. S. Sanders & Company

NASHVILLE

To my Mother and Father

Library of Congress Catalog Card Number:
91-62455

ISBN: 1-879941-02-3

Published in the United States by
J. S. Sanders & Company
P. O. Box 50331
Nashville, Tennessee 37205

J. S. Sanders 1991 Edition
Second printing February 1993
Third printing March 1995
Fourth printing May 1997

Manufactured in the United States of America

Contents

Preface

Allen Tate wrote *Stonewall Jackson: The Good Soldier* in 1927 when he was living in New York with his wife, Caroline Gordon, and their small daughter. An anti-romantic in literary theory and sensibilities, he was attempting to be that most romantic of all things—a man of letters who survives on what he writes. It was just as difficult a role to fulfill then as it is today, and Tate wrote quickly whatever brought in quick cash: book reviews and essays, and—only when he could allow himself the luxury—an occasional poem. (It must also be said that during this period, the Tates lived rent-free in their Greenwich Village apartment in exchange for which the poet-essayist performed certain janitorial duties, including the firing of the furnace.)

During the 1920s, biographies sold well—better, on average, than novels—so Tate agreed to write a biography of Stonewall Jackson for Minton, Balch and Co. It is difficult to believe that the publishers knew what they were doing when they allowed him to choose his subject. In Northern literary circles, Tate was usually polite and circumspect about regional controversy. Writing for the *New Republic* and friendly with intellectuals of the Left, he could even be deprecating about the South in casual conversation—at least about obvious Southern peccadillos and affectations. But a careful listener might have caught the irony in his voice and wondered about the use of such phrases as "the War between the States." His editors did not listen carefully and ended up publishing a book that is still something of a literary scandal.

For by 1927, Tate—along with John Crowe Ransom, Donald Davidson, and Andrew Lytle—had begun to resent Northern attacks on the intelligence and integrity of their region and were in the process of planning a counterattack which would be published three years later as *I'll Take My Stand*. In a sense, Tate's biography of Stonewall Jackson (published in 1928) was the first assault in a war to regain Southern self-respect, the literary equivalent of the firing on Fort Sumter. It was bold, aggressive, and merciless—not unlike Stonewall Jackson himself, who ordered his men to fire at the bravest Yankee officers and to shoot Confederate stragglers.

In many ways Jackson epitomized what Tate and the Agrarians believed was virtuous and enduring about the South. In the first place, he was from a family of small farmers rather than a member of the privileged planter class. Tate, Ransom, Davidson, Lytle, and the other Agrarians (with the exception of Stark Young) never believed in the existence of a Southern "aristocracy"; and Tate says of the region in his own time that it was inhabited by "a whole people ... sorely afflicted with the delusion of ancient grandeur." Jackson, not Pierre Gustave Toutant Beauregard or even Robert E. Lee, was the Good Soldier, a mountain man who was well-mannered but unpretentious, loyal to his own kind but never proud. Tate and the others understood Jackson quite well. They had come from such people themselves.

Second, Stonewall Jackson never suffered a significant defeat. Like Nathan Bedford Forrest, whose biography Lytle would later write, Jackson was a consistent winner, largely because he knew how to move troops quickly, instinctively understood when and where to attack, and was calm and rational under fire. Of Jackson, Southerners could easily say, "Had he not been killed, we would have won the War." For Tate, in 1927, the War was still winnable.

Third, Jackson was a deeply religious man. A skeptic himself at this stage of his life, Tate nonetheless recognized the importance to society of a religious vision, a supernatural mythos to give order and meaning to life. He well understood the degree to which the South was informed by such a vision, and he also was convinced that the North was committed to a radical materialism that threatened the survival of the Old Republic. Jackson was a man whose entire life, including his military career, was guided by religious conviction. He was utterly oblivious to danger because, like any good Calvinist, he believed he was as safe on the battlefield as in his own parlor, until his time came. Tate admired that certitude and probably envied it. After a long struggle with doubt, he would eventually become a Roman Catholic. In the meantime, he understood that it was the hardshell beliefs of people like Jackson that gave the South its essentially sacramental understanding of nature, history, and society.

These qualities combined to make Jackson the perfect Southern paradigm, the ideal figure for the region to commit to memory. Radcliffe Squires, in his otherwise excellent literary biography, reproves Tate for not capturing the tragedy of the War. But Squires fails to understand that in Tate's narrative, Jackson is not intended to be tragic but rather epic, a hero of the past—writ large to teach latter-day Southerners who they were and how they should behave. Tate didn't want to be Seneca. He wanted to be Vergil. Squires, who understood everything else about Tate, failed to understand his Southern sensibilities, which were very finely honed in 1927, in part because of the ridicule of the South growing out of the Scopes Trial, in part because Tate had been living in New York City for several years and was tired of being patronized. (During those years he was known by his Northern acquaintances as a man who used his courtly manners as an aggressive weapon.)

Squires might have examined more carefully the proportions of Tate's chronicle, which was not the story of a man's life so much as the account of his deeds in battle. Tate tells us as little about Jackson's private life as he can. There is virtually nothing about his loss of one wife and the all-too-hasty courtship of another; his bumbling, pedestrian career as a teacher; his personal idiosyncrasies; his chronic indigestion. These are the ingredients of a man. Tate gives us the portrait of a hero, because he believed that was what the South required at a moment when it was beginning to forget its past.

As for his chronicling of battles, Tate also follows epic rules rather than the rules of conventional biography or modern fiction. We see battles as grand strategies rather than vignettes of personal experience, rendered through interior monologue. It is the action that is important rather than the thought and sensibilities of the participants. The book is closer to the *Iliad* than it is to *The Red Badge of Courage*.

But Tate departs from the pure epic mode in one significant respect: he devotes several long passages to the political background of the War, its causes, the beliefs and ideals that fueled it. Such passages were necessary by the late 1920s, because, even with a handful of Confederate veterans still alive, the world in which the War was fought was rapidly disappearing, inevitably destroyed by the triumph of raw industrial might and a new American pragmatism. Tate felt he had to instruct a late generation of Southerners concerning the society of their grandparents, if only to counteract the simplistic version of 19th century history they were reading in their high school textbooks.

His own account of the circumstances surrounding Secession constituted the chief scandal of the volume. He stood the conventional explanation on its head. According to this version:

- The Yankee industrial society had its own form of slavery: "This [the Northern] atmosphere was beginning to be charged with commerce and industry. Commerce and industry required a different kind of slave. He would be a better slave; he would have the illusion of freedom."

- The North rather than the South bred the real rebels against the United States and their Constitution: "The Northern revolutionists chose to interpret the Constitution through some mystical sense that had no exact correspondence with the letter of that document. 'The spirit' (because it is irresponsible) 'killeth; the letter giveth life.' They interpreted it by abstract right. The South interpreted it historically, literally."

- The North declared war on the Union: "On the 15th Lincoln called for 75,000 volunteers to put down the 'rebellion.' No one need be deceived by the word. A revolution is not started by the party that fires the first shot; a revolution is a question of ideas.

  "It was now a living fact that the North was trying to destroy the social and political structure of the United States by force of arms."

To Northerners of the late 1920s, these ideas seemed either blasphemous or hopelessly eccentric. Today they probably appear so to most (if not all) Southerners. Yet they were the accepted version of the War to many Southerners of Tate's generation—and probably to virtually all who lived in the South before the turn of the century. Only after several generations of textbooks published in Boston and New York did the War take on the simplistic look it has today—a crusade to free the slaves from cruel and rapacious masters.

Aware of the Yankee myth and its growing acceptance, even among Southerners, Tate decided to disturb the pure narrative texture of his epic to remind his readers that the South had its own version of the "irrepressible conflict" and that the heroism of a man like Stonewall Jackson could only be understood in terms of a commitment to that political view. Jackson, after all, believed that slavery was immoral, owned no slaves, and had little in common with the rich planters who did. If you wanted to understand why he was willing to fight and die for the Confederacy, you had to see the war in terms other than those defined by the victor.

Had Tate written this epic account even thirty years later, he might have presented his arguments in more detail—and with corroborating evidence from the letters and memoirs of 19th century Southerners. Certainly he would have adopted a more moderate tone. For the narrative is full of insolent asides calculated to quicken the pulse of sympathetic readers and drive up the blood pressure of nearly everybody else. It is unabashedly partisan, and for some, unbearably so.

Yet this tonal quality, like the political commentary, was calculated to accomplish a specific purpose with a chosen audience. It was apodictic rhetoric, the kind of language used in preaching to the choir. We still hear it employed by keynote speakers at political conventions. Its intent is not to convince or to instruct but to excite and to unite in common cause. If you are a Democrat at a Republican convention, you find such language tiresome at best, bloodboiling at worst; but when you go to your own convention, the same kind of rhetoric magically acquires meaning and immediacy and power.

Tate was writing *Stonewall Jackson: The Good Soldier* for a mystical convention of Southerners in his generation—an audience of far-flung delegates that had the capacity to make common cause against an enemy they still confronted, still saw as hostile. Southern politicians of that day routinely referred to carpetbaggers, scalawags, the Republican Party in terms of contempt; and they still gathered at cemeteries on Confederate Memorial Day, though in diminishing numbers. As late as 1948, candidates for office in the eleven states of the Confederacy could wrap themselves in the Stars and Bars and win a lot of votes. Tate understood the public uses of such rhetoric and chose it for his epic narrative because during that era it was the language instinctively adopted in talking about that War, those heroes. If it seems strident and reckless today, it is because we have lost the context in which it was first cast. In 65 years, the current accounts of the civil rights struggles will probably seem just as quaintly partisan.

In the final analysis, however, *Stonewall Jackson: The Good Soldier* is still a first-rate piece of work by a first-rate literary artist. The same year Tate also published *Mr. Pope and Other Poems*, a volume that contained some of his standard anthology pieces, like the title poem and "Ode to the Confederate Dead." A year earlier he had published "Poetry and the Absolute," his first important critical essay. He was in the process of establishing a formidable literary reputation. And while the attitudes he struck in this volume were not calculated to ingratiate him with the New York crowd, the book did add breadth to his reputation as a man of letters. It showed that he could manage narrative prose and that he knew politics and history as well as literary theory.

It must be said, however, that for all its narrative virtues—its spare, serviceable prose; its lack of irrelevant lore; its attention to the dramatics of a good tale—*Stonewall Jackson: The Good Soldier* was a young man's book. It was recklessly conceived. It was half-heartedly researched. It was impudent to the point of being fool-hardy. In his choice and treatment of his subject matter, Tate was throwing down the gauntlet to the Yankee scholars who thought they had laid the Southern cause to rest.

However, in a literary world that was "liberal" but less "politically correct" than our own, he was able to survive and prosper because he was a modernist in his esthetics and because being aggressively Southern was considered quainter and less wicked than it is today. No one was ostracized for flying the battle flag, and the Lost Cause was treated with some respect on the stage and in films.

However, it is doubtful that Tate would have undertaken the same project twenty years later or that he would have treated it in the same cavalier way. The mature Tate would have been more prudent and more arch. He would have been less epic and more discursive. And his irony would have been shaved more finely—so finely, in fact, that those who read the book might not have recognized it at all. Twenty years later Tate was no longer regarded as a "Neo-confederate" but as a cosmopolite, a citizen of the Republic of Letters, that international community of artists that has no geographical or linguistic boundaries.

Soon Tate would be quarreling with Donald Davidson over the latter's "Lee in the Mountains," saying that the emotions expressed in that poem were extra-literary, that no one could or should make a poem that had as its purpose the fostering of regional piety. It was essentially an esthetic rather than an historical argument, but it provides us with some insight into Tate's literary persona as it developed in later years. As far as the Republic of Letters was concerned, he was no longer Stonewall Jackson; he was a Frenchman, observing American regional conflict from his studio with a critical detachment, a latter-day Marcus Aurelius (who in his *Meditations* thanked a mentor for teaching him not to care whether the blue team or the green was victorious).

At least, to the literary world this is what Tate seemed to be.

To those Southerners who knew him in later years, he was someone quite different. A cynical partisan might have said he was a sutler, one of the mercenary traders who came to the battlefield before and after a great conflict and sold goods to both sides. For Tate was the modern man of letters when he was in the North and still an unregenerate, if somewhat politic Confederate when he was among his old friends in the South.

But cynics notwithstanding, he was actually something better than a sutler. He was more like a spy, who lived among his enemies, adopting their ways and rhetoric while still retaining a loyalty to his own country. In this role Tate was able to define the essential complexity of his region and its history—and to be listened to by some of the most influential people of the time. And when he was at home with people who understood all these matters, he could speak more freely—and not always without risk.

One example should suffice. In the early 1970s, when he came to the University of Texas at Arlington to address a literary gathering, he was frail and aging. He had to ask the younger men who met him at the airport to walk more slowly, because he had difficulty catching his breath. (The disease that would eventually kill him was beginning to take charge.) As the group entered the Robert E. Lee Room where Tate was scheduled to speak, one of the local faculty members mentioned that the school had just banned the Confederate battle flag from the campus, despite the fact that the city had been named for the Lee-Custis house and the school athletic teams had always been known as "The Rebels."

"As a matter of fact," he said, "the battle flag hung in the blank space on that wall until only yesterday."

Tate's eyes flashed quickly, but his expression didn't change. He seemed to listen to the information with no more than perfunctory interest.

"Everyone is still boiling over the matter," said the faculty member. "The university's president sided with the small band of protesters. Caved in at the first sign of trouble."

At the ensuing luncheon Tate found himself seated next to that same president, a fussy little man who didn't quite know how to respond to the famous poet's distant and precise courtesy. Finally, after the meal, Tate was introduced and rose to speak.

"As some of you may understand, I feel very much at home here in the Robert E. Lee Room," he said. "It's nice to know that at least in this place, the South's heroes are still remembered."

The silence deepened and all eyes turned to the president, sitting beside Tate, beginning to shift in his chair.

"But there is something missing," Tate said. "There's a huge white space on the wall back there."

He looked down at the president with a cold eye and pointed.

"I would hope to see a large Confederate flag hanging right there."

The assembled students gasped, then burst into applause.

It was not just a jest or a random impulse that caused Allen Tate, near the end of his life, to stand up once more for the old Cause. He had been reared in an era when the memory of Lee and Jackson and a hundred other heroes was still alive in a society not yet defeated by progress and uniformity and Yankee practicality. His generation, as he himself wrote, was the last that could turn backwards toward the past and see the South as it once was—and at the same time look forward to see what modern ideologues were urging it to become. He had lived, he said, in a "moment of self-consciousness," and out of that moment had come the enduring vision of the South—preserved in poems, novels, criticism, and narrative history—the greatest literary outpouring in modern America. And it was that enduring South to which he paid tribute in his brief but deliberate breach of propriety. The man of letters and the Southerner were at peace with one another for a moment in a darkening twilight where he had a few friends close at hand.

It was that man—frail, fighting for breath, but with a hard glint in his eye—who, almost a half century earlier, had given this extraordinary gift to his people: this epic account of their great military hero.

Falls Church, Virginia   THOMAS LANDESS

Stonewall Jackson

Stonewall Jackson

STONEWALL JACKSON

I

JACKSON'S MILLS

ONE summer day Tom Jackson climbed up from the river bank into the road that ran by his uncle's mill. He was barefooted; he wore ill-fitting homespun pants held up by striped bed-ticking galluses. Over his shoulder, on a forked twig, hung a big pike he had caught in the mill-pond. As he came to the road, Colonel Talbott, a gentleman of the county, stopped him.

"That's a nice fish you got there, Tom. What'll you take for him?"

"The fish is sold, Colonel Talbott."

"But I'll give you a dollar for it."

"I can't take it, sir. The fish is sold to Mr. Kester."

"Now, Tom," the Colonel said, "I'll give you a dollar and a quarter. Surely he won't give you more'n that."

Tom said: "Colonel Talbott, I have an agreement with Mr. Kester to sell him fish of a certain length for fifty cents apiece. He has taken some too short. Now he's goin' to get this big one for fifty cents."

Tom must have made his speech quite solemnly, in his

eyes the humorless fixity that people knew later as the sign of an unswerving will.

In the late afternoons of the summer Tom, a book in his hand, lay by the mill-race gazing at the water as it poured down on the wheel and turned it around. Another book lay in the high grass close by.

The boy had been reading *Francis Marion* by Mason Weems, a man known to fame in his time as the Parson. This Parson had written books about patriots of the first American Revolution; Tom had heard of the others but had never seen them; so he read about the Swamp Fox again and again. He had borrowed the book from his friend Joe Lightburn. The book lying in the grass was the Bible. He read a little in the one, then a little in the other. They were about all he had to read. He liked to read about soldiers. Parson Weems somehow made them seem very luminous, very far away and heroic. Young Jackson's ancestors had lived and fought when the Parson's heroes lived and fought. His ancestors were noble men. How good it would be to be like them. . . .

It was a good place to read and think. You could hear only the water in the mill-race or the slow, steady trickle of the overflow of the dam. He lay in the shadow of the old grist mill. The mill stood at the nose of a peninsula made by the winding Monongahela River, in Lewis County, Virginia. About three miles north of the town of Weston the river turns dead east for a half-mile, then northwest. The land hemmed in by the water is black and fertile. On this land lived a hardy frontier gentlemen by the name of Cummins Jackson.

Mountains, high and thick-wooded, shut the valley in on all sides. It was a little world to itself, cut off from the old civilization of the seaboard. Tom Jackson was happy there. His Uncle Cummins was a kind man.

It was new land, taken up only a generation ago. Tom must have thought it old. The past seemed far away; he must not have heard it mentioned very often. Not far from Jackson's Mills his grandfather had fought the Indians. Not much was said about it; but it wasn't long ago. . . . . It was now only about 1835.

Up at the big house, which stood back a few hundred feet from the mill, Uncle Cummins was the head of the family. Tom's step-grandmother and some of his aunts lived there. Ten or twelve slaves lived on the place, in cabins. Most of them were domestics; only a few worked in the fields or drew timber from the forest. There were not many slaves, yet Cummins Jackson was a well-to-do man. His acres ran over ten thousand. He was a farmer, a miller, a lumberman, a breeder of horses, a rider to hounds. He was the sort of man that people in the old part of Virginia called a yeoman; they were still ruled by English ideas. He worked with his hands. Everybody on the place had to work.

In the late afternoon, when the day's work was over, Tom could take his two books down to the mill-race.

When the day's work was over, Uncle Cummins sometimes went up to the big house and tapped a keg of hard cider, and had a pitcher brought up to friends who might be stopping in on the way home; or lingered at the mill to talk politics or farm business with the last visitors of the day. Once Tom saw his uncle hoist up a big barrel of cider and, on a bet, drink from the bung. He could carry a barrel of flour out of the mill under each arm. Uncle Cummins was a powerful man.

Nobody knows whether Tom Jackson tippled with the godless mountain boys. He must have known the taste of liquor. He said one time that he liked it, that he always had. That was why he let it alone. There were other diversions for boys. In the autumn Uncle Cummins got out the hounds and for weeks the fox hunt kept the neighborhood in an uproar of shouting and baying and cursing. Then, just before Christmas, the deer season opened. Tom hunted deer and 'coon over the hills. He once killed a big 'coon in the tall chestnut that stood in the yard of the home place. People in those days called their dwellings the big house or the home house or the home place.

Tom rode over the hills and through the thickets of Lewis County clad in drab or butternut homespun. He rode hard. He did everything hard. He had a queer "stomach complaint" that had to be fought off with exercise.

One day Mr. Lightburn and a friend had just splashed through the ford on horseback when they heard a thin wail that sounded like music. The road turned sharply from the ford. Around the turn came a procession of seven or eight boys in column of twos. Joe Lightburn and Joe Jackson headed the column, armed with wooden guns; the other boys followed; two or three little niggers brought up the rear, one of them carrying a rusty old gun. As the army came up to the two mounted gentlemen, the general, who was Tom Jackson, called a halt. Not a word was spoken; no one even smiled; the two men looked on with complete gravity. Then, after a moment, General Jackson, whose side arm was an old fiddle, struck up "Napoleon's March", and the column swung, in perfect step, into the other fork of the road. As it disappeared the two horsemen could have observed that the uniform of the leader was butternut.

Tom began making his own clothes from earliest childhood. The sheep upon which the rough woolens grew were his special charge. He cropped them and took the wool to his kinsman David Hays, who had a carding mill at Jane Lew. He brought it home, and the aunts made it into homespun. The little flax raised on the place Tom broke with the rude flail of the time. It was woven into coarse linen. Tom was a responsible man at the age of thirteen.

Then, Uncle Cummins put him in charge of the sawyers and niggers. There was a great deal of timber on the great tract of land. But Tom had time for other things. Fishing and jockeying took time.

In the autumn of 1836 the quiet round of living at the Mills Tom broke with a visit to his brother Warren. The two boys went to see their sister Laura, at the Neales', near Parkersburg. Then, their visit running out, they worked their way down the Ohio into the Mississippi. Stopping on an island they cut wood and sold it to passing steamboats, the big side-wheelers that pushed barges of coal and timber, or carried great cargoes of cotton and grain. The fuel trade was good,

but the climate and the mosquitoes were too much for
the mountain boys. They returned in the spring of
1837, both full of malaria but the better each of them,
for the adventure, by the possession of a new trunk.
Tom got back in time to do some surveying for Major
Bailey.

There were godless pleasures on the frontier. Horse-
racing came in with the spring. Uncle Cummins took
his horses all round the country. They seldom lost a
race. One day in the summer—it was 1839—a great
race was arranged at the Simmons farm a few miles
away. A neighbor owned a fine horse, the only racer in
the county that could make it interesting for Cummins
Jackson's Kit. The night before the race Uncle Robinson, the old negro hostler, got Kit to the track to meet
his rival for a secret run. Next day Robinson whispered the result to his master. His master, so tipped
off, put up the limit of his cash on Kit. Then Cummins
Jackson, whom the pious Doctor Dabney spoke of as
a "kind of sporting gentleman", grew excited. Tom,
as usual, was at hand to jockey his uncle's horse. But
Uncle Cummins, taunting his opponent and boasting in
a loud voice, decided to ride for himself. He was too
heavy for Kit. Kit lost the race; Cummins Jackson
lost his money and his head. The contest ended in a
fight and the fight persisted as a local feud for a number
of years.

Uncle Robinson's zeal for his owner did not always
bring on such ignominious conduct. He was a devoted
servant, and he particularly loved young Marse Tom.

He was always doing something for Marse Tom.

Across the mill pond a thick grove of sugar maples
stood out in a kind of solitary magnificence. It may
have seemed to Tom that they had been put there to
give the country on the southern side of the river a
special and, to the initiate, an unmistakable significance.
He used to lie at the edge of the pond, reading his books.
But he must have looked often at the trees on the other
side, so often that the act of seeing was lost in an inten-
sity that, as time went on, ceased to be physical awareness. . . . When the sap began running it was Tom's
business, every year, to draw it off. Uncle Robinson
helped him. But in the spring it was hard to get across
the river. The Monongahela was a smaller stream then
than it is now; the forests had not been cut down to
build houses for men who should never get used to them;
but the water spilled over the banks in the spring. At
high water the only ford in the river at Jackson's Mills
was over a boy's head. It was hard to get over the river
to the maples. And the sap ran when the spring thaw
came on and the stream reached the flood.

Uncle Robinson helped Tom find a big log. Timber
was plentiful but boards were scarce and too expensive.
They made a dug-out canoe. They pulled the log to
the river bank and Tom burnt out the inside and soon
had a sturdy boat of the kind much in use by the
pioneers. In the hollowed-out boat Tom ferried his
friends Joe Jackson and Joe Lightburn over to the
maple grove. Once, when a spring freshet made a
sudden torrent in the river, Tom was caught up and
washed over the dam. He had to swim ashore.

In the evening and of a Sunday Tom played on his

fiddle. He played negro songs and sang them. Sometimes he went to church, to the Methodist Episcopal Church or the Harmony Methodist Church; perhaps to the Broad Run Baptist Church. His Uncle Cummins must have thought religion womanish; at least his neglect of it gave Tom a freedom of choice in the matter of denominations that kept him, for years, from choosing at all. But Tom was religious in a way that probably kept people from seeing that he was. He certainly had no feeling for orthodoxy. He was quiet and very serious. His material existence was not quite precarious, but he was an orphan. His living was due to the kindness of his Uncle Cummins, not to the usual and assumed order of family dispensations. He must have been driven, from the time of his mother's death, to wonder, without knowing what he was doing, at the source of human order and fixation, and later at the source of all power and influence. He was an orphan, moreover, who had became introspective and reticent.

That his hypochondria was due to his "obscure stomach complaint" is not the profound thesis of this narrative. Nobody knows what it was due to, and it is not interesting enough to enquire about. Tom Jackson was almost painfully aware of his social predicament and of the decline of his branch of the Jackson family. But even from his childhood he must have been an extraordinary person. There would be no common solution to his problem. The will to property may require only a submissiveness to that symbol of order which is the local church. But the will to power sometimes becomes the will of God.

On Sundays, at home, the old negress Granny Robinson read and preached from the Bible. When Tom was about fifteen she held a revival meeting. She was the leader of the slaves—she could read and write. Cecilia, her devoted apostle, expounded her doctrine to Tom and the other children of the neighborhood. But Tom did not spend all his time with pious slaves. Most of it, when he was not at work, went to log-rolling, cornhuskings, apple-peelings; to hunting, fishing, riding, reading.

Tom could read easily from an early year. He went to school occasionally to itinerant masters, but never regularly or for long. In 1839 a certain Colonel Withers, a gentleman Latinist from eastern Virginia, opened a school in Weston. Tom rode to school every day on horseback.

He read the few books he could get. He read by the light of pine knots that he stuck in the jamb of the fireplace. One of the slaves swapped the knots for lessons in reading and writing. When the slave had mastered his signature he signed it to a pass, and got off to Canada on the Underground Railroad.

By 1840 Tom Jackson was ready to make all the money he could. Money in large sums could not be earned by a boy in western Virginia. Among the landholders even, it was scarce. For it was hardly a necessity. Most of the local business was carried on by swapping corn for oats, wool for leather, cattle for hogs. Every plantation of any size was an economic unit. Food, clothing, and shelter, the three necessities, were provided by the yieldings of the farm. Not only on the frontier but in the South as a whole, metaphysical wealth such as we accept unquestioningly since the Civil War was unknown. Wealth as numerical operations that are no longer symbols but intrinsic values of themselves would have been unintelligible to an ante-bellum Southerner. Wealth was a collection of physical objects; money could have been dispensed with if another device of exchange had been invented. The Southerner valued money because it permitted him to exchange one object—so many pounds of cotton—for another object—a team of horses.

Tom Jackson had no physical objects, no possessions whatever. Without possessions a man did not morally exist. The idea of the "inner life", held by the Calvinist people in far-off New England, had no meaning. In the South, the man as he appeared in public was the man: his public appearance was his moral life. The nearest equivalent to the "inner life" was "private affairs". The New Englander was mystical, religious; the Southerner, practical, materialistic. Private affairs were not enquired into and they had no public value. A man's property was his character. Tom Jackson must set about getting property or a substitute for it. One of the substitutes was education—not learning for itself but as a means. For learning has never been respectable in itself.

All the people round Jackson's Mills knew that Cummïns Jackson's nephew was ambitious. They respected him. One of these was Colonel Alexander Scott Withers, the Latinist recently removed to Lewis from Fauquier. One day the colonel, dressed with the ele-

gance of the piedmont gentleman, called upon the
Jacksons. At the mill he bought a small poke of meal.
But the scholar refused to carry it. Joe Lightburn,
who had spent the day with Tom, offered to carry it
home for the colonel.

"No," he said, "gentlemen from Fauquier have servants for such tasks and work their heads instead of their
hands."

"Well," said Tom, "when you've got the money to go
to William and Mary College then you know how to
work your head."

The colonel said: "Some day I will get you a job
so you can earn some money."

The day's work being over, perhaps Tom and Joe
Lightburn, and Joe Jackson if he was there, went down
to the mill pond to read a little, or just to lie on the
bank by the dug-out boat and gaze absently across the
river at the maple grove. Perhaps Tom or one of the
other boys, growing restless, said:

"Let's cross over the river and rest in the shade of
the trees."

II

ELIZA AND JOHN

IN the city of London, in the year 1748, a handsome
blonde, six feet tall, beautiful as well as handsome,
had made up her mind to leave England. The young
lady, besides being beautiful, was vigorous.

She had thrown a silver tankard at the head of her
step-father. Her own father had just died. Her mother
had married his brother. Miss Eliza, being more reso-
lute than Hamlet in Hamlet's predicament, had acted
with greater resolution. And Mr. Cummins—to
suppose for a moment his thoughts—must have reflected
with some bitterness upon the fickle character of respectability. He owned, even if he did not personally
conduct, a public house at the sign of the Bold Dragoon.
As a moral offset and, in God's providence, a financial
support to the Bold Dragoon, a landed estate in Ireland must have instructed the worthy man's conscience
in the higher things. His niece and daughter had flung
the tipsy Dragoon at the head of the sober Estate.
She was in disgrace.

Being so, she had no money for passage to the Colonies. But she was a resourceful girl. She took out
papers of indenture to a prosperous family bound for
Maryland. The period of the indenture is unknown;

it must have lasted, as we shall see, for five or six years. Elizabeth Cummins became one of those numerous indentured servants from whom a great many respectable families of the Southern States are descended.

About a half-century before this incident occurred in the history of Scotch-Irish emigration, a great number of families bearing the Jackson surname were settled in the Province of Ulster. Some of the Jacksons had got hold of land and risen to power. In the first two decades of the eighteenth century the Hon. Richard Jackson held lands from the Irish Society of London. He had grown rich, and influential in politics. The Society didn't like it; it raised his fees. Landlord Jackson, in turn, raised his tenants' fees. The worthy farmers of Coleraine, County Londonderry, felt the pinch of high rents; they decided to do something about it. In 1728 great hordes of the Scots whose ancestors, a century before, had fled, persecuted, to Ireland, now took ship for the Colonies. They began pouring into Pennsylvania and Virginia.

Some of them went to England before they faced the perils of an unknown wilderness. At least, in 1729, right after Richard Jackson raised his tenants' rents, one of the Jackson families embarked from Port Rush, Ireland, for London. This family had a son John, aged ten. The parents' Christian names are unknown. They died, supposedly, in England.

In 1748 John Jackson was twenty-nine. He took passage for America. Elizabeth Cummins took passage in the same ship.

The Jackson tradition holds that John fell in love

with the handsome lady at sight, that he wanted her to marry him at sea. She withstood the impetuous suit of her lover for seven years.

In Cecil County, Maryland, John and Eliza settled, for a time, to live their separate lives. Not until 1755 were they married. Eliza, as an indentured servant, cannot be imagined as having gained a foothold in the society of tidewater Maryland. Not that indentured persons were always deficient in respectability; they often became respectable in their own right, and even more often founded reputable families. They were deficient in opportunity. This was particularly true in Maryland, where a small, powerful aristocracy, different from the looser feudal order of Virginia, had got hold of immense tracts of land and shut out the small farmer. The early history of John Jackson is obscure. It is not likely that he had prospered in the seven years of his residence in Maryland.

For, shortly after their marriage, John and Eliza moved westward to the south branch of the Potomac, in Pendleton County, Virginia. Thirteen years later the Jackson family, increased by the sons George and Edward, pushed farther into the West. They settled on the present site of Buchhannon, West Virginia, patenting land along a small creek called Turkey Run. It was a wild region, on the very extremity of the colonial frontier. For years their house was called Jackson's Fort.

When the Scotch-Irish began coming to Virginia about 1730 they found the country, not thickly populated, but divided up into vast estates. These, under the laws of entail, could not be broken up to make room for the immigrants. The vast extent of an old Virginian plantation could barely be imagined by the contented English squire who never came over to get one of them for himself. Such an area conceived as fixed productive property rather than as negotiable wealth, brings no image whatever to the modern urban mind which thinks, not in space but in time; for Time is Money. The Washingtons owned several counties; the general himself was one of the first speculators in western lands, and he clearly anticipated the Jeffersonian heresy by making way for the small farmer. The immigrant ancestor of Colonel Fielding Lewis had entailed upon his descendants a tract of thirty-three thousand acres, besides large holdings elsewhere. The founder of the Carter family owned so much land that local history calls him King Carter. In between the large estates small landowners, relatives of the great proprietors or men who had served out their indentures, had got a foothold. They were either independent farmers or tenantry to the squires: negro slavery was not much developed before the Revolution. But by the middle of the eighteenth century most of the small plantations of a few hundred or a thousand acres were taken up. Many of the owners were respectable minor gentry. Others had sunk to the squalor they have not got out of to this day. They were the poor white.

Poor white and gentry alike were mainly of English extraction. When the Scotch-Irish arrived, finding no decent land to settle on and being ambitious, they were unwilling to take bad lands that would have made them less secure than the well-housed and well-fed negroes. They moved on from place to place, settling down in the end in the wilderness west of the Blue Ridge. Sir Alexander Spottiswoode had opened up the valley of the Shenandoah in 1716. His fellow explorers each received for their prowess a small golden horseshoe and the knighthood of that emblem. The men of Ulster came over and took the land.

John Jackson had little trouble getting as much land in western Virginia as an Englishman, a generation before, could get on the banks of the James. At first the land was worthless. It had to be cleared. And the Indians had to be fought. At all events the clearing of the land could not have been a profitable business. Timber was still plentiful in eastern Virginia; transportation from the frontier was difficult. The Jacksons lived in the daily struggle against the wilderness that all the pioneers had to face. John Jackson was an Indian fighter; so were his sons; and Eliza, their mother, could load and fire a musket as coolly as a trained soldier.

To John and Eliza were born eight children. The second son was Edward, born in Maryland in 1759. He was a large man of muscle and will, who was indubitably his six-foot mother's child. In his father's house in western Virginia the first court of Randolph County had convened, and in time he was appointed Justice of the County, captain and colonel of militia, Commissioner of Revenue, high sheriff; he later represented the County of Lewis in the Virginia Assembly. There was nothing distinguished about Colonel Edward Jackson; he was an able man, probably ambitious and certainly honorable. Like the men of his place and time he was bent upon subduing the American frontier. They are not to be blamèd because the beating down of frontiers got to be not a means, but a habit, a way of life.

At the age of twenty-four Edward Jackson took to wife Mary Hadden. Her family had emigrated from New Jersey before the Revolution.

Their third son was Jonathan Jackson, born at Jackson's Fort in 1790. Jonathan did not become a strong man. All races, on the frontier, were to the swift, all battles to the strong. Men had got into their heads the image of a wilderness to be conquered. They never got it out of their heads again. Jonathan Jackson was not one of these.

Jonathan went to school to academies in Clarksburg and Parkersburg. He was still a schoolboy when in 1801 his father, Colonel Edward Jackson, left Turkey Run to take up land for himself. The place he chose was in Lewis County, a fertile peninsula made by the winding Monongahela River. . . . There were six grants of land including nearly eleven thousand acres. At the nose of the peninsula, back from the river a few hundred feet, Colonel Jackson built a hewn-log manor house with an ell. Seven years later he put a dam in the river and set up a mill house. Across the mill-pond stood a cluster of sugar-maple saplings. Colonel Jackson called his new home Jackson's Mills.

By 1810 Jonathan Jackson had finished reading for the Harrison County bar in the office of his cousin,

John G. Jackson, of Clarksburg. He was a promising, kindly, urbane young man. He was soon appointed Commissioner of Internal Revenue. It was a small office but it had a dignity at that time. It was the day of local autonomy in politics; the country had not learned to look up to the town. Jonathan Jackson was able but not ambitious. He prospered; and his father gave him various properties.

In 1818 he was married to Miss Julia Beckwith Neale of Parkersburg, a lady of "admitted beauty." She had dark hair and blue eyes. She was educated to read and write; not all the beautiful women of her time could read and write. Julia Neale came of a respectable family of the tidewater. Nothing we know of her indicates that she had any pioneering in her blood. She was sensitive, shy, not very robust.

Jonathan and Julia his wife went to live in a new three-room cottage that Jonathan had built on Main Street of the village of Clarksburg, Virginia. It had a small inserted porch and a half-attic, gabled. The site was a large piece of land to put a town house on. A fine apple tree stood in the yard.

This was still 1818. Jonathan Jackson said he would some day use the cottage as a law office. He would build a big house farther back from the dusty street.

To Jonathan and Julia Jackson were born four children. Elizabeth was born in 1819; Warren, in 1821; Laura Ann, in 1826. Thomas Jackson, third child of Jonathan and Julia Jackson, was born on January 21, 1824.

In February, 1826, Elizabeth, the eldest child, fell

ill of typhoid fever. Her father had to nurse her. On
March 5th Elizabeth died. Jonathan Jackson, who had
been infected through his daughter, took the disease.
He died on March 26th.

On March 27th his wife gave birth to another child,
Laura Ann.

The widow Jackson and her children were in a bad
way. Yet they had no reason to be concerned with the
material future. Jonathan Jackson had made money
and had it given him. A few weeks after his death,
when Julia Jackson had got over her confinement, the
lawyers told her that not a cent of money, not a foot
of land, had been left.

Jonathan Jackson had gone on the notes of too many
of his friends. He had played cards. The stern business of subduing the wilderness and keeping it well in
hand had relaxed in his grip.

The Masonic Fraternity came to the rescue of the
indigent family. It provided them a small one-room
cottage to live in. The ladies of the town gave the
widow their sewing. They urged her to open a day
school for children. The session was three months. She
had three children of her own to look after, one an
infant in arms.

So matters went. . . . .

It is the year 1830. In the four years of her widow-
hood she had got a little help from her husband's family and her own; but not much. . . . When the attach-
ment began one cannot say. By 1830 it was well-
known in the kind of town where everything is well-
known, that Captain Blake Woodson was "payin'

court" to the good-looking widow. Captain Woodson was a respectable man but he had not got on. Her connections opposed the match. They came forward now with generous offers of support. All we know is that she turned them down. The least we can remark is that she exhibited something of the fine conscience that distinguished the career of her son Thomas.

On November 4, 1830, Captain Blake Woodson and Mrs. Julia Jackson were married. They left Clarksburg to live in Fayette County. It was a new county, cut out of a large old one. Captain Woodson had been appointed clerk.

Warren was sent to live with his kinsman Alfred Neale, of Parkersburg. Tom and Laura Ann lived only a few months in the Fayette home. They went to live with their uncle, Cummins Jackson, who had fallen heir to Jackson's Mills upon the death of his father, the colonel, in 1828.

In less than a year, in 1831, the children were called to the bedside of their mother. She had given birth to a son, Wirt Woodson, and she died on September 4, 1831. Tom and Laura Ann returned to Jackson's Mills.

Uncle Robinson, an old slave belonging to Cummins Jackson, came for them on horseback. He was a good old negro. He was always doing something for Tom.

III

CONSTABLE AND CADET

COLONEL WITHERS knew Tom Jackson well. There was something distinguished about the boy that a distinguished character, like the colonel, could understand. Colonel Withers had been his teacher. He had found Tom an ignorant and fumbling student, who knew only how to read; but very much in earnest. Tom's logical categories were not tightly partitioned off; he could not think out quantities in mathematics quickly or clearly. Yet the colonel knew this was due to deficient schooling. He knew too that Tom never fumbled in matters of plain judgment. Tom could not be fooled. He knew his own mind.

Perhaps Colonel Withers had heard the story of Tom, Colonel Talbott, and the fish. Perhaps he didn't need to know that particular story.

Colonel Withers had made Tom a promise. Making it, as we have seen, he had displayed one of the typical old Virginian prejudices. He was now to exhibit some of the old Virginian distinction in the judgment of character.

In 1841 Governor Thomas Gilmer appointed the colonel justice of the peace. A justice of the peace became a member of the county court. The court elected constables for the several districts of the county.

A constabulary was vacant. Colonel Withers urged the appointment of Tom Jackson. Tom's rival, one Richard Hall, otherwise unknown to fame, was elected. But for some reason Hall was not sworn in. Tom Jackson was sworn into office June 11, 1841. He had appeared in open court and taken out a security bond of two thousand dollars. Cummins Jackson signed it. He got the office after all, but nobody knows how.

Tom was almost too young for the job. He was only seventeen. But he did it well. He had to collect bad debts, serve notices, attach property. Nobody likes a collector of debts, a server of notices. But Tom Jackson made no enemies. He was inflexible; at the same time he was just.

A widow living south of Weston had sold some goods to a neighbor. He couldn't be made to pay her. Tom went round to see him a few times, but the debtor, whom we must all forgive, always put him off. One day Tom stood in front of the livery stable in Weston. The man rode up to Benny Pritchard's blacksmith shop, across the street. Tom saw his chance.

In those days there was an unwritten law that a man's horse could not be seized for debt while he was in the saddle.

But this man had got off his horse. Tom ran over to seize the bridle. The debtor was too quick for him, leaped back into the saddle. Tom, in his turn, was too quick for the debtor. He grabbed the bridle and led the innocent beast toward the low open door of the shop. The debtor lashed the constable with his whip. The constable held on. At the low door the man had to dismount or get his head bumped. He dismounted. Tom claimed the horse. The debtor promptly redeemed it by paying the debt. Tom was inflexible. At the same time he was just.

For a year Tom performed his duties. Clad in homespun, he rode horseback over the hills and through the thickets of Lewis County. His clients were scattered and hard to reach. He must have heard all kinds of talk. People in those days talked of little but politics; in Virginia they talked of nothing else. Already there were rumors and some evidence of a powerful revolutionary party growing up in the North. This party as yet had no name of its own, but a great many people shared in a general feeling that would soon require a name. There were people in New England who wanted to destroy democracy and civil liberties in America by freeing the slaves. They were not very intelligent people; so they didn't know precisely what they wanted to destroy. They thought God had told them what to do. A Southern man knew better than this. He knew that God only told people to do right: He never told them *what* was right. These privy-to-God people were sending little pamphlets down South telling the Negroes, whom they had never seen, that they were abused.

Time was passing. Tom was eighteen and he had made very little money. His education was remote as ever.

In the spring of 1842 Congressman Hays had his turn appointing a cadet to West Point. Tom saw his opportunity and became one of four candidates. He borrowed books from his kinsman, Captain George Jackson; he began to study for the preliminary test, to be held in Weston. Only one of the four could go.

Tom was weak in mathematics. And Gibson Butcher won the appointment. Tom settled down to his defeat. But in a short time Gibson Butcher came home from West Point, saying he couldn't stand the discipline and would never get used to such a life.

Tom went immediately to see Captain Jackson and Mr. Jonathan Bennet. They agreed to write letters in his behalf to Congressman Hays. Captain Jackson wrote a letter to the Secretary of War himself. Tom's supporters believed in him, but they were dubious.

For they were concerned about his lack of good schooling. They were afraid he would never pass the entrance examination after he got to West Point. Mr. Bennet was particularly concerned. But Tom said:

"I know I am very ignorant but I can make it up in study. I know I have the energy and I think I have the intellect."

One morning early in June, 1842, Tom Jackson set out for Clarksburg to catch the stage for Washington. He was dressed in a full suit of homespun. He carried the rest of his clothes in a pair of saddlebags. He rode horseback from Jackson's Mills to Clarksburg. A little nigger boy rode with him to bring back his horse.

He missed the stage. Here Tom failed to do one of the things he ought to have done; but not knowing that he was Stonewall Jackson he couldn't be expected to do it. He failed to walk through the mud all the way to Washington. He simply rode on to Grafton and caught up with the stage. At the Green Valley Depot, east of Cumberland, Maryland, he got out of the stage and rode for the first time on a train. He had never even seen an engine before.

He was green as grass. Full of wonder, he arrived in Washington on June 17th. He went immediately to see his Congressman.

Mr. Hays was most cordial. He had received two petitions for the appointment of young Jackson, signed by thirty-one of his most interesting constituents, many of them members of the Jackson family who were the most powerful clan in western Virginia; Colonel Withers, the gentleman from Fauquier, had signed it too. Mr. Hays asked the Secretary of War to put Jackson in Gibson Butcher's place. He took Tom to see the Secretary. That official, possibly for the moment forgetting his manners but not his principles, must have noticed the young man's clothing. He voiced his principles thus:

"Young man, you have a good name. If anybody at West Point insults you, give 'em a good beating and charge it to me."

The Secretary of War issued a provisional warrant of appointment on June 18, 1842. In the warrant Tom gave his name as Thomas *Jonathan* Jackson. He was ambitious; but he was evidently willing to take the name of an unsuccessful parent and vindicate it. Mr. Hays wrote a letter to the Superintendent at West Point, saying his man was not well-prepared. But he spoke more at length of his seriousness and ambition.

All the business being done, he invited Jackson to

stay a few days in Washington. It was Tom's first trip
to a large town of fifteen thousand people. But he was
worried about his coming examination at West Point.
He declined the invitation. The one pleasure his Congressman could induce him to take was a climb up the
unfinished dome of the Capitol.

There he could see, across the Potomac, the home of
Captain Robert Lee. and farther still, the rolling hills
of northern Virginia. To the west, barely visible, lay
a dull blue ridge, almost lost in the horizon.

To the southwest stretched the plains of Manassas.

IV

WEST POINT

EARLY in July, 1842, three young men stood at the main entrance to the West Point Military Academy. They were talking in a desultory way. But they were evidently young men of high spirits. Their faces showed the ruddy complexion, the fine modeling of sons of Virginia country gentlemen. They had just arrived from Virginia to begin their military careers. They were watching with mild curiosity the other new cadets as they came up to the gate.

While they stood there two figures defined themselves some distance away, and became gradually more distinct. The first figure was a cadet officer; he was walking very briskly, head erect, shoulders thrown back. At his heels followed a slender boy of eighteen, dressed in a full suit of homespun, over his shoulder a pair of saddlebags containing his meagre wardrobe. He put one foot before the other very evenly, very precisely; yet the precision of his gait seemed to exaggerate its shambling awkwardness and to make conspicuous the large clumsy feet.

As this striking figure came near the three young men, they could see his face. He had a high sloping forehead. His eyes were grayish blue, clear and rather

introspective.   He had high cheek bones, almost gaunt.
His mouth was a single line of compressed lips.   His
jaw stuck out heavily.   When he had come up to where
the cadets were standing he looked straight ahead, not
at any certain object but as if into space.

George Edward Pickett, Ambrose Hill, and D. H.
Maury, the three young men, were silent.   Then one
of them, suddenly turning, said:

"That man looks as if he had come to stay."

Tom Jackson had come to stay, though he was at
that moment by no means sure of it.   He was ignorant.
He had failed in the preliminary examinations at home.
And if he had failed there in a country town, could he
reasonably expect to do better at a place like West
Point?   But he did do better.   He was accepted as a
cadet. . . . .

Time went on and young Jackson was known as a
silent fellow.   He made few friends.   The boys in his
own class and those in the classes above him probably
gave him little heed, but he was marked by a kind of
silent opinion as an eccentric.   Occasionally he was
singled out by the upper classmen as the appropriate
butt for their practical jokes.   All their attempts upon
the dignity of the victim ended in failure.   The con-
spirators hanged themselves in their own strategems.
Tom Jackson remained unmoved.   They decided to let
him alone.

There is always, in every school, at least one boy
whom the students do not like.   Young men are ex-
tremely conventional, and run like wolves in a pack;
respectful of the crowd, fearful of the single people who

make it up. They will not let any of their fellows be unlike them. Probably half the eccentrics are what the good fellows take them to be—mediocrities, cranks, fools. The other half are men of some character and a few are men of genius. Cadet Jackson was easily classified; he was a fool. Cadet Jackson cared no more for what people thought of him than a rhinoceros cares for the birds that live on his back and peck at his hide.

His one purpose was to distinguish himself. He obeyed all the rules laid down by the officials. He obeyed none of those established by tradition and enforced by the cadets. He went where he pleased; he did as he pleased. He spoke to whom he pleased—a great heresy; he picked friends because he wanted to, not because any interest of the moment required it. He met a few of the cadets in personal friendships; he indulged in the general conviviality of the place not at all.

He knew he had to study hard. He barely passed his first regular examinations. From these he received the rank of fifty-one in a class of seventy-two. When he arrived at the Point he was given three weeks to learn the English grammar. He learned it.

Jackson never studied the day's lesson; he studied the subject. Often he was three days or a week behind his day's assignment. He would not study the next lesson until he had mastered the preceding one. As a result he was marked low in his classes; in the end he knew his subjects better than those who received high grades. In fact, he literally mastered every study he undertook.

At night, when taps had sounded, the boys all went
to bed. Tom Jackson, who always obeyed the rules,
turned off his light. He piled anthracite coal upon the
grate until it blazed up to a high flame. He lay on the
floor in the unsteady light, his book before him. French
verbs and the theorems of geometry he fairly burnt
into his head. In the daytime he sat up to a table on a
stool, bolt upright. He had an obscure stomach complaint; he was afraid of cramping his internal organs.

Nearly every afternoon he took a short walk. He
walked fast. Then suddenly he would stop. He would
stand for half a minute or longer, very still, one hand
raised in the air to the level of his face, the palm turned
out, a detached far-away look in his eyes. Then, suddenly as he had stopped, he would resume his walk.

Sometimes one of his friends came to his room.
Jackson would be staring into space, a far-away look in
his eyes. . . . Only repeated helloes from the friend, or
a nudge at his elbow, could bring him back to awareness
of a present world. The power of concentration, of
self-forgetfulness, he had developed instinctively since
his childhood. It lacked an object then and it was only
revery. Now he was learning to control it, to set it
tasks; it had become intellectual power of a high order.

All the stories of Jackson's boyhood take form and
meaning after he arrived at West Point. The average
boy tells a few unnecessary lies without becoming a
liar, or sells a fish for more than his due profit without
becoming a swindler. Jackson did neither of these. His
rigid devotion to the point of honor was, in a child, an
eccentricity. It is a popular tradition which the Roman-

tic school is responsible for that only writers and artists
are eccentric. Distinction of any sort is an eccentricity.
Character, being the quality that sets a man off from
his contemporaries, is not character if it is immediately
understood.

Great men who are men of action seldom have more
than one idea, and because this idea exists as a limit,
the various means of realizing it become ends in themselves. Nearly every man once in his life can summon
enough knavishness to make a fortune or overthrow a
state; his idea is not a limit, it is a confusion of ends
with means. If Jackson had been one of these he would
have looked upon his studies at West Point as mere
tools, the eventual utility of which he might have
doubted. They were ends in themselves. Jackson was
one of those distinguished persons whose ambition is so
far-reaching that a single object, outside themselves,
cannot contain it. The impulse is thrown back upon
itself; not the achievement of a simple end, but the
exercise of character for its own sake, becomes the
unconscious aim of such men. It is the paradox of the
great that the most ambitious are the most disinterested.
Thomas Jackson was one of these.

Late in 1842 Jackson began making a list of maxims.
Some of them were original; that is, as original as he
could make them. There was nothing new about them.
His character and conduct were usually more interesting than what he said. He could even, with a serious
face, copy out for his meditation the pious saws of a
book entitled "Politeness and Good Breeding". He
meant to overcome his awkwardness in society: it was

an obstacle to distinction. But his own moral system reached further.

> That friendship may at once be fond and lasting, there must not only be equal virtue in each but virtue of the same kind: not only the same end must be proposed, but the same means must be approved.

In short, ambition will have no other ambition before it. But perhaps this is better:

YOU MAY BE WHATEVER YOU RESOLVE TO BE.

Jackson wrote this slogan in his notebook after he had been at West Point only a few months. His mind was made up. To the hour of his death he never changed it. There is more of Jackson's character in the maxim than in anything else he ever said.

In the summer of 1844 Jackson was given a furlough. Always in the back of his head lurked the image of Jackson's Mills, perhaps of the grove of sugar maples across the pond. He had been writing home of his homesickness, and to his sister letters that touched upon his feeling of loneliness, written in a kind of stilted bad English that doubtless came to his pen to disguise his emotions. At home, he saw all his relatives and friends. He saw his cousin Sylvanus White. He said to him: "I tell you I had to work hard. Not for all Lewis County would I fail to go back to West Point. I am going to make a man of myself if I live. I can do anything I will to do."

Back at West Point, he learned that he had been made a cadet officer in his absence.

Cadet Jackson was thinking intensely of his future. At about this time he wrote a long letter to his sister Laura Ann, telling her what career he thought he would choose. He told her he didn't think much of the profession of arms. But he might follow it for a while. He knew that the army in time of peace was no place for an ambitious man. There was no prospect of war. There were harangues in Congress about Texas and the balance of power between North and South. A cadet could not be expected to look very far ahead in these matters. He wrote home to his sister:

> I look forward with no small degree of satisfaction to the time when my circumstances will allow me . . . to share with yourselves the ineffable pleasure of domestic circles.

He wrote this in November, 1845.

On April 23, 1846, he wrote as follows:

> Rumor appears to indicate a rupture between our government and the Mexican. If such should be the case the probability is that I shall be ordered to join the army of occupation immediately.

On June 30, 1846, Cadet Jackson was commissioned Brevet 2nd Lieutenant of Artillery. He was graduated on July 1st from the Military Academy, with the rank of seventeen—an advance of thirty-four over his rank at entrance. People said that Jackson had a good mind but neither an active nor a quick one; that he was an honest, admirable fellow of whom not too much was to be expected.

He went home for a few weeks. Then he reported for service to the First Artillery, Captain Francis Taylor, at Fort Hamilton, Long Island. He was joining "the army of occupation." The Mexican War had begun.

V

MEXICO

B Y the middle of April, 1846, General Taylor had
moved his troops forward to Fort Brown on the
Rio Grande. General Ampudia lay opposite him at
Matamoras. The Texan and American politicians took
the hopeful view that Taylor was on American soil.
The Mexicans said the southern boundary of Texas
lay farther north, and they had a little the better of
the argument. The disputed strip of land was not fit
to raise hell upon; and even if it had been, the cactus
and the dust would have choked it out. However, a few
American soldiers, reconnoitering, were caught by the
Mexicans and captured.

On April 23rd President James K. Polk in an ecstasy
shouted that "war exists, and, notwithstanding all our
efforts to avoid it, exists by the act of Mexico herself."

The "notwithstanding" was sheer fiddle-de-dee.
President Polk was a myopic Southern politician who
failed to see that the acquisition of western lands
was not precisely the way in which the South could
maintain a balance of power with the North. Calhoun
had compromised everything but his honor to acquire
Texas: Texas restored the balance of power between the
sections. But he had bitterly opposed the Mexican

War. He knew it would mean new territory. He knew just as certainly that the North would never let slavery go farther than Texas. He held that Texas was the last slave State, and he was right. He felt that the institutions peculiar to the South might be preserved; they could never be extended. Indeed, he said, the genius of the South lay, not in an extension of her institutions, but in maintaining the existing order of a stable, landed society.

The idea of stability, however, had not got much headway in the western States. They were new. The Atlantic States, in 1850, were more than two hundred years old. Tennessee, Kentucky, Alabama, and Mississippi had not turned a century. Andrew Jackson, fifteen years before, had struck the first hard blow against Southern society, by suppressing the Act of Nullification in South Carolina. Jackson, as a Westerner, hated everything in the East. Jackson had been born in South Carolina. But South Carolina, except for the fact that there were a great many Democratic votes there, meant no more to him than Massachusetts. He hated wealth, if it brought leisure, and he hated institutions, by means of which a society devotes its leisure to culture. As a matter of fact, Andrew Jackson had an instinctive hatred of gentlemen; at least his dying words evinced a good deal of hate for Calhoun. It is just possible to see Calhoun and Andrew Jackson as the Christ and Antichrist of political order in the United States.

Polk was no Antichrist. He was an imperialist; a not very intelligent imperialist. The revolutionary

party in the North would never permit American society
to expand in the terms of the Constitution. The
North, with respect to history and all decent traditions,
was wrong. Andrew Jackson had been ignorant and
unscrupulous. But Polk had simply not been very
intelligent. Instead of slaves in the new Western
States to count as two-thirds their number, there would
be white men, counting all three-thirds, to vote down
southern rights in the East.

The institution of slavery was a positive good only
in the sense that Calhoun had argued that it was: it
had become a necessary element in a stable society. He
had argued justly that only in a society of fixed classes
can men be free. Only men who are socially as well as
economically secure can preserve the historical sense
of obligation. This historical sense of obligation im-
plied a certain freedom to do right. In the South, between White and Black, it took the form of benevolent
protection: the White man was in every sense responsible for the Black. The Black man, "free", would
have been exploited.

In the North, the historical sense was atrophied, and
the feeling of obligation did not exist, The White man,
"free", was *beginning* to be exploited. Men, whose
great-grandfathers had sold the Indians to the West
Indian traders and had got negroes in return, whom
they sold to the Virginians, did not feel themselves to
be involved in the transaction. The Northern men did
not feel responsible for this procedure; lacking the historical sense, they could repudiate it in the name of
morality. They had come to believe in abstract right.

Where abstract right supplants obligation, interest begins to supplant loyalty. Revolution may follow. When such a revolution triumphs, society becomes a chaos of self-interest. Its freedom is the freedom to do wrong. This does not mean that all men will do the wrong thing; only that no external order exists which precludes the public exercise of wrong impulses; too much, in short, is left to the individual. It was such a revolution that the Northern States were now moving towards.

Of these affairs Lieutenant Jackson thought little. His political theories were never to become very interesting. His view of slavery was always that of the orthodox Virginian, or of any respectable citizen of the border states. He had always believed that the slaves should be free. He didn't know how it could be done. He knew it could not be done quickly.

Moreover, a soldier had no business thinking about politics. His aim should be first the carrying out of the ideas of the politicians; then the attaining of distinction for himself. A second lieutenant had no part in the former; so his business became solely the latter. Lieutenant Jackson was determined to distinguish himself.

Accordingly, without realizing that the Mexican War was to be the first campaign of the Northern Revolutionists, organized by the stupidity of the South, against his native State, he left Fort Hamilton on August 19, 1846, to join the army of General Taylor in Mexico. He accompanied his command, Captain Taylor's company of thirty men and forty horses. They went to

Pittsburgh, then down the Ohio and the Mississippi to New Orleans. They went from New Orleans, by sea, to Point Isabel. The campaign of General Taylor was over. Point Isabel became a dull military post, where men came with stories of battles they had been in.

Jackson was restless. There was nothing for him to do. One day Captain Taylor was walking up and down the beach. At his side, walking with him, was Lieutenant Daniel Hill, from North Carolina. A short distance away Jackson walked, alone, stopping to look at the sea, then resuming his walk.

"There's Lieutenant Jackson," said Captain Taylor, "a most efficient and talented officer. If the course at West Point had been a year longer, he would have been graduated at the head of his class."

Jackson came up to the two officers. He was introduced to Hill. Hill said something about the battles, fought earlier in the year, at Monterey and Palo Alto.

Jackson drew himself up to his full height. The gray-blue eyes, dull in repose, now gathered light, and flashed.

"Oh, how I envy you men who have been in a battle! If I could only be in one battle!"

Jackson did not see active service until the spring of 1847. General Taylor's army had been organized for an invasion of Mexico from the north. In March, 1847, General Scott was ordered to get together an expedition against Vera Cruz; the route to Mexico City by way of Vera Cruz reduced the line of advance from 600 to 260 miles. Scott started out with 13,000 men. In due time this army was landed on Mexican soil, and

on March 27th the city of Vera Cruz surrendered to
the Americans. Jackson was promoted to the rank of
first lieutenant, and the brevet rank of captain. He was
already distinguished, but he was not satisfied.

After some delay, Scott began his invasion. At the
mountain pass of Cerro Gordo the Mexicans held a
strong position; but Captain Robert Lee, a talented
officer of the Engineers, discovered a hidden line of
approach. The position was carried by the Americans.
Captain John Magruder of the Artillery captured a
light field battery.

Nearby was a small Mexican town called Jalapa;
it was on Scott's line of communications. He had to
garrison it before he could leave it behind. For this
duty Lieutenant Jackson was detached from his command. Jackson had spent seven months on garrison
duty. Now, when action was at hand and distinction
was in his grasp, he was assigned to garrison duty again.
It was a blow.

Scott's army marched on. Jackson could do nothing
but obey orders. The melancholy optimist now almost
despaired. His ill-fortune was not an accident, he
thought; he decided it was a part of the divine plan.
He wrote his sister:

> I throw myself into the hands of an all-wise God. . . . It
> may have been one of His means of diminishing my excessive
> ambition.

One need not subscribe to the lieutenant's theology to
be aware that this particular revelation of it contained

a great deal of self-knowledge. He could not be fooled, even by himself. He knew his own mind.

In a few days Providence reversed the decision. Captain Magruder needed men for his captured battery. Now Magruder was an ill-tempered officer, strict and hard to please; no one wished to be under his command. No one but Jackson. Jackson saw that this was his chance. Magruder was a gallant and fearless soldier; his men were always in the midst of a fight.

At the battle of Chapultepec, in September, Jackson commanded a section of the new battery. The Mexicans held an almost impregnable front. Jackson moved his command up close to the breastworks, supporting the 14th Infantry. The Mexicans poured down a hail of bullets and cannon balls. The infantry scattered, melted away. Jackson's own men skulked in a ditch. Single-handed he dragged one of the guns across the ditch into firing position. His men still skulked. In a storm of bullets he walked up and down in front of the gun shouting that there was no danger. Finally a sergeant screwed up his nerve and came to help him. The two men began loading and firing the gun. General Worth saw him in his isolated position, and ordered him to retire. Jackson sent back word that with a company of regulars to support him he could carry the Mexican works. The general was impressed. He sent forward a whole brigade. The Americans poured over the breastworks and put the Mexican army to flight. Jackson was brevetted major for his services.

Some one asked him if he had been afraid standing alone under fire of the whole Mexican army.

"No, the only anxiety I felt was that I might not meet enough danger to make my conduct conspicuous."

After a series of battles Scott's army on the 14th of September entered the city of Mexico. Jackson was quartered with the other officers in the National Palace. In a short time General Scott held a levée for his officers. Jackson came up to be introduced. The general said in a loud voice so that everybody in the room could hear: "I am not sure that I can shake hands with Major Jackson. But if he can forgive himself for slaughtering those poor Mexicans the way he did I suppose I can."

Jackson's blush we may suppose was not due to the rather unfortunate joke, but to the fact that he was being distinguished in public by the commander-in-chief.

The young major settled down to the pleasant routine of an American army officer in Mexico. The Americans were received on the whole with respect. He began going into society. He rose at nine and had a cup of chocolate, brought to his bed by a Mexican peasant girl. He dressed and went to his company drill. He was then at leisure.

His letters to his sister—who had by this time been married to a Mr. Arnold—tell us what he did with his leisure. He cultivated the society of his brother officers, and he was received, he said, by some of the best families of the city. The manners of the Spanish Americans charmed him; but they were, he felt, barbarians, very backward and corrupt. His sister was shocked at the money he spent, but the young major replied that he had to appear as a gentleman if he expected to be received as one. Sunday evenings he danced with the lovely señoritas. There was one whom he fell in love with. He decided not to see her again. Mexico was a place where an innocent man could find innocent pleasure, or an ambitious man his fortune, but somehow one should not be drawn deeply into its life. No Christian should; and young Jackson, who could dance on Sunday because he had not yet found a rule against it, because he had no doctrine, was a Christian. Protestants only were Christians. His Protestant blood flowed steady in his veins.

He wrote letters describing the architecture of the country, the habits of the people, their dress; and he wrote one very solemn, very literary letter to his brother-in-law, whom he addressed in literal conformity to the best etiquette as Dear Sir, in which he catalogued nearly every object and custom that he had observed. Major Jackson probably understood little he saw (the young backwoodsman thought the Mexicans barbaric), but he saw everything. He could have *used* his observations to advantage.

He learned Spanish. He read, in Spanish, Humboldt's History of Mexico; he read Chesterfield's letters in Spanish. The tongue might be useful—if he made up his mind to try his fortune in Mexico—and it would be a mark of cultivation at home. He took his self-imposed tasks with great seriousness; he did them well.

He was beginning to be serious about religion; he was eager to find out the truth; and as his attitude became more and more definite—it did rapidly after he had come to Mexico—he devoted the same ponderous energy to the Catholic Church as he had given to his studies at West Point. He was trying to find out what he thought about the God who had at first disappointed him and then awarded him "distinction." He decided, after living in a monastery for some weeks, after discussing points of doctrine with the Archbishop of Mexico, that he did not think as the Catholics did. He must look further.

Then, at last, after nine months in Mexico, the major was ordered home. The Mexican War was over; the United States had got, by the victory, vast territories. Jackson thought not much about it. He had done his duty, and he arrived at Governor's Island, in August 1848, a distinguished young officer. But there was nothing for him to do. As a soldier he was probably distinguished as he would ever be; an army post, as he knew, was a sterile place. He said little, but he did not like it.

VI

THE PROFESSOR

MAJOR JACKSON was now sent to Fort Hamilton on Long Island. It was a small military post. There was nothing to be done there except to perform the light duties of drill and of making reports to superior officers. Jackson was still subordinate to his old commander Taylor, who was now a colonel. Colonel Taylor was an old-fashioned Virginian, who was probably more pious than the generation of his grandfather had been, and less given to cock-fighting and horse-racing. With the colonel, the young major passed his dull time discussing points of religious doctrine. He was already very religious. His health was not good; the hypochondria that had settled upon him had turned his mind inwards. But he knew his mind so well that he couldn't make it up in a hurry.

At last he "applied for baptism" in the Episcopal Church of Fort Hamilton. It was understood that he was not obligated to join that particular Church at any time. He merely wanted to be sure of being a Christian. And a Protestant. He believed that Catholicism was anti-Scriptural.

Time passed: it was almost two years since he had come back from Mexico. The excitement of the war

was over, and so was the small fame of Major Thomas
J. Jackson. And at about this time a most interesting illusion took shape in his mind. Doubtless much
of his desire for personal distinction rose in the dis-
crepancy between his inherited family pride and the
poverty that had humbled his branch of the Jackson
family. The Jacksons of western Virginia had been
respectable people; they still were. Thomas Jackson's
illusion made it out that the whole family had gone into
a decline: it thus became his self-imposed duty to restore
it. As a matter of fact, the Jacksons, more numerous
now than at the time Thomas' grandfather Colonel
Edward was alive, held more positions of honor than
ever before. While Thomas Jackson was at Fort Hamilton his kinsman William Jackson was elected to the
Virginia Constitutional Convention. The major com-
mented on it in a letter to a relative:

> Indeed, I have some hopes that our ancient reputation
> may be revived.

If Major Jackson should happen to live to the year
1900, he will see a whole people, some of them deprived
of their birthright, but all of them sorely afflicted with
the delusion of ancient grandeur.

From Fort Hamilton Jackson was transferred to
Fort Meade, near Tampa Bay on the west coast of
Florida. Fort Meade he liked even less than he had
liked Fort Hamilton. His health there was no better
than it had been. He became more and more restless.

In the Valley of Virginia, in 1839, the Virginia Military Institute had been founded. It was modeled upon West Point. The instruction, the equipment, and the discipline were of a high order. In the same town— the small market town of Lexington—stood the halls of Washington College. Here young Major Daniel Hill was an instructor. He had heard that the Military Academy needed a new professor, that Major Thomas Jackson was being considered for the place. He went over to the Academy and urged the appointment of the young officer whom he had met four years ago at Point Isabel.

Other men than Jackson were being considered too— McClellan, Reno, Gustavus Smith, Rosecrans. But Jackson was appointed. On March 27, 1851, he became Professor of Natural and Experimental Philosophy and Artillery Tactics. He got the place because his record in the Mexican War had been impressive. Besides this he was a Virginian. Some one asked him if he were not afraid to try to teach such advanced subjects—he had been away from his West Point studies so long. He answered:

"I can always keep a day or two ahead of the class. I can do whatever I will to do."

When Jackson took the position, he believed if war ever came he would have a better chance for distinction by getting out of the army in time of peace than by staying in. His academic work would give him a chance to increase his information and to develop his intellectual power. Jackson reported to Lexington for duty in July, 1851.

The young professor had severe ideas of military

and intellectual discipline. The boys did not like him.
They saw no use being so exact about everything. A
citizen of Lexington said that Major Jackson was as
"exact as the multiplication table and full of things
military as an arsenal." He was in his twenty-seventh
year; but the boys called him "Old Jack."

On August 4, 1853, he married Miss Eleanor Junkin, daughter of the President of Washington College.
A year later she had a still-born child, and died.

The major's habits became very familiar to the citizens of Lexington. He amused them. He was not
aware of this. He was aware of his duty only. One day
when the weather had become intolerably warm and
the cadets and the other instructors appeared in summer uniforms, Major Jackson appeared in the class-
room in the heavy woolen garb of a soldier dressed for
a winter campaign. Some of the boys asked him why
he didn't make himself more comfortable. He replied:
"I have received no order not to change my uniform,
but then I have received no order to change it, and
until I do I will go as I am." One winter evening when
snow covered the ground and it was bitter cold, the
Superintendent of the Academy sent word to Jackson
that he wanted to see him in his office. Jackson arrived
precisely on time; he was asked to sit down. Then the
Superintendent, remembering something he had to do,
rose and told Jackson to remain seated until he returned.
The worthy Superintendent meant to be gone only a
few minutes but he got into conversation with some
people and forgot all about Jackson. It was very late
when he remembered him. He supposed Jackson had

waited a reasonable time and gone home. But coming into his office next morning, he saw Jackson sitting bolt upright in the same chair as he had sat in the night before. Major Jackson interpreted the Superintendent's polite request that he remain seated for a few minutes, as a military order for him to remain there until he was relieved. Major Jackson never disobeyed an order.

In the summer of 1856 he sailed for Europe. He went to France and England. He looked at pictures, at cathedrals; he did his duty by all the historical places. He was improving his mind. The young backwoodsman who had thought the Mexicans barbaric because of their religion could not have thought the Europeans less so because of their art. But there was one thing he really understood. He understood the battlefields. He was a close student of Napoleon's "Maxims of War." He went over every foot of the field of Waterloo. Major Jackson knew that wars were not all won by bravery. They were won by intelligence.

On July 16, 1857, Major Jackson took him another wife. She was Miss Mary Anna Morrison, of North Carolina, whose sister had married Major Daniel Hill. His home life in Lexington now really began. His house was run like a battalion of artillery. There was a time for everything and everything had its place. The major was up before seven to get the household to family prayers as that hour struck. The servants had to be there too. If anybody was missing when prayers began he forewent their benefit. After prayers he had breakfast. From eight to eleven he taught his classes.

He was not a very good teacher; he had a perfect mastery of his subjects, but he could understand them only in one way. If a pupil struggled to get hold of a problem in a way that had not occurred to the major, the major could only repeat it over again as he understood it himself. (Jackson had written: "Not only the same end must be proposed, but the same means approved.") At eleven o'clock he walked briskly home. For two hours he pored over his books, standing at a high desk so that his discomfort would make him attentive. He read the Bible and made notes; then he studied his texts; he not only understood what he read; his visual memory was so retentive and accurate that, finishing a book, he knew every word of it by heart. He read widely in history. He knew every movement of Napoleon's principal campaigns.

He lunched at one. After lunch he took a long walk. He walked very fast. Suddenly he stopped; he raised his left hand to the level of his eyes, the palm turned to the front. He seemed to be looking at something far away. Then, suddenly as he had stopped, he resumed his walk. Sometimes he went to work with the negroes on his farm. He was not still ruled by English ideas; he worked with his hands.

His eyes grew weak; he could no longer read by lamplight. He spent his evenings, two hours of them, staring at the wall. He rehearsed the materials of his study for the day. He developed great power in the holding of complex, interrelated quantities before his mind. Chess-players have this power, and great strategists.

He became a member of the Presbyterian church, then a deacon. He took his duties very seriously. He started a negro Sunday School; he taught it himself. If his pupils were not on time, they didn't get in. After a while they were always on time. The major was very much interested in the negroes. His own were part of his family. He had bought one slave to get him out of the hands of an unworthy master. If Major Jackson met on the street a gray-headed negro who lifted his hat to him, the major took off his in return, making a most respectful bow.

The major had not outgrown his awkwardness in society. He couldn't speak in public, but he wanted to learn how; he had no doubt of his ability to learn. He joined the Franklin Society of Lexington, which met for debating; he asked to be put on the programme; and he worked very hard preparing his debate. He knew it perfectly; he could probably have said it backwards.

The Society was assembled. It was Major Jackson's turn to speak. He rose and stood behind his chair. He began to speak. . . . He spoke two or three sentences, and stopped. . . He began to speak over again; when he got to where he had stopped before he stopped again. He repeated this three or four times. . . . He could not get beyond the unhappy word. But he showed no embarrassment, no concern for the embarrassment of the audience. He walked round from behind his chair and sat down. He had done his duty; he had prepared his debate; he had learned it; he had been on time to the meeting of the society; he had

made an honest effort to speak. He would have preferred to succeed in his speech, but he was quite satisfied with having tried. He had sat down in full complacency. In a few minutes—as was his habit of recent
years when he had no particular duty to perform—he
fell sound asleep.

The citizens of Lexington made a simple judgment
upon the major's behavior. They thought he was a
crank at best; at worst a fool. The stories of his courage under fire they still heard, but even this was an eccentricity; it couldn't be real courage. Major Jackson was a man of small ability. His job as an unimaginative teacher of science suited his capacity; he
would never get further. A man who obeyed nothing
but rules, who told the literal truth about the smallest
matters, boring his neighbors, could never be a distinguished man. Why, one day he had walked in the rain
to a friend's house a mile away; in conversation he had
stated a fact inaccurately. He couldn't rest until he
had corrected the error. A mistake was a lie; it might
mislead.

In 1855 Major Jackson had refused to lend his
brother Wirt Woodson, then in Ohio, enough money to
buy some land. Whatever all his reasons may have been,
the reason he gave was a good one. He did not care to
invest in property that might be confiscated by the
State of Ohio. This would surely happen if there came
about a war between the sections. Calhoun had fore-
told such a war ten years ago.

The revolutionary party in the North was gaining in
power. The Abolitionists, as the most unreasonable

men were called, kept sending more and more pamphlets to the negroes. They held meetings and discussed the negro's wrongs. They helped runaway negroes get away to Canada. They openly disobeyed the laws of the United States. The Fugitive Slave Law required Northern men to return wandering Southern property to their owners. The Northern men refused. The case of a negro named Dred Scott, who had been taken by his owner to a Northern State, became famous. Scott asserted his freedom. The Supreme Court decided the case. It decided against Dred Scott. Still the North refused to obey the law. A political party was formed called the Republican Party. They were against slavery. They were ready to defy the Dred Scott Decision, which confirmed a law of the United States in an interpretation of the Constitution. These men were a minority but they talked and made a great deal of noise. The Southern people and even the Northern Democrats called them Black Republicans.

Even before the new Republican Party was formed in 1856—it was quite anti-republican because it came to believe in violence and tyranny—there had appeared a queer book by a lady named Harriet Beecher Stowe. Mrs. Stowe had never been in the South: she had spent a few days in Kentucky, just south of Cincinnati. Her book was a picture of Southern plantation life. It had great influence on the popular imagination of the North. It was very minute in detail. Somebody asked her how she knew about Southern life. She said she didn't need to know. She said God had given her all the scenes in a vision. Mrs. Stowe had come from New England,

where her theocratic ancestors had urged the selling of
the Indians into slavery. That was a kindness, they
had said. The Indians were practitioners of the Black
Art. In New England God was never wrong. The
name of Mrs. Stowe's book was *Uncle Tom's Cabin.*

There had been trouble in Kansas. When new western territory was opened up, immigrants from each
section scrambled wildly across the country to get
there first. If slaveholders got there in greater numbers
they controlled politics; the territory would later on
become a slave state. It was the idea of "squatter-sov-
ereignty." This would not happen if the Northern
men won the race. Kansas contained about equal numbers from both sections, and the struggle in Kansas
had amounted to a real civil war. Under the protection
of civil disorder a great many fanatics and scoundrels
had robbed and murdered the honest men who were
trying to set up the political order they believed in.
A man named John Brown had been the leader of a
gang of Abolitionist fanatics in Kansas. He had a
great many holy killings to his credit.

After he killed a slave owner he cut off his fingers; of
one "the skull was split open in two places. . . . A large
hole was cut in his breast, and his left hand was cut off,
except a little piece of skin on one side." "Without the
shedding of blood," Brown said, "there is no remission
of sins."

In the summer of 1859, supported by contributions
from the Abolitionists, he came east to strike at the
heart of the slave empire in Virginia. He had set up
a "provisional government"; he and his followers all

took fancy titles. On October 17th he led a party of twenty-two armed men from Maryland across the Potomac into Harper's Ferry, Virginia. He captured the town. He meant to use the Harper's Ferry arsenal as a base of operations. He wanted to arm the slaves with muskets or long-handled, sharp-bladed pikes; with these at a given time in the dead of night the slaves were to fall upon their masters and murder them. Brown believed it was right to do this. God had told him it was. Brown was from New England. Now the remarkable thing about men in New England was their equality. An illiterate fanatic like John Brown was as privy to God as the Reverend Lyman Beecher. But John Brown, as one of his biographers points out, stirred the whole continent to a great "spiritual questioning." At Harper's Ferry Brown added a few more murders to an already respectable list.

In New England, educated and ignorant alike believed in the same things. Men who had gone through the museum of European culture and then written respectable essays on the English poets, now saw nothing irregular in the antics of a homicidal maniac. But Lincoln said: "That affair corresponds in its philosophy with the many attempts. . . .at the assassination of kings and emperors." Lincoln was not a New Englander.

In the North men believed and came even more devoutly to believe, that the Civil War was fought by the South because the men of that section had got hold of a few mistaken ideas.

Brown had made an old engine-house his headquarters. He was soon surrounded and besieged. Militia companies arrived. After two days a company of marines, commanded by Colonel Robert E. Lee and Lieutenant J. E. B. Stuart, came from Washington. The marines took the engine-house by assault. Brown and six of his followers were captured, and were taken to the jail in Charlestown, Virginia, to await trial.

The whole state of Virginia was in great excitement. Brown was charged with murder, treason, and the attempt to incite a servile insurrection. People in the North thought he was a hero. If he were sentenced trouble might be expected. The jail at Charlestown was put under a heavy guard. Major Jackson took a company of his cadets to Charlestown to form part of the guard. Brown was convicted and executed.

A few months later, early in 1860, Jackson spent a few days in Washington. He wrote home to his wife: "What do you think about the state of the country? I think we have great reason for alarm."

VII

TO ARMS!

THERE was reason for alarm. The reason grew stronger as the spring of 1860 came and went. In May, Abraham Lincoln was nominated for the Presidency on the Republican Ticket. Lincoln was not well-known. He was called the rail-splitter; he could bend an iron poker between his fingers; he had been to Congress; he had debated with Stephen A. Douglas; he could tell, so in the South the rumor went, amusing dirty stories. He had two ideas—his character proved to be greater than any idea he had—and they were the Union and the restriction of slavery to its present limits. There was little Abolitionism in him. He believed in the Union because he was a Westerner; the Western States were parasitical communities, looking to the East economically and spiritually. They could not believe in the right of secession; they could have no desire to cut themselves off from the section they depended on— New England. He believed slavery was wrong, without being fanatical about it. The idea was a part of the atmosphere he lived in. This atmosphere was beginning to be charged with commerce and industry. Commerce and industry required a different kind of slave. He would be a better slave; he would have the illusion of freedom.

Lincoln's two ideas, if they came to power, meant revolution. The Northern revolutionists chose to interpret the Constitution through some mystical sense that had no exact correspondence with the letter of that document. "The spirit" (because it is irresponsible) "killeth; the letter giveth life." They interpreted it by abstract right. The South interpreted it historically, literally. This interpretation guaranteed the South a continuation of its historical rights. The North, as represented by the Republican Party, was not willing to stand by the Constitution. Secession was not revolution; it was Constitutionalism. People said that the South was about to break away from the government. In the North there was the underlying idea (even Lincoln had it), rationalized and given rhetorical dignity, of the "government" as a collection of public buildings, as a political machinery, that had for some obscure reason to be preserved. The South said that the only government was the Constitution, and that the North was about to tear it asunder. For Lincoln, with his two ideas, had been elected, on November 6, 1860, to the Presidency of the United States. Since the Revolution two nations had grown up; they could no longer pretend to be one. The "irrepressible conflict" was about to begin.

South Carolina seceded from the Union. This was on December 20th. The election of Lincoln was a virtual declaration of civil war upon the established order of the States. Other Southern States seceded in quick succession.

In Charleston harbor lay Fort Sumter. Major

Anderson continued to occupy it with "government" soldiers. Their presence there after December 20th confirmed the Northern declaration of war.

On February 4, 1861, a Convention of the seceded States met at Montgomery. They adopted a Constitution and they elected Jefferson Davis President. The border States still held out for the Union, hoping that some compromise might be found. Virginia was the most important border State. In temporizing, it did not repudiate the right of secession; it merely hoped that it might not have to use that right.

Governor Pickens of South Carolina had sent repeated warnings to the Northern rebels in Fort Sumter. The Confederates, commanded by General Beauregard, opened fire at sunrise on April 12, 1861. Major Anderson surrendered on the 13th. On the 15th Lincoln called for 75,000 volunteers to put down the "rebellion." No one need be deceived by the word. A revolution is not started by the party that fires the first shot; a revolution is a question of ideas.

It was now a living fact that the North was trying to destroy the social and political structure of the United States by force of arms. Virginia had made that structure two generations ago; she would stand by it now.

The whole state was alive with opinion. Virginia believed in the Union she had created. She had always upheld the right of secession; though she had not been the first to try to exercise it. In 1814, at the Hartford Convention, some New England States had threatened to secede. Virginia would not secede without thinking it over.

Lincoln's 75,000 men put an end to thought. Union opinion, which had been strong in Virginia, collapsed. There was one cry:

To arms! To arms!

Virginia passed an Ordinance of Secession on the 17th of April. Major Jackson argued all night with Doctor Junkin, president of Washington College and formerly his father-in-law. He was trying to convert him to State Rights. Doctor Junkin was not a Virginian. Major Jackson was. He dreaded war. He had seen war, and he called it the "sum of all evils." But he was a Virginian. He had only one decision to make. He said: "If I know myself, all I am and all I have is at the service of my country."

Just before Virginia seceded, some cadets had pulled down the Federal flag in the court-house yard at Lexington. There was still Union sentiment. Local militia restored the flag. Other cadets marched out to tear it down again. The authorities of the Academy recalled them. Feeling was high. Jackson addressed the cadets:

Soldiers, when they make speeches, should say few words, and speak them to the point. I admire, young gentlemen, the spirit you have shown in rushing to the defense of your comrades; but I must commend even more the readiness with which you listened to the counsel and obeyed the commands of your superior officer. The time may come when your State will need your services; and if that time does come, then draw your swords and throw away the scabbards.

The hour had come. Jackson had lately suggested to his pastor, Dr. White, the idea that war might be averted if all the Christians of the two sections could be prevailed upon to unite for a day or two in prayer. The plan was not put into effect; we cannot say if it would have succeeded. It was too late now even for prayer. The war had come. Jackson said: "Why should the peace of a true Christian be disturbed by anything man can do unto him? Has not God promised to make all things work together for good to those who love him?"

Jackson was one of those unusual men who are superior to circumstances. For ten years he had been superior to the obscurity of his life as a professor. He would be superior to the fullest achievement of his ambition.

On April 21st Major Jackson led a battalion of cadets to Richmond. On March 6th, two days after Lincoln's inauguration, Davis had called for 100,000 volunteers. On the 17th, the day Virginia had seceded, he had issued a call for 32,000. About 300,000 all over the Southern States had answered the two calls. Only a few had been accepted. The supply of muskets, of ammunition, of uniforms, of war materials of all kinds was meagre. Many of the men who had been mustered in were armed with old-fashioned fowling-pieces or flintlocks. There were plenty of competent field-officers to command these men, but they could not be spared to teach the rank and file how to drill. Major Jackson's cadets were going to Camp Lee, near Richmond, to drill the thousands of raw recruits that were pouring into Richmond from all parts of the south.

The major had received his orders without a moment's notice. April 21st was Sunday. Major Jackson, who would not mail a letter on Sunday, preferred not to engage in secular business on that day. But he always obeyed orders. On Sunday morning his cadets were ready to move.

He was very busy but he was very calm. At one o'clock his boys were to begin their march to Staunton, where a train awaited them. Jackson asked Doctor White to come over and offer a prayer at the parting ceremony. In the midst of his duties he walked quietly home to say good-bye to his wife. In their bedroom they knelt together; they prayed. Then he read from the Bible:

> For we know that if our earthly house of this tabernacle be dissolved, we have a building of God, a house not made with hands, eternal in the Heavens.

He rose and left his house. He never entered it again.

Doctor White purposely closed the religious service fifteen minutes before the time set for the departure. A subordinate officer asked Jackson if they had better not start at that moment. It was ten minutes to one. Jackson pointed to the clock. He shook his head. He was a humorless, unimaginative man, exact as the multiplication table. When the clock struck one, he called out: "Forward, march!"

Arrived in Richmond, the cadets were distributed where they were most needed. Jackson was without a command. He had not a provisional rank in either the Confederate Armies or the Army of Virginia. He was given little attention. Most people had never heard

of him; except for a few, those who knew him thought
he might command a company, possibly a regiment. He
did not seem to be very military. He uttered no bomb-
bast; he spoke little of himself; and he wore no military
regalia.

For a few days he was given a desk job in the En-
gineering Corps. Many people thought that was what
he should do—a compass and ruler were just the thing
for an unimaginative man. A map would give him a
chance to exercise his talent for dull exactitude.

He had accepted the work, but all the time he was
looking for a better place. He had a few friends in
the Virginia Assembly and in other public offices, who
believed in him; and they were working in his behalf.
On April 26th he wrote to his wife:

> Last night Governor Letcher handed me my commission as
> Colonel of Virginia Volunteers, the post I prefer above all
> others, and has given me an independent command. Little
> one, you must not expect to hear from me very often, as I
> expect to have more work than I ever had in the same time
> before.

The independent command was the post at Harper's
Ferry. By the last of April about 1000 men from several States had been gathered there under the command
of General Harper. Harper held his commission in
the Virginia Militia, not from the Confederate government.

Harper's Ferry was the gateway to the Shenandoah
Valley from the North; it had to be guarded. The
machinery of the arsenal had already been sent to Rich-

mond to be used for the making of Confederate rifled muskets.   Forces were gathering elsewhere—at Manassas Junction, to protect the Orange and Alexandria Railroad; at Aquia Creek to hold the Richmond and Fredericksburg Railroad.   Manassas gave the Confederates "interior lines"; using the railroads, they could quickly rush their scattered troops to a threatened point on the line.   Besides the road from Manassas to Gordonsville through Orange Court House, another ran over to Front Royal in the Valley.   It was called the Manassas Gap Railroad.   General Beauregard, the "hero" of Fort Sumter, was in command of the main Confederate army gathering at Manassas.   (See map, p. 115.)

Jackson went to Harper's Ferry the first week in May.   Military affairs at Harper's Ferry were suffering from "the pomp and circumstance of glorious war".   General Harper and his staff, dressed in gold lace and mounted on fiery steeds, galloped every afternoon through the town, in the admiring view of the women and children.   There was hardly a man of the thousand who could present arms; there was hardly an officer who knew enough to tell him how to do it.   Colonel Jackson had orders to supersede General Harper in the command.

The general and his militia officers were enraged.   Officers like them throughout the south were enraged.   All men in the militia above the rank of captain had been reduced.   The Confederate government—one of the wisest things it ever did—was filling their places with all the trained soldiers it could get.

The soldiers at Harper's Ferry were not much impressed with Jackson. He wore no gold lace. He still had on the dingy blue uniform of a professor in the Virginia Military Institute. He wore his old cadet cap pulled down in a very unmilitary fashion over his eyes, so that the vizor almost touched his nose. He issued no manifestoes; he made no speeches in which he pointed out that all Yankees were cowards; and he held no parades for the women and children. He told nobody his plans; so people thought he hadn't any. He issued a few orders from his ill-furnished headquarters on the second floor of a small hotel.

Within a week the garrison of Harper's Ferry took on new life. The men were learning how to drill, the captains of companies to manoeuvre them. The commanding officer did not feel himself above giving the minutest instructions to men in the ranks. He was patient with ignorance; he was implacable with unwillingness to learn. The men learned quickly, for they were intelligent.

But in general it was hard to find officers. The Virginians thought it a greater honor to serve in the ranks. There was one company at Harper's Ferry in which more than a third of the rank and file were expert in Latinity but ignorant of war.

Colonel Jackson wrote very few letters to his wife. She had gone to North Carolina. There was not much chance that the Yankees would be able to capture a letter sent to North Carolina. But he would run no risk even when there was no risk to be run. When he wrote her—she had asked for news—he told her there was no news, at least none that he would send. He told her how he felt, or that he loved her, or exhorted her to renewed fervor in prayer. Once he described the roses blooming at the window of his temporary quarters, saying he often looked up at them from his work—"but my sweet little sunny face is what I want to see most of all."

New companies came to Harper's Ferry and new regiments, until in a few weeks the colonel had about four thousand men. He was busy trying to give the raw troops discipline. They were hard to discipline. For they were free men; they had been brought up to believe in personal liberty. Many came from large plantations; others, from small farms; all of them intensely felt their independence. A majority of them were not slaveholders at all; they were fighting for their country, for the principle of local self-government that for generations had given them their independence. They were fighting for State Rights.

Meanwhile the Federal Army had been quickly approaching something like organization. Besides the 75,000 men Lincoln had called for in April, there were 65,000; the Yankees now had about 150,000 men. 80,000 of them were being stationed in the East. The main Federal Army was being gathered and trained at Washington under Brigadier-General Irvin McDowell. This army was meant to form a column for the invasion of Virginia through Manassas Junction to Richmond, which had recently become the Southern capital. Manassas was only thirty miles from Washington. Another army, under Major-General Patterson, lay near

Chambersburg, Pennsylvania, two days' march from Harper's Ferry. Neither of these armies up to the middle of May had shown any sign of advancing. But on the 24th McDowell sent a detachment across the Potomac to occupy Arlington Heights, which commanded the city of Washington.

The Confederates under Beauregard had been thinking too much about defense to take this important point. From the beginning President Davis didn't want the South to win its own war; he wanted it to act upon a noble and martyred defensive, so that Europe might be moved to intercede. In 1860 the South had $500,-000,000 worth of baled cotton. It was never exported. It would have given the South more cash to run the war on than the North had. A false set of values got into the head of the Confederate President at the start. He wasn't a revolutionist, but he proceeded with revolutionary psychology; he didn't want to give the appearance of waging an offensive war, a war of aggression. An offensive war would have meant only a suppression of the Northern revolutionists; it wouldn't have been a war of aggression at all. Washington should have been occupied by the Southerners as their own capital, as the capital of the United States, before the Northern revolutionists could put Lincoln there and get their country up in arms. The South should have done many things it did not do. It is easy now to see what the South should have done.

Colonel Jackson spent most of his time drilling his recruits, getting in stores, collecting muskets and horses, and seeing—so unorganized at that early period was the Confederate Ordnance Department—seeing himself that cartridges were made for his men. But sometimes he would ride out to places east and west of Harper's Ferry. He usually rode alone, or with a single staff officer. He instructed his men not to recognize him. If the Yankees, across the river, found out that Colonel Jackson was reconnoitering a position, they would think it valuable because he did, and might start useless trouble.

The Baltimore and Ohio ran by Harper's Ferry and it would have been a great strategical feat to destroy it. But the allegiance of Maryland was in doubt; it was not wise for the Confederates to destroy property upon which the commerce of that State depended.

But the South needed cars and engines. One day Colonel Jackson sent a message to the president of the railroad saying the coal trains passing Harper's Ferry day and night disturbed the rest of his troops. The president, remembering his tracks had not been torn up, was eager to please the colonel. He arranged to have all trains, going in both directions, pass between eleven and one. Jackson headed them all off, took the cars and engines, and sent them to Winchester. Teams of horses and mules pulled them over the dirt road.

This was Jackson's sole exploit at Harper's Ferry before he was relieved of the command by General Joseph E. Johnston, the able officer who had been in charge of the Richmond forces. Johnston was needed at the front. When he got to Harper's Ferry, Jackson at first would not give over the command; he had received no orders to do so! But he saw by chance an order in which General Lee referred to Johnston as his successor. He immediately yielded.

It was Johnston's purpose to wait on the defensive. He was committed to the President's defensive policy, not for political reasons but because he was a cautious officer. He proposed to fall back from Harper's Ferry to Winchester. The Ferry, he said, could not be held against assault. By the 8th of May Johnston had 11,000 men. But even these could not hold the post against Patterson's 14,000, should that general attack. Patterson would not attack; he thought Johnston had 32,000 men; but Johnston didn't know this.

On the 8th of June all the State troops were mustered into the Confederate Army. The regiments were organized into brigades. When Johnston arrived Jackson hoped he would be given another independent command in western Virginia, his native section, where the Yankees, under General McClellan, were getting control of his people. But he was retained in the Valley Army, still subordinate to Johnston. He was given the command of the First Brigade.

All the men in his brigade were Virginians. It was the only all-Virginia brigade in the Army of the Shenandoah. There were five regiments.

At this time he was using every influence to get promotion. He wrote a remarkably candid letter to one of his political friends at the capital. Next day, he wrote a second letter—fearing the first might get lost in the mails!

On June 15th Johnston fell back from Harper's Ferry to Winchester. Across the Potomac a high bluff

called Maryland Heights looked down upon Harper's
Ferry. Across the Shenandoah, to the east, Loudoun
Heights, a high wooded mountain, commanded the town.
Jackson thought Harper's Ferry should be held, for
moral effect upon the South, with the spirit of the
Greeks at Thermopylae; so did Lee, who despatched
his opinion from Richmond. It is hard to see any tactical reason. But from the outset Jackson and Lee
had one mind.

Johnston left the First Brigade at Harper's Ferry
to observe the movements of General Patterson. He
thought the leader of this brigade could be depended
upon. On the 20th of June Jackson marched westward
to Martinsburg, and burnt the Baltimore and Ohio
shops.

At the end of ten days it was obvious that the Federals meant to advance all along the line. McDowell's
army was getting ready; the Northern politicians and
newspapers were crying it on. And Patterson was cautiously feeling his way into Virginia.

On July 2nd he crossed the Potomac at Williamsport. Johnston pushed the main body of his army up
to Darksville, half-way from Winchester to Williamsport. Jackson led the advance and at Falling Waters
he deployed about 300 men against the head of Patterson's column. There were a few men killed and
wounded on each side. Jackson captured about 40
prisoners. Patterson recrossed the Potomac and wired
General Scott that the Confederates had attacked him
with 3,500 men. Patterson thus became merely a
ghostly menace to the Army of the Shenandoah: one

skirmish at Falling Waters, and the ghost was laid. And General Scott was depending upon Patterson to keep Johnston interested, so that McDowell could crush, with 40,000 men, Beauregard's 20,000 Confederates at Manassas. Patterson was to keep Johnston from joining the main army, from using the "interior lines".

On July 3rd Colonel Jackson received from General Lee the commission of brigadier-general. The small success the day before, at Falling Waters, had nothing to do with it. It was politics: Jackson had repeatedly urged his friends in Richmond to get him promoted, and they had succeeded.

Johnston's army went back to Winchester, where the men had two weeks of hard drilling. They were not hard to discipline in this way—after they got into their heads the necessity of it. But there was very little saluting of officers. There was too much social equality between the privates and officers for that.

On July 15th General Patterson tightened up his nerve and advanced to Bunker Hill, nine miles from Winchester, where he lost it again. He turned off to Charlestown two days later. There was nothing to fear of him for a week or two at least.

Meanwhile, all through July, General Beauregard had been getting information from Washington. On July 4th his outposts had captured a courier bearing despatches that exposed the numbers with which McDowell might soon be expected to attack him. They were roughly 50,000. He had 20,000. There was a very remarkable secret service, too, that supplied the

Confederates with the innermost thoughts of people
high in the Federal command. The most important
person in this service was a Mrs. Greenhow, a respectable Southern woman who had the confidence of senators, cabinet members, army officers. The Federal
plans, from hour to hour, from day to day, she reported
by cipher to Beauregard. She lived within musket
shot of the White House.

On the morning of July 16th there appeared at her
house a strange man. He handed her a piece of paper
which bore two words in cipher: *Trust Bearer.* Mrs.
Greenhow immediately wrote out, in a code that she
alone in Washington could understand, the message:

> Order issued for McDowell to march upon Manassas
> tonight.

The strange man took the message, got a horse and
buggy, and drove down the east bank of the Potomac
until he came to a certain ferry. There he crossed the
river and delivered the message to a waiting cavalryman.
It was in General Beauregard's hand by nine o'clock
that night. The general sent out orders to his pickets
to fall back from Fairfax Court House and Centerville
to the line of Bull Run.

General Beauregard wired President Davis, urging
him to send the Army of the Shenandoah to his support. This was on the morning of the 17th. President
Davis had had the chance to know as much about war
as any politician of his time; he had commanded troops
in the field, after graduating from West Point, and
he had been Secretary of War under Pierce. His

knowledge of war enabled his personal pride to keep him from realizing he knew nothing of it. He wired, after waiting fifteen hours, timid and uncertain *advice* to General Johnston. If McDowell's army had been organized and efficient, it could have destroyed Beauregard's by the time Johnston got his permission to help him. He never got orders; he got permission. Events in the next few days would have been different had not General Johnston's character been superior to his circumstance.

After midnight of the 17th General Johnston issued orders to his army to march south from Winchester. The march began at dawn. Jackson's brigade took the lead. The men were very quiet. They didn't know where they were going. They were low-spirited because they thought they were leaving the enemy behind. The column of nearly 9,000 men in bright new uniforms, mostly gray but some of them blue, spun out on the road for seven miles. (See map, p. 115.)

A few miles south of Winchester the head of the column could see, to the east, the long smooth back of the Blue Ridge. Ten miles away, southwards, the beetling forehead of Massanutten stuck out of the rolling valley of the Shenandoah. Jackson's men thought they were marching towards Massanutten to the right, up the Valley Turnpike; they thought they were retreating. Suddenly the column was halted. The regimental officers along the line read a general order:

Our gallant army under General Beauregard is now attacked by overwhelming numbers. The General Commanding

hopes that his troops will step out like men, and make a
forced march to save the country.

The column turned east towards Ashby's Gap.

All day in the hot July sun the Confederates marched.
Their well-shod feet kicked the dust up in clouds. Their
feet fried in the dust. Some of the men shouted; some
sang. People along the road cheered them, ran out
with buckets of water and baskets of food. Old women
wept. Young girls in hoops waved handkerchiefs.
General Jackson rode at the head of his brigade, on
a little sorrel horse. He said nothing. The men
marched steadily on.

General Beauregard knew that the army from the
Valley had set out for Manassas on the morning of
the 18th. He didn't think it would arrive in time to
save him from defeat. By the morning of the 18th Mc-
Dowell's whole army had passed through Fairfax
Court House; it was concentrated at Centreville, three
miles from the fords of Bull Run, the line of Confederate defense.

With the Federal Army had come a mob of specta-
tors and adventurers. Congressmen and senators had
driven thirty miles to see the "rebels" defeated, captured, perhaps hanged on the spot. Sutlers had come
with their wares priced high. Pickpockets slid in and
out through the crowd. Fancy-women, in pairs, stood
on corners in the village. Ladies in fine dresses and
plumes sat in their carriages.

General McDowell was hopeful. General Scott had
promised him that Patterson would not let Johnston

get out of the Valley: with this understanding McDowell had undertaken the campaign. On the morning of
the 18th Johnston had not arrived. McDowell did not
know he had started. Colonel J. E. B. Stuart, of the
Confederate Cavalry, fooled Patterson, from the 18th
to the 20th, into believing Johnston was still at Winchester. Patterson telegraphed General Scott that
Johnston (with his 32,000 men!) was still before him.
The Yankees under McDowell had great hopes of
success.

On the morning of the 18th McDowell sent Tyler's
division to feel out the Confederates at Blackburn's and
Mitchell's Fords. Tyler advanced Richardson's brigade
to Blackburn's Ford. Richardson fought a small battle
with Longstreet's brigade and was driven back. One
regiment was routed and demoralized. Both sides exaggerated the importance of the engagement, and Beauregard's men thought it was a great battle, which they
had won. The Yankees, rank and file, felt they had
been severely repulsed. General McDowell decided he
couldn't send a raw army to a frontal attack across a
deep creek against abattis and intrenchments. For the
Confederates held in force every ford of Bull Run on a
line eight miles long.

McDowell intended to wait a few days to look over
the ground. Many of his undisciplined men had thrown
away their rations, and he had to wait till their haversacks could be filled. Transportation was slow. All
organization was muddled. But he meant now to attack one of the Confederate flanks. By the night of the
18th he had already decided that the Confederate right

flank, at Union Mills, was too well protected by woods
and bad roads; he would attack the left side of his
enemy's line at the Stone Bridge or above.

All day, on the 18th, the Confederates of Johnston's army marched. Before them, rising like a great
wall, stood the Blue Ridge running northeast and southwest beyond vision. As the hours passed it rose higher
and higher. Then at dusk the head of Jackson's column
stepped into the green water of the Shenandoah; the
tall Valley Virginians stepped in to their armpits and
waded across. Now they were at Ashby's Gap. In an
hour they were going on a winding road down the slope
into eastern Virginia. Twenty miles away rose another
range. It was Bull Run Mountain, running north and
south from the headwaters of Bull Run, which, they
knew, flowed southeast. Twenty miles the other side
of Bull Run Mountain lay their comrades, confronting
the Yankees under General McDowell. They were
almost too late.

After midnight the First Brigade halted at the village
called Paris. The men, worn out, stacked arms and
fell asleep by the roadside. A staff-officer reminded
Jackson that he had not ordered out a sentry for the
night. Jackson said:

"Let the poor fellows sleep. I will guard the camp
myself."

All night he walked round the camp.

VIII

THE STONE WALL

EARLY next morning the First Brigade took the lead again. The sun had risen in a clear sky. The men at the head of the column could look back up the road; far as they could see, the glittering rifles of their comrades wound back endlessly into the mountains.

Half-way from Paris to Piedmont, Colonel J. E. B. Stuart, who had fooled Patterson long enough, rode by the First Brigade at the head of his cavalry regiment.

The colonel smiled and waved his hat. His hat, broad-brimmed and shallow-crowned, was fawn-colored; a dark brown ostrich plume dangled from the left side; the right side of the brim was pinned with a gold star to the crown. His coat was gray; the collar and cuffs were white serge and the sleeves were ornamented with gold braid. His riding gauntlets were a spotless white. He rode a large, spirited horse.

All along the column of the First Brigade Colonel Stuart yelled out his greeting to men he recognized. Or he joked with an old friend. When he smiled he showed his even white teeth; his eyes lit up and the blood rose in his cheeks. Under the full brown beard his skin was soft and pink as a baby's. Colonel Stuart was a daring, careless fellow. He feared neither man nor devil, but he feared God. He was pious; he neither swore nor drank.

Stuart's dashing horsemen vanished in a cloud of dust. Jackson's foot-soldiers trudged on. At eight o'clock they halted at Piedmont, a station on the Manassas Gap Railroad just below the slopes of the Blue Ridge. Crowds of people had gathered to see them. The crowds cheered. The soldiers climbed into the empty box cars, or let their legs dangle over the side of flat-cars; some got up on the cow-catcher of the engine.

Baskets of food and jars of milk the people gave the soldiers. Negro women came through the crowd, balancing trays of fried chicken on their heads. Some of the young people sang popular songs. Near the station an old man was down on his knees, praying. Four or five little niggers stood by, wondering. They looked very serious.

Then the train started. Only the infantry were on the train. The artillery, the cavalry, the ammunition and supply wagons kept up the march by road.

At four o'clock in the afternoon of July 19th Jackson's brigade of the Army of the Shenandoah arrived at Manassas Junction. The throngs of onlookers crowded in and milled like cattle at the station. Sisters and wives and mothers of the volunteers were looking for their men.

Jackson's brigade marched north on the road to Mitchell's Ford, about four miles away. There was the 2nd Virginia, led by Colonel J. W. Allen; Colonel J. F. Preston's 5th Virginia was in line; and the 27th Virginia under Lieutenant-Colonel John Echols; then the gallant Colonel Kenton Harper, who had been a general in gold lace, now a brave regimental commander, with his 5th Virginia; under Colonel A. C. Cummings the 33rd Virginia marched. Jackson's men came to a halt about a mile from Mitchell's Ford.

By the next afternoon, July 20th, three of General Johnston's four Shenandoah brigades were on the field. Brigadier-General Kirby Smith's brigade had not been able to get a train. There were rumors that a traitorous engineer had wrecked some cars so that the debris would block transportation. But, besides Jackson, General Barnard Bee was there with his men; General Bartow, with his. These three brigades, nearly eight thousand men, General Beauregard placed on the Bull Run line in reserve. Bee's and Bartow's men were stationed between McLean's and Blackburn's Fords, to support Jones and Early, who held the front line at McLean's, and to support Longstreet, who guarded Blackburn's. Jackson halted his men between Mitchell's and Blackburn's Fords, about a mile from each place. As night fell on the 20th of July, 1861, the Confederates had 29,000 men of all arms to meet the attack of 35,000 Federals.

But Beauregard, shortly after midnight, received news that made him decide to take the offensive himself. His scouts reported that McDowell was deploying his forces on the Warrenton Turnpike. It meant only one thing: the Yankees were about to attack his left flank by way of the Stone Bridge. Beauregard thought he would checkmate the movement by attacking McDowell's left flank, by way of the lower fords of Bull Run, where most of the Confederate army was concentrated. He issued orders for this attack at four-thirty in the morning. He expected two small brigades, under Colonels Cocke and Evans, to hold the Yankees in check at the Stone Bridge, while his main force advanced to Centreville and cut McDowell's communications with Washington. He hoped to destroy McDowell's base, and line up on his route of retreat.

Generals Ewell and Holmes, who held the extreme right of the Confederate line at Union Mills Ford, were supposed to march first; they had the farthest to go. The brigades at the center of the line, before Blackburn's, Mitchell's and McLean's Fords, where Jackson, Bee, and Bartow stood in reserve, had orders to follow the advance of Ewell. Johnston and Beauregard rode to the top of a hill behind Mitchell's Ford to see the Confederates advance to the attack. Its success depended upon its getting started before the Federal attack at the Stone Bridge had gone too far. It was now eight o'clock, July 21st.

Johnston and Beauregard kept on waiting. Nothing happened. Johnston thought Bee and Bartow and Jackson should reinforce Evans. He ordered them to march to the Stone Bridge.

Colonel Evans, since five o'clock, had been skirmishing with Tyler's Federal division at the Stone Bridge. He expected an overwhelming assault at any time, but by eight-thirty it hadn't come. Then suddenly he saw great clouds of dust rising north of the Warrenton Turnpike. The clouds rolled away from him towards Sudley Ford, five miles up Bull Run from the Stone Bridge. He believed the attack at the Stone Bridge to be a feint. The Yankees, he thought, were fooling him there, while they marched to the rear of the Confederate army. He left four of his ten companies at the Bridge, and marched across the Warrenton Turnpike to place himself on the line of Federal advance from Sudley Ford; then he deployed his small force on the crest of the Matthews Hill. This height commanded the road from Sudley. Behind him lay the valley of Young's Branch, a small creek flowing east into Bull Run. On the far side of Young's Branch, to the south, stood a high flat plateau called the Henry House Hill.

General Bee had, early in the morning, told his Captain of Artillery he was sorry to march away from the battle, which he was sure would be fought north of the fords where he and Jackson had been stationed at first. He had told Captain Imboden his men would have a good chance to eat and rest after their long march from the Valley.

Johnston and Beauregard still waited on their hill. It was now nine-thirty. Nothing happened. Their attack somehow was not coming off on time.

At nine forty-five the Yankees appeared before Evans, coming down the road from Sudley. Evans had about 600 men. The Yankees were about 12,000, with 24 cannon. Evans had 2 howitzers. The Yankees came out of the woods and formed for the attack in the open ground in front of the Matthews Hill. A fierce combat followed. But Evans held the Yankees in check for an hour.

Johnston and Beauregard still waited on their hill. General Bee, near the Stone Bridge, heard the increasing volleys of musketry and the roar of cannon away to the north across the Warrenton Turnpike. He marched to the sound of the guns. He gained, with his brigade and Bartow's, the summit of the Henry House plateau, and saw Evans' battle. He sent word to Evans to retreat to the Henry House Hill. Evans sent back word to Bee to reinforce him on the Matthews Hill. Bee advanced at once. But he advanced against his better judgment.

The fight on the Matthews Hill was now desperate. The volume of the firing had been increasing steadily for an hour. Jackson, impatient at the Stone Bridge a mile away, ordered his men to march in the direction of the battle. By eleven o'clock his brigade had reached the flat summit of the Henry House Hill. Instead of advancing his men to the northern edge of the summit, so as to receive the Yankees just as they got to the top, he drew them back to the southern edge, into a pine thicket. There, the Federal artillery could not reach him; if it came into sight, it would be only five hundred yards away; his infantry could shoot down the Yankee gunners before they fired. The First Brigade lined up just inside the stretch of pines. The battle kept raging a mile away. Soon it came nearer.

For, while Jackson's men were resting on their arms in the pines, General Heintzleman hurled two fresh brigades against Evans' and Bee's men. Outnumbered about five to one, their ranks depleted, the Confederates broke and fled in rout into the valley of Young's Branch, then up the slopes of the Henry House Hill. Most of them came up a shallow, wooded ravine to the east of the hill, and poured, panic-struck, into the open field beyond.

General Bee followed his defeated troops, vainly trying to stay the rout. All organization was lost; no man knew where his command was. The Yankees pressed on in pursuit. They were massing for a renewed assault in the rear, in the valley of Young's Branch.

Captain Imboden, with his guns, had been left behind. General Bee had told him to hold his position at the side of the Henry House, nearly two thousand feet in advance of the line that Jackson took, until he got orders to retreat. General Bee had sent the orders; they had been lost; the courier had been shot. At last Imboden's ammunition ran out. He limbered up, and retreated south over the plateau. He ran into Jackson taking position in the pines.

Captain Imboden explained his plight. He swore, saying General Bee had forgotten him. Jackson looked displeased at the swearing, but ignored it. He said:

"Unlimber right here. I will support your battery."

General Bee galloped by, shouting to his men. He rode up to Jackson.

"General, they are beating us back, they are beating us back."

Jackson was perfectly calm. He replied:

"Then, sir, we will give them the bayonet." His thin lips closed to a straight line.

Bee dashed off into the midst of two thousand yelling, panicky men. He waved his cap on his sabre. Riding up and down he pointed his sabre at Jackson and his men standing quiet and in order in the pines.   He shouted:

"Look there at Jackson standing like a stone wall. Rally behind the Virginians!"

By this time Johnston and Beauregard had heard sounds on their left flank that convinced them there was a battle in that quarter.   At eleven-thirty their attack on the right had not begun.   General Ewell, who was to lead the attack, had never received his orders. They immediately set off at a gallop for the scene of action.   They ordered Early and Bonham to follow them.

They got there just as Bee's men were trying to rally to their leader's shout.   The Federals had been successful.   They had surprised the Confederate left flank.   They had joined hands with the rest of their army at the Stone Bridge.   The Confederate left wing, only 6,500 men including the scattered regiments from the immediate rear, was almost annihilated.   The Federals were confident of victory.   They now had 16,000 men ready to cross the plateau.

There was a momentary lull.

Bee's men had begun to rally.   Beauregard rode up and down in front of the line cheering the men and calling to them to form line on their colors.   The Federals were now pouring in a heavy fire of shells and musketry.   The Confederates rallied just as the Yankees charged across the plateau.

McDowell, to encourage his infantry, had sent a battery up close to Jackson's pine thicket, on the left side of the Confederate line.   Colonel Stuart, without waiting for orders, with 150 horsemen charged the battery and took it.

In the struggle that came on for the possession of the Henry House Hill, this battery was taken and retaken three times. The carcasses of the horses, the splintered caissons stood as a challenge to both armies. On the bare plateau, between the fighting lines, men lay face down, motionless, sprawled in ungraceful postures; so casually prone that they might rise at any moment to rejoin the yelling devils a hundred yards away. Where Jackson's men waited the thick smoke and dust eddied into the pines. A salty sweet stink filled the air. Shells burst over their heads.

Jackson rode up and down. Here and there he called to his men.

"Steady, men. All's well. Steady, men."

Captain Imboden asked permission to take his battery to the rear. Fresh guns had come up. Jackson's face was composed. But his eyes blazed; the battle was just hot enough to make him feel right. He stared at Imboden, nodding his permission. He raised his left hand to the level of his eyes, the palm turned out. He jerked it down. Blood trickled from his finger. He pulled a spotless handkerchief out of his breast pocket and quickly tied it on his finger.

"It's only a scratch," he said. Then he wheeled and galloped off to the other end of his line.

After several charges the Yankees had got hold of most of the plateau. They outnumbered the Confederates now more than two to one. The Yankees were very brave men; they had never been in a battle before but they ran right up to the muzzles of the spitting rifles of the Confederates. They ran up in small groups; if their officers could have made them all come together they would have driven the Confederates down the southern slope of the hill. They were about to drive them anyhow. They were gathering on the left flank of the Confederates who had no men there to oppose them. The Confederates were being forced back.

A Confederate officer, hatless, his face plastered with dust and sweat, rode up to Jackson. Pointing to the Yankees gathering on the far side of the plateau for another charge, he shouted:

"General, the day is going against us."

"If you think so, sir," said Jackson, "you had better not say anything about it."

The Federals were now coming, firing as they ran. Jackson said to his men:

"Reserve your fire till they come within fifty yards, then fire and give them the bayonet. When you charge yell like furies."

It was now almost three o'clock. The time had come. Jackson's men had lain in the woods, peppered by shrapnel and bullets. When the Yankees came near they rose, and a sheet of flame burst out of the thicket. Then they yelled and rushed at the blue rebels. They stuck them with bayonets; they brained them with the butts of their muskets. The Yankees turned and fled across the plateau.

At the same moment to the left and rear of the Confederate line a column of 1,700 men were marching to the field. They moved in plain view of the Yankees.

The marching men had on blue uniforms. The Federals thought they were their men: they held their fire. Just as Jackson's men were pursuing the broken Yankees across the plateau, these new men fell upon the right flank of the Federal line. The new men were General Kirby Smith's missing brigade, just arrived from the Valley. The whole Federal army on the Henry House Hill broke, and ran down the northern slope.

A second line of battle, drawn up in the rear, could not bring them to order. McDowell ordered a general retreat. The Yankees marched off the field.

It was not yet a rout. A battery of the old Regular Army covered the withdrawal. The retreating Yankees poured in disorder over the Stone Bridge towards Centreville. It was not a rout until the Confederates began dropping shells in the confused mass of soldiers, pickpockets, supply wagons, elegant ladies, sutlers, Congressmen, that choked the road beyond Bull Run. Colonel Stuart's cavalry picked up prisoners and captured wagons, but his regiment was too small to do greater damage. The Yankees ran and fought one another to get away from a spectral enemy. Beyond Centreville Colonel Stuart did not dare pursue.

General Johnston sent orders to the brigades on the right to cross the creek and march to Centreville. Before they received this order he had heard a rumor that a large body of Yankees was advancing against the lower fords of Bull Run. As dusk fell, the body of Yankees turned out to be Jones' Confederate brigade, dressed in blue, coming back from an advanced position on the road to Centreville. All pursuit of the Yankees stopped.

The Yankees didn't know this. When they got to Centreville they rushed on, a frenzied mob, to Washington, thirty miles away. The fear-crazy men bringing up the chaotic rear sent forward rumors of "Cavalry! Cavalry!" and "Masked batteries!" There were neither. Fear drove the men on. McDowell's raw volunteers, by the morning of July 22nd, when they appeared at the Long Bridge over the Potomac, had marched more than forty-five miles.

Just as the Yankees were fleeing down the Henry House Hill, President Davis rode with his staff to the field. That night he talked with Beauregard and Johnston. He said nothing of pursuing the Federal Army; perhaps he didn't think it necessary. He seemed well satisfied. He congratulated his generals. He was a very dignified man. Had not the invader been driven back? Let's stand on a dignified defensive. If the Yankees return later it will not be our fault; we will have been virtuous.

While the Yankees were retreating over the Stone Bridge, Jackson went to his surgeon. As Major McGuire dressed his wound, Jackson, jerking his head excitedly, kept saying:

"Give me 10,000 men and I will be in Washington tomorrow morning."

In Washington on the morning of July 22nd "all was chaos and despondency; the city was filled with intoxicated stragglers, and an attack was expected. The troops were less than 50,000, many of whom were so demoralized and undisciplined that they could not be relied upon for defensive purposes. . . . Sufficient and fit material of war did not exist. The situation was difficult and fraught with danger."

President Lincoln was scared; he knew that the capture of Washington by the people he was pleased to call rebels would be the downfall of the North.

Jackson with 10,000 men could have ended the so-called Civil War. But who was Brigadier-General Jackson that he could ask for such a command? His men had fought well. Not all the officers of the Southern Army understood that Jackson, by his coolness, his superior tactical knowledge, his intellectual grasp of the relations existing at every moment among the complicated forces of the battle, had won it. General Beauregard thought *he* had won it. That kind of thinking was likely to become a habit with General Beauregard.

Jackson's had lost more heavily than any other brigade. 561 men of 2,500 had been killed or wounded. At nightfall he led the battered Stonewall Brigade back to its camp south of Mitchell's Ford. They had a well-earned rest.

Silence came down on the hot stench of the battlefield. Many of the officers and men, not receiving orders, celebrated the victory. There was whisky and apple brandy. There were pretty girls and dancing at houses near the field. The soldiers had picked up handcuffs the Yankees had dropped on the field. They were fine trophies.

Jackson got up at sunrise. Before breakfast he wrote a letter to his pastor in Lexington. A few days later Doctor White, recognizing Jackson's handwriting as he took the envelope out of the postoffice, said to some standers-by, that here was some real news of the great battle. He read:

In my tent last night, after a fatiguing day's service, I remembered that I had failed to send you my contribution to our colored Sunday School. Enclosed you will find my check for that object, which please acknowledge at your earliest convenience, and oblige

Yours faithfully,
T. J. JACKSON.

IX

WHAT WAS SAID AT FAIRFAX COURT HOUSE

THE capture of Washington seems now to be inevitable; during the whole of Monday and Tuesday it might have been taken without resistance. The rout, overthrow, and demoralization of the whole army were complete." The Monday and Tuesday to which Secretary of War Stanton referred were July 22nd and 23rd, the two days following the battle.

Through these two days and the next, General Jackson kept his men under arms and supplied with cooked rations for service in the field. He was awaiting the order to march. His brigade, as we have seen, had suffered more heavily than any other unit in the Confederate army. But it was ready to move. President Davis had not considered attacking Washington. But his generals, Johnston and Beauregard, cannot be excused on this ground. What their reasons were we shall never know. Later on Johnston asserted that the Confederates were "more demoralized by victory than the enemy was by defeat"; but if Jackson's battered troops, the day after the battle, were an example of the condition of the whole army, this assertion is false. There were 20,000 Confederates who had hardly fought in the battle at all. There were other excuses—the lack of transportation, the inadequate stores at Manassas Junction, the fortifications in front of Washington that barely existed. Besides the 20,000 men who had been only slightly engaged, Johnston, a few days after the battle, received 10,000 more. He had an army of nearly 40,000 men eager to move.

His army was badly organized. The officers were inexperienced. The men lacked discipline. All this was true. Jackson knew it as well as any other officer on the field. But he also knew the condition of the enemy. It was worse.

The orders to march did not come. On the third day he put his men in camp near Centreville. He was dissatisfied. But he said nothing. If Jackson exacted obedience and loyalty of his subordinates, he gave obedience and loyalty to his superiors. They did not ask his opinion. His opinion was not given. He went quietly about his duties.

On the morning of the third day after the battle Captain John Imboden came to breakfast in Jackson's quarters, a farm house near Centreville. He had been with Jackson when he received his wound; he had heard it was worse; he came to inquire after it. Mrs. Jackson was there. The battle was the only topic of discussion. Captain Imboden said:

"General, how is it that you can keep so cool, and appear so utterly insensible to danger in such a storm of shells and bullets as rained about your head when your hand was hit?"

Jackson looked very grave. He said:

"Captain, my religious belief teaches me to feel as safe in battle as in bed. God has fixed the time for my death. I do not concern myself about that, but to be always ready, no matter when it may overtake me."

After a pause he added:

"Captain, that is the way all men should live, and then all would be equally brave."

The summer wore on. Jackson spent his time drilling his men and looking to their comfort. He wrote frequent letters to his wife. She thought her husband had not been praised enough for his part in the battle of Manassas. On July 22nd he had written her:

Whilst great credit is due to other parts of our gallant army, God made my brigade more instrumental than any other in repulsing the main attack. This is for your information only—say nothing about it. Let others speak praise, not myself.

On August 5th he wrote her more fully on the subject:

It is not to be expected that I should receive the credit that Generals Johnston and Beauregard would, because I was under them; but I am thankful to my ever-kind Heavenly Father that He makes me content to await His own good time and pleasure for commendation—*knowing that all things work together for my good.*

General Jackson could afford to ignore the immediate satisfactions of glory.

The summer wore on, and the Confederate army under Johnston at Manassas, on paper 40,000, dwindled

to little more than half that. Thousands received fur-
loughs. Mr. Benjamin, the Southern Secretary of War,
granted most of them; he knew more about military affairs, of course, than his field officers did. At least, as
a politician, he feared his constituency.

The victory at Manassas led people to believe that the
Yankees were cowards. Vigilance relaxed. Jackson
had no such belief. The Yankees were townsmen, it was
true, and most of them, before Manassas, had never fired
a rifle; they might be awkward in the field for a time, but
they were brave as any soldiers had ever been. The Confederates, not used to camp life, came down, nearly a
third, with summer sicknesses. But not Jackson's men.
He looked to the comfort and health of every private.
He held his men ready for immediate action.

Meanwhile, thirty miles away, the Federals, instead
of being paralyzed by defeat, were gathering and organizing the most powerful army ever seen on the American
continent. The day after the Federal rout of July 21st,
Congress had voted Lincoln 500,000 men. Lincoln
called to their command, under General Scott, the
"Young Napoleon," Major-General George Brinton
McClellan, who had won small victories in western Virginia over badly organized Southern forces. But he
was the only Northern officer who had won any victories
at all. He was a charming, industrious man. It will be
seen whether he was another Napoleon.

General Johnston did not like the Southern war policy, but he saw little he could do. In the last week of
September, however, he suggested to Mr. Davis that he
come to Fairfax Court House to discuss military pros-

pects with him, General Beauregard, and General Gustavus Smith. The President came. The Confederate officers pointed out that McClellan should not be permitted to organize at leisure an overwhelming force and then to march out, again at leisure, and crush the Confederates. The President sadly and politely agreed. He asked how many men Johnston needed for an invasion of Maryland. Johnston said 60,000—20,000 more than he had. The President said there were that many troops but that they were needed at other threatened points. At that time there were *no other threatened points whatever.*

Even if there had been, a victory over the main army of the North would have relieved them. But Davis had still another idea. As late as September he held to a belief that had something to do with his passivity in July. He felt that an invasion of the North would consolidate the Northern people. If they were not roused, the Confederates could virtuously remain on the defensive, and France and England would recognize them. It never occurred to President Davis to use his eyes, to see that the Northern people were already thoroughly alarmed. The war had been brought on by a fanatical minority; but one battle had been enough to gather sensible men, the majority, to the Northern cause. Davis may be excused for his military blunders as such; but most of them were due to political blindness. The blunder of not invading the North in 1861 was due to the fact that Davis, as a politician, could not grasp a political idea.

Shortly after the conference at Fairfax Court House,

Jackson was promoted to major-general in the Confederate Army. All through the summer he had been thinking what should be done. Perhaps his increased rank would give him more influence, and remove the impropriety of his attempting to advise the commanding generals. One day in October he went to General Gustavus Smith's tent. He had not mentioned his ideas before. He would mention them now.

He found General Smith lying on a cot, sick. He started to withdraw; Smith urged him to stay. Jackson told him he had a subject of great importance he wanted to discuss. Hesitating, he at last sat down on the ground and began.

"McClellan will not attempt to come out against us this autumn. If we remain inactive they will have greatly the advantage over us next spring. Their raw recruits will have then become an organized army, vastly superior in numbers to our own. . . . If the President would reinforce this army by taking troops from other points not threatened, and let us make an active campaign of invasion before winter sets in, McClellan's raw recruits could not stand against us in the field.

"Crossing the upper Potomac, occupying Baltimore, and taking possession of Maryland, we could cut off the communications of Washington, force the Federal Government to abandon the capital, beat McClellan's army if it came out against us in the open country . . . subsist mainly on the country we traverse, and making unrelenting war amidst their homes, force the people of the North to understand what it will cost them to hold the South in the Union at the bayonet's point."

Jackson asked General Smith to urge Beauregard and Johnston to offensive warfare. Smith replied that it would do no good. Finally Smith said: "I will tell you a secret." "Please don't tell me any secret," Jackson said; "I would prefer not to hear it."

"But I must tell you. I am certain it will not be divulged." Then General Smith told Jackson what had been said at the conference at Fairfax Court House.

Jackson slowly rose, and shook hands with Smith, He said:

"I am sorry, very sorry."

He mounted his horse and rode away.

The Confederate army in Virginia, after October 21st, occupied three districts: the Potomac District, at Centreville, under Beauregard; the Aquia District, under Holmes, guarding the mouth of the Potomac and the possible line of Northern invasion through Fredericksburg; the Valley District, covering the threatened points of the Shenandoah Valley from Harper's Ferry to Staunton. The whole army now became known as the Army of Northern Virginia.

On October 26th Jackson was ordered to take command of the forces in the Shenandoah Valley. His headquarters would be at Winchester. Doctor White, his Lexington pastor, was present when the order came. Jackson said:

"Had this communication not come as an order, I should instantly have declined it, and continued in command of my brave old brigade."

Yet he was eager to get an independent command. He would be subordinate to Johnston; but he would be sixty miles away from Centreville; he could within limits use his own judgment. He was now certain that there would be little action in eastern Virginia until the Federals chose to initiate it. The people of the South and their political strategists believed that the Confederates, standing behind the earthworks of Centreville, could win the war.

Only a few days remained to Jackson at Centreville. He knew he was leaving. But his discipline did not relax. In a way he did not want to give up his Stonewall Brigade. He had become attached to it. The men were attached to him. But they thought he was a peculiar man. They saw him walking in the woods round Centreville, alone. He would raise his left hand to the level of his eyes, the palm turned out; he would stand for a long time in a kind of fierce revery. But he kept his eyes open. He would walk on, still in revery. He found he could pray as devoutly with his eyes open as he could with them shut. He told Doctor White he had found nothing in the Scriptures prohibiting prayer with open eyes. This was a great advantage: he could walk and pray at the same time.

Jackson said: "Every thought should be a prayer. The attitude of prayer should become a habit."

The young officers of his brigade, their coat collars adorned with gold bars, their waists girdled with blue or red sashes, spent their idle time talking about good horses and good dogs, or wondering when they would get into another battle. When they came near Major-General Jackson's tent, they heard strange words. They were not of horses and dogs, not of politics, nor even of strategy. Jackson always had a preacher near him. He was always arguing the Redemption or Predestination. He was learned in such uninteresting problems. He held long debates with Doctor White. Major Dabney, his chief of staff, was a Presbyterian minister. His artillery officer, Captain Pendleton, was a minister. He was always near. The four pieces of one of the captain's batteries were called Mark, Matthew, Luke, and John. They spoke the true gospel, the men said. General Jackson was respectful and humble in the presence of his divines. He was always asking questions. He thought the ministry the noblest of professions. The young men in blue or red sashes were puzzled. Jackson was still the professor of mathematics; he still wore his dingy old coat and mangy cap. But the young men had seen him riding up and down on the Henry House Hill.

Jackson was ready to leave in the first week of November. He called out his brigade. He mounted his horse and rode to the front of the line to say his farewell to the men.

I am not here to make a speech, but simply to say farewell. . . . Throughout the broad extent of country through which you have marched, by your respect for the rights and property of citizens, you have shown that you are soldiers not only to defend, but able and willing both to defend and protect. You have already won a brilliant reputation throughout the army of the whole Confederacy; and I trust, in the future, by your deeds in the field, and by the assistance of the same kind Providence who has hitherto favored our cause, you will win more victories and add lustre to the reputation you now enjoy. You have already gained a proud position in the future history of this our second War of Independence. I shall look with anxiety to your future movements, and I trust whenever I shall hear of the First Brigade on the field of battle, it will be of still nobler deeds achieved, and higher reputation won!

The praise was prepared and formal. Then, giving way to his impulse, he stood up in his stirrups, and raised his voice.

In the Army of the Shenandoah you were the First Brigade! In the Army of the Potomac you were the First Brigade! In the Second Corps of the army you are the First Brigade! You are the First Brigade in the affections of your general, and I hope by your future deeds and bearing you will be handed down to posterity as the First Brigade in this our second War of Independence. Farewell!

The Stonewall Brigade became the most famous organization in the Confederacy.

X

GENERAL JACKSON RESIGNS HIS COMMISSION

O N the evening of November 5, 1861, a lady accompanied by an "absent-minded old clergyman", got out of the Strasburg stage and walked into Taylor's Hotel in the town of Winchester, Virginia. The lady had just come up from North Carolina. She seemed to be looking for some one. But she hardly expected to find the person she sought. In the stage she had been told that General Jackson, her husband, had gone off on an expedition. She walked on up the stairs, but turning round she saw a group of soldiers. One of them came quickly towards her, muffled to the eyes in a great military cape. She was not sure she knew him. Suddenly he threw his arms round her and kissed her.

"Why didn't you come to meet me when I got out of the coach?" she asked.

"Well," said the general, "I didn't want to blunder into kissing somebody else's *esposa!*"

The general had a weakness for exactitude. The stanch Presbyterian put his affectionate words into Spanish. It is not hard to see why.

The Jacksons went to live with the family of the local Presbyterian minister, Doctor Graham, who gave the hero of Manassas a good welcome. Jackson was the

especial hero of the Valley people. Their sons had filled
the ranks of the Stonewall Brigade. They had written
many letters to Secretary Benjamin, asking him to let
Jackson and Jackson only command the soldiers provided for their defense. In the old Presbyterian manse
the general found just the kind of society he liked—simple, pious people. He spent his evenings asking Doctor
Graham questions on points of doctrine. He always
listened most respectfully; yet Doctor Graham said he
himself learned more than he taught. Then, the earnest
conversation being over, Jackson might have been seen
running down the stairs, a child riding on his back.

The Stonewall Brigade, arriving shortly after Jackson, would not have believed that their reticent and often
abrupt commander could have unbent to amuse a child.
His justice was often tempered by mercy, but his mercy
was hardly ever made human by mirth.

When Jackson came to Winchester he found only a
few unorganized, badly disciplined companies of militia.
With these he had to defend the extreme left of the Confederate lines. Between him and Beauregard and
Holmes, on the extreme right, lay General Daniel Hill
at Leesburg, holding the center. It was Jackson's business to observe the enemy, but he had to keep in touch
with Hill and Beauregard; he must be ready at a moment's notice to march to Manassas to the support of
the army there should McClellan decide to attack, just
as he had done earlier in the year. This was the limita-
tion put upon his movements. He could interpret "observe the enemy" as he pleased. The best way to observe
him, thought Jackson, is to march in his direction.

He started making his plans. Johnston had decided to reinforce him with his old Stonewall Brigade. When it got to Winchester he had all told nearly 4,000 men for his ambitious schemes. It was a handful. In his district, bearing upon his position from the north, northwest, and west, were about 50,000 Federal troops. They were scattered over a large area. But they were there. General Banks, an eminent Massachusetts politician, held the north bank of the Potomac with 18,000 men. To the west General Rosecrans held western Virginia for the Union with 27,000 men; in the early autumn General Lee had tried to drive him out and had failed. At the village of Romney, thirty-five miles from Winchester, in the valley of the South Branch of the Potomac, General Kelley commanded 5,000 men.

Jackson made up his mind to attack this isolated detachment. He saw that Romney, weakly held, was the key to his strategic situation. By routing or capturing Kelley's force, he could separate Banks from Rosecrans, and drive a wedge into western Virginia. There may have been sentiment in his desire to retake that section: it was his home. But sentiment cannot explain the vast plan that lurked in the back of Jackson's head. This plan looked ultimately to an invasion of Pennsylvania by way of the Monongahela River and Pittsburgh. While the Valley Army performed this feat, the army under Beauregard was to march through Maryland and unite with Jackson at Harrisburg, Pennsylvania; whence together they would attack Philadelphia, Baltimore, and Washington.

But Jackson knew the temper of the powers at Richmond. He explained his ultimate designs only to a few trusted friends. Of the authorities, who seemed to fear any plan that might promise victory, if it involved risk, he asked merely reinforcements that would permit him to take Romney and hold it. He asked for the use of General Loring's idle division of 7,000 men. He asked for Colonel Edward Johnson's brigade stationed at the head of the Valley near Staunton. General Johnston recommended that both forces be sent to Jackson. President Davis approved the sending of Loring's division only. Colonel Johnson had had a skirmish with a small force of the enemy; his position was evidently a "threatened point."

Jackson spent the month of December trying to give his troops a few ideas of discipline. The Stonewall Brigade still had much to learn. On Christmas Day, 1861, General Loring's division arrived. Loring was an officer of the old army, but his troops were little better than a mob of uniformed civilians.

The westward march of Jackson's reduced force of 9,000 Confederates, 2,000 being sick, began on New Year's Day. The weather was mild. Like raw troops the men threw away their blankets and coats. Next day it rained; by nightfall the rain had turned into sleet; the temperature dropped to zero. The men complained. Jackson paid them no attention. By January 5th the Valley army had passed through Bath and stood before the village of Hancock. Jackson bombarded the town —in retaliation against a useless Federal bombardment of Shepherdstown, Virginia—but his motive was not entirely revenge. Under cover of the shelling of an unim-

portant village, a detachment of his men wrecked the
Baltimore and Ohio bridge over the Great Cacapon
River. Jackson now intended to push on toward Grafton, breaking up the railroad; he would destroy the line
of General Kelley's supply and cut General Banks'
communications so that Banks could not invade the
Shenandoah Valley for a long time.

Suddenly he had to abandon this part of his scheme.
The grumbling of the men grew fierce. They had
marched over ice-covered roads. They had no tents.
The supply wagons, because the horses were not rough-
shod, could not keep up with the column. The Stonewall Brigade grumbled a little. But Loring's men were
at the point of mutiny. Loring had outranked Jackson
in the old army. He was now serving under him. He
encouraged the complaints of the men.

Jackson was not sympathetic with their complaints.
He had one fixed idea: the success of the Southern cause.
Hunger and cold were nothing. The Southern volunteer, early in the war, thought that success was not in-
compatible with comfort.

One morning some members of the Stonewall Brigade, rising, shook off the blanket of snow that had
thoughtfully come down upon them while they slept.
They cursed the leader that had let them suffer. They
said he was mad. The whole expedition was insane.
Then they saw a not unfamiliar figure get up and shake
off his snow-blanket; the figure approached them. He
called out a pleasant "Good morning!" He had been
lying only a few feet away and he had heard them.

What kind of man was General Jackson? He had

not uttered a word of sympathy for their suffering. He
had issued harsh and peremptory orders. But he suffered exactly as they did.

On January 14th the Valley Army marched into
Romney. The garrison of the enemy, because Jackson
had not been able to get in its rear, escaped to the north.
Jackson decided to leave General Loring with his division at Romney on the outpost. It was a position of
honor. It was isolated. It was nearer the enemy than
the Stonewall Brigade would be at Winchester. (See
map, p. 115.)

On the 24th Jackson came back to Winchester with
the Stonewall Brigade. He was on the whole satisfied
with his hard campaign; though he had not done all he
wanted to do. He had restored three fertile counties to
the Confederacy. He had driven a wedge into the enemy's line. The advanced position at Romney could
be used later on as a point of further advance.

He received, on January 30th, an order from Secretary of War Benjamin:

> Our news indicates that a movement is making to cut off
> General Loring's command; order him back immediately.

Loring had permitted his subordinates to send a petition
to the War Department. They dilated upon their suf-
ferings, upon their exposed position. The honor of the
exposure had not entered their heads. These wise officers expressed the opinion that "Romney was a place
of no strategical importance" and that they "might be
maintained much more comfortably, at much less ex-
pense, and with every military advantage, at almost any

other place." There was no movement whatever to cut off Loring. Jackson's far-reaching work was undone.

On the last day of January General Jackson wrote the following letter:

Headquarters, Valley District,
Winchester, Va.:
Jan. 31, 1862.

Hon. J. P. Benjamin, Secretary of War,

Sir,—Your order, requiring me to direct General Loring to return with his command to Winchester immediately, has been received and promptly complied with.

With such interference in my command I cannot expect to be of much service in the field, and, accordingly, respectfully request to be ordered to report for duty to the Superintendent of the Virginia Military Institute at Lexington, as has been done in the case of other professors. Should this application not be granted, I respectfully request that the President will accept my resignation from the army. . . .

People said that Jackson's resignation was about equally due to wounded vanity and a capricious eccentricity. Who was Jackson? He had won some fame at Manassas, but there were other officers as famous who were not such fanatics and madmen. What if the resignation should be accepted? The war would go on, and so far Jackson had done little to make him indispensable; he would not be missed. He would bear the stigma of disloyalty to his superiors, of unwillingness to work with them for the common good. Later people would forget him. Was this the conduct of a merely ambitious man?

Johnston did not like having orders sent over his head

to a subordinate, but he wrote Jackson that "the danger in which our very existence as an independent people lies, requires sacrifices from us all who have been educated as soldiers."

"Sacrifices!" cried Jackson. "Have I not made them? What is my life here but a daily sacrifice? Nor shall I ever withhold sacrifices from my country, where they will avail anything. I intend to serve here, anywhere, in any way I can, even if it be as a private soldier. *But if this method of making war is to prevail, the country is ruined.* My duty to Virginia requires that I shall utter my protest against it in the most energetic form in my power, and that is to resign. The authorities at Richmond must be taught a lesson, or the next victims of their meddling will be Johnston and Lee."

In the end Jackson's resignation was not accepted. It is a question whether he ever performed .a greater service for his country than that which his threat of resignation achieved. Meddling, to a certain extent, continued; but Mr. Benjamin, taken to task by Governor Letcher, saw his mistake. He had not meant to undermine the confidence of the rank and file in Jackson's authority; as a politician he had simply yielded to the public clamor.

Jackson, ambitious though he was, could have repudiated all chance of "distinction" for the principle he believed in. Whatever may have been the original motive back of his present conduct, the aim of that conduct was unmistakable. Perhaps he had an inferiority complex; perhaps his glands needed attention; it was likely that some of his religious ideas, under psycho-analysis, would reveal very, very significant complexes. It was certainly a quaint idea that, above all other earthly ends, the independence of Virginia stood first. Most of the young Confederates hoped to attain this end as an accident of the wearing blue or red or yellow sashes. A man who resigned his commission because officers in blue or red or yellow sashes felt uncomfortable was clearly a fool. He should have been willing for them to be comfortable. What else could be expected from an eccentric professor of mathematics who refused to mail a letter on Sunday . . .

So the talk ran. But if Jackson heard it nobody knew. The difficulty he had had with Richmond was on every tongue in Winchester but Jackson's; he had mentioned it to no one. Nor did he, after it was over, explain it. He had won his point with the central authorities. And he settled down to a quiet life in the Presbyterian parsonage.

But all day he was with his troops. He was still drilling them. Detachments were sent off into the surrounding country to gather information. He had spies everywhere. He had a woman spy. She was Miss Belle Boyd. . . . He made regular reports to Johnston. . . . He was eagerly awaiting the coming spring; the roads would get firm, the sun warm; action would begin. . . . There was no time to lose. The great Federal army near Washington was growing every day. By February General McClellan had nearly 200,000 men.

The future looked almost hopeless for the Confederate arms. In the West General Albert Sidney Johnston had, so people whispered, mismanaged his army. He had let Fort Henry and Fort Donelson slip away from him. The Yankees were overrunning Kentucky and Tennessee. The Confederates were retreating into Mississippi. In the East, to oppose 200,000 men, General Joseph E. Johnston, at Manassas, had 32,000.

In February McClellan decided to invade Virginia by way of Aquia Creek and Fredericksburg. Johnston had to fall back from Manassas to keep him from getting in between his own army and Richmond. He fell back to the line of the Rapidan River. He could meet McClellan if after all he marched overland from Washington; he could turn to the east to meet him if he came down by water, either to Aquia Creek or to the peninsula between the James and York Rivers.

If Johnston's 32,000 were a forlorn hope against the hordes of McClellan, Jackson's 4,600 ill-armed men were equally outnumbered.

On February 27th General Banks crossed the Potomac at Harper's Ferry. He had 38,000 men and 80 guns. His crossing was a phase of the general plan of Federal campaign. All the armies were ordered to move upon the "enemy." Johnston expected Jackson to fall back, and conform to the line his own army had taken. Jackson asked permission to hold his ground.

He also urged Johnston to send him reinforcements. The request was almost unintelligible. Why should the army defending Richmond release men to the Valley Army, where there was no critical defense to be made? But Jackson had his own plans. He told them to no one. They were far-reaching; he always tried to make the immediate ends of a campaign attractive enough to get permission to undertake it. He had been told to "keep the enemy occupied" so far as his handful of men would let him. He asked for more men for this ostensible purpose. He meant to do more than occupy him.

He intended nothing less than the destruction of all the enemy forces in his district. More than this, he had seized upon an idea that went beyond the marching of men to a battlefield. President Davis had been elected to his office that he might have the official duty of grasping such an idea, but he hadn't grasped it so far; it may be doubted if he saw its meaning even after Jackson and Lee had set it before his eyes. To the unfolding of Jackson's idea upon the hills and roads of the Valley, and by the waters of the Shenandoah, the reader will now turn.

"Events," said President Davis, "have cast on our arms and hopes the gloomiest shadows." There was no shadow of gloom upon the arm of Jackson.

For, as Banks with 38,000 men advanced to Winchester, Jackson, with barely 4,000 effectives, marched north to meet him. It was his idea of a retreat.

XI

BY THE WATERS OF THE SHENANDOAH

GENERAL BANKS had an overwhelming force, but in the ten days following his crossing into Virginia he had advanced only as far as Charlestown. He had heard that Jackson had about 11,000 men and that his position at Winchester was fortified. He moved forward cautiously. On March 7th Jackson had marched his small army out to confront him. On the 7th and on the 11th he had offered Banks every opportunity to attack him. That general had declined the gage.

The people of Winchester were excited. The Yankees were at last about to occupy their town. Jackson could not hold it against such odds. Then Jackson decided, 4,000 against 38,000, to take the initiative himself.

But, on the evening of the 12th, after dinner, Jackson said to his host, Doctor Graham: "I will dine here tomorrow as usual." The Yankees were now only four miles north of Winchester.

Leaving Doctor Graham, Jackson went to meet his officers to complete the arrangements for a night attack on the army of Banks. "By the vigorous use of the bayonet, and the blessing of divine Providence," he believed he could defeat him. His men were to fall upon

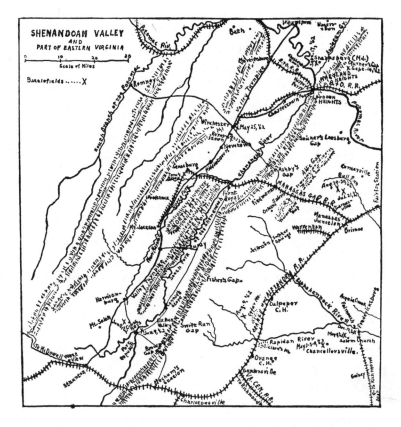

This map shows the entire theatre of Jackson's campaigns except the Seven Days' Battles. The author refers the reader to it only when the sense of the text seems to demand it; but constant reference to it will greatly clarify the narrative. To keep the map simple, the line of Jackson's marches has not been drawn in. The reader may thus have this pleasure to himself.

Banks' undisciplined men just before dawn. But at
the council of war it became obvious to Jackson that
some of his subordinates had blundered.

The supply and ammunition wagons had been fool-
ishly sent eight miles south of Winchester, and the men
had been sent after them to get their rations. The night
attack would involve a march of twelve miles before the
onset against the enemy. Jackson was in a rage.

There was nothing to do but make the accidental
withdrawal of his troops an actual retreat. As he rode
south with Major McGuire, he fiercely said: "That is
the last council of war I will ever hold." It was the last.

Next day Banks entered Winchester. Jackson retreated to Strasburg, eighteen miles up the Valley.
Banks lay idle until he got orders from Washington,
which urged him to keep Jackson under observation.
Then, on the 18th, he sent Shields' division of 11,000
men to Strasburg. Jackson fell back again. He now
camped at Mount Jackson, twenty-five miles above
Strasburg. It was his purpose to lure Banks up the
Valley away from his communications. But Banks now
felt that there was no danger of an attack from Jackson;
he had at last found out Jackson's real strength; and
4,000 men were not to be taken seriously. Banks in a
few days would be free to act for the defense of Washington or in direct coöperation with the main army under
McClellan. His army as an independent unit would
cease to exist and would be merged with the forces about
to press directly or indirectly upon the Southern capital.

Jackson's small army was getting a little larger every
day. They were a rough, determined, careless set. A

year of war had taught the Confederate private that bright buttons and high, polished boots put no extra speed in his bullets or in his legs. He wore heavy brogans. If he had no buttons, bright or dull, on his jacket, he fastened it with a string. He no longer wore the smart coatee. He liked better the short, single-breasted jacket. He liked any sort of trousers he could get, and if leather was scarce he made a belt out of rope, or used a convenient old rag as galluses. One of Jackson's regiments, at a distance, looked all gray; but up close the men had on every shade of gray and brown. Some, if they had been careful, still had on the light blue of a year ago. Others, the mountaineers and woodsmen from the Blue Ridge and the Alleghenies, wore the butternut homespun that their wives and mothers had clothed them in for years. There was no uniformity, and on route step they looked like an armed mob. Only a few carried knapsacks; they rubbed the skin off a man's back. Cartridge box, haversack, blanket-roll slung over the left shoulder and tied on the right side at the waist, a musket rubbed bright with water and wood ashes—these were all the equipment that a Confederate private could be depended on to carry. He carried his rations in his stomach. If three days' rations were issued, he cooked and ate them at once, rations being lighter in the stomach than on the back.

Jackson's men in camp at Mount Jackson had time to amuse themselves. All but the cavalry. The regiment of Colonel Turner Ashby's dashing light horse desired no rest and had none. There was no fun resting. Ashby had about 600 of the best riders in Virginia, and the best

riders in Virginia were the best in the country. They
had been brought up in the saddle. They could jump
their horses over fences; they could ride as easily through
fenced fields and woods as they could canter down the
great, shining Valley Turnpike. There was even less
uniformity in their appearance than in the infantry. A
young man rode into camp in his own clothes, on his
own horse, with his own pistol, his own shotgun or car-
bine, and "jined the cavalry." Ashby never drilled his
men; there was very little discipline; but there was a
high degree of efficiency. The men had friends and
kinsfolk in every village; they knew every hollow and
hill in the Valley. Even when they were most effective
they were having a good time. At night they sang
round the campfires.

> If you want to have a good time
> Jine the cavalry . . .

No matter how far Jackson might be camping from his
enemy, Ashby's men always camped within rifle shot of
the Federal outposts. They exchanged shots with the
enemy cavalry day and night, and then scampered away;
the Yankees were such bad riders that they were afraid
to leave the roads; Ashby's men invariably outdistanced
them. They always knew what was happening in the
Federal camp. One of these reckless horsemen said they
thought no more of galloping through the camp of the
enemy than they did of riding over their fathers' farms.

Jackson found Ashby indispensable. But he wished
that his men were better disciplined.

Ashby reported to Jackson on March 21st that the

Yankees at Strasburg were retreating. They were not retreating because they were afraid of Jackson. Although the Confederates were not then aware of it, McClellan was moving his great army by ship to Fortress Monroe, whence he meant to advance up the Peninsula towards Richmond and, after a brilliant assault, capture the city. The invasion of Virginia through Aquia Creek and Fredericksburg had been abandoned. Its success would have depended upon Johnston's remaining at Centreville and letting McClellan march to his rear; but Johnston had withdrawn to the Rapidan. General Shields was withdrawing to Winchester because the two other divisions of Banks' corps were moving into eastern Virginia to join the army protecting Washington while McClellan was away in the Peninsula. Sedgwick's division was on the way to Manassas, where General McDowell commanded the Washington troops. Williams' division had left the day before Ashby reported Shields' retreat.

President Lincoln had agreed to let McClellan go to the Peninsula if a force of 72,000 men was left for the defense of Washington. McClellan knew that the best defense of Washington would be an attack on Richmond, but Lincoln was not convinced. As time passed, Lincoln said he would send McDowell to the Peninsula by way of Fredericksburg—that is to say, overland; he could join hands with McClellan and form the right wing of McClellan's army north of the Chickahominy River. McClellan thought that Johnston had more than 100,000 men (Johnston had less than half that many), and he needed or supposed he needed 155,000 to make his victory over the Confederates decisive.   Lincoln kept urging McClellan to action, lest delay permit the Confederates to hoodwink him and march upon Washington before he could get there.   Lincoln was yielding McDowell's corps of 40,000 men with extreme reluctance. He was afraid of what Johnston might do.   He did not once think of Jackson.   An ex-professor of mathematics, isolated in the Shenandoah Valley with 4,000 men, could not affect the movements of a great host of 200,000.   A force only slightly larger than his own would be enough to keep him quiet.   And so Shields' division, now 9,000 men, was to remain in the valley to watch Jackson (he only needed watching), to guard the Baltimore and Ohio Railroad and to protect from cavalry raids the repair work in progress on the Manassas Gap Railroad; 9,000 could perform these simple duties with ease. Meanwhile McDowell could move quickly to the Chickahominy, and McClellan could make a rush upon the seven-hilled capital of the Confederacy, the stronghold of the people whom Mr. Lincoln was pleased to call rebels.   Jackson, the ex-professor of mathematics, after the fall of Richmond, would be scooped in as an afterthought.

Johnston, of course, had hoped that Jackson might be able to hold Banks' corps in the Valley, since every man who left the Shenandoah would shortly appear before him, but this was clearly impossible.   To hold Banks, thought Johnston, Jackson would have to defeat him.   Neither General Johnston nor Mr. Lincoln believed, the one fearing and the other hoping, that Jackson could do this.   Jackson was simply counted out.

Ashby's reports on the 21st led Jackson to think that Banks' whole corps was leaving the Valley. On the morning of the 22nd Jackson rode forward with three companies of infantry to Ashby's support. There was in the morning a brisk skirmish at Kernstown, a village of five or six houses four miles south of Winchester. Jackson had ordered the rest of his army forward; it arrived at one o'clock after a march of fourteen miles. The men had marched twenty-two miles the day before. They were dead-tired. They were not in condition to fight. But Jackson would not wait until the next morning. (See map, p. 115.)

Ashby had said there was only a rear-guard at Kernstown, that the main body of Banks' corps, the divisions of Sedgwick, Williams, and Shields, were well out of the Valley. Jackson meant to crush the few companies left behind. Banks might get scared and send back a large detachment from his departing army. Jackson wanted the detachment sent back after he had attacked the rear-guard, not before; so after giving his men a little rest he attacked at once.

At half-past three 2,000 Confederate infantry moved north on the left side of the Valley Pike to turn the unprotected right flank of the Federals. In the center of the battlefield, across the Pike itself, the Federals stood behind a bank. The attack on the Federal right was successful; colors were captured; several blue regiments were cut up and sent back to the shelter of the woods in the rear. But in the center, behind the embankment, their number steadily increased. Jackson saw solid masses of blue infantry coming up. He was puzzled.

Suddenly, when the Confederate onset appeared to be entirely successful, 3,000 Yankees hurled themselves in a counter-stroke against the depleted and worn-out Confederates. The counter-stroke put the Confederates to rout. Jackson sent some guns to the front to cover the retreat, and as night fell these guns and Ashby's men kept the Yankees off till the infantry got away.

Jackson had fallen into a trap and been defeated. It was the first defeat he ever suffered; and it must be said, out of order, that it was the last. Ashby had been deceived. Shields' whole division of 9,000 had lain hidden in ambush.

Jackson was whipped on the field, which he yielded to the enemy. But this enemy was badly shaken. The Confederates, outnumbered more than two to one, had killed and wounded as many men as they had lost. Shields did not follow the Confederates. He knew he had outnumbered them, but he supposed that Jackson would not have dared attack him without having reinforcements close by. This was the first mistaken supposition of Federal generals about Jackson. It was not the last.

Jackson's infantry had looked forward to an easy victory. That night, in their camps near Newtown, a few miles south of the battlefield, the men fell in their tracks, discouraged, and slept where they fell. Jackson stood looking at his campfire. One of Ashby's troopers broke the silence by daring to speak to his general.

"The Yankees don't seem willin' to leave Winchester, General!"

The general looked at the boy. He said:

"Winchester is a very pleasant place to stay in, sir!"

The trooper was very young. He said:

"Somebody said they were retreatin', but I guess they're retreatin' after us."

Jackson kept his eyes on the fire. Slowly he said:

"I think I may say I am satisfied, sir!"

Then, gazing at the burning logs a moment longer, he turned quickly into the dark and disappeared.

Probably not another man in the Confederate States could have understood the satisfaction Jackson felt. Why should a man feel satisfied with defeat even if he had managed to give the enemy a battered head in the fight? President Davis had been elected to understand such things, but he didn't.

News of Jackson's fierce onslaught upon Shields' division came speedily to Banks at Harper's Ferry. He halted Sedgwick's division and ordered Williams's division to countermarch to Shields' support. Blenker's division, a part of McClellan's army, was ordered to march to the Valley to serve under Banks if that officer needed further reinforcements, or, if all became quiet on the Shenandoah, to march on to join Fremont's army in western Virginia. President Lincoln went even further. He had heard that the troops for the defense of Washington were not up to standard, and since so many men were needed in the Valley to crush Jackson, he told McDowell to hold his corps near Washington. At the moment McClellan was organizing his campaign against Richmond and required, or thought he required, more than 150,000 men to defeat Johnston's "100,000,"

Lincoln withdrew from his command over 46,000 men. All this was done because Jackson had been defeated at Kernstown. The operation of the main Federal army was brought to a standstill.

Evidently, at Kernstown, Jackson had touched Lincoln at some quite sensitive place. 4,000 men had suddenly grown important. They swelled so large in Lincoln's vision that he made Banks independent of McClellan so that he could devote all his time to them. Nor was this all. McDowell in front of Washington was assigned to an independent command. Fremont in western Virginia was freed from the orders of McClellan. All the armies had been under the control of a trained soldier. Now they were independent of one another, and depended for joint action upon the telegraph wires, at the far end of which stood two civilians, Lincoln and Stanton.

The Southern people, however, saw Kernstown as another disaster; it was another Fort Donelson and Fort Henry. There was little to be expected of an ex-professor of mathematics.

Before dawn of March 24th the defeated Confederates had begun their march up the Valley. They took their time. Banks, when he got to Winchester to look the situation over, telegraphed Lincoln that Jackson's "15,000" had been cut up and demoralized, and that their retreat up the Valley was a flight. But for some reason the pursuit went no farther than Woodstock. And the Federal outposts were withdrawn to Tom's Brook, seventeen miles south of Kernstown. Ashby pushed his men up to the Yankee pickets, and the main

Confederate body went on to Mount Jackson, far in the rear.

Banks was urged on to the pursuit, but for a whole week he lay idle. He had 19,000 men. "The superb scenery of the Valley," wrote a Federal officer, "opened before us—the sparkling waters of the Shenandoah. . . ." The Federals were contented with admiration of the landscape. For it seems that Banks had heard that reinforcements were being sent to Jackson from Gordonsville, where the left wing of Johnston's army lay. Banks could not be sure of this or anything else; his cavalry, the "eyes of the army," were such bad riders that they brought him little information and that little wrong. Banks wired Stanton on March 25th: "Reported by rebel Jackson's aide [a prisoner] that they were assured of reinforcements to 30,000, but don't credit it."

He merely feared it. Next day he wired Stanton again: "They [Confederates] are broken, but will rally." The 30,000 men were doubtless a ruse. Jackson's watchword was to deceive and mystify the enemy. He put little faith in numbers. He put his faith in God. The higher criticism of this faith is that Jackson relied upon his intellect.

Banks, on April 2nd, at last pushed Ashby southwards, crossing Tom's Brook, and entered the village of Edenburg, ten miles away, that evening. The change of scenery was evidently satisfying. He went no farther.

Banks on the 4th of April, still inactive, wrote the Federal Secretary of War that he intended immediately to "strike Jackson an effective blow." The eminent

Massachusetts politician evidently looked at all affairs, military included, *sub specie aeternitatis.* Immediately to him turned out to be two weeks. He moved his main body not an inch until April 17th.

He was in a difficult position, even if on the surface of operations he had defeated Jackson and pursued him. He had been urged by his superiors to push Jackson hard, and he should accordingly have pressed Jackson back beyond New Market. So long as Jackson held that town Banks' communications were in danger: Jackson might slip down the Luray Valley and get in his rear by way of Front Royal and Strasburg. He had been drawn, by a "defeated and demoralized" enemy, into an embarrassing situation. The Massanutten Mountain cut him off from the support of McDowell in eastern Virginia; the Alleghenies, on the west, severed him from Fremont's 25,000 men, now gathering for a campaign against Staunton and the railroad connections there. If he had been bold as a victorious general should have been, he would have forced Jackson from Mount Jackson and occupied New Market. From that point he could have thrown a detachment across Massanutten to Luray, and blocked Jackson's access to his base. Over the mighty barrier of Massanutten, in its entire length, ran only one road, the road from New Market to Luray. Jackson held it. (See map, p. 115.)

The interval of rest that Jackson's men now had improved their spirit. The snail-like pursuit of Banks had made up for their defeat at Kernstown. Not only they but people everywhere were beginning to understand that their defeat had the consequences of victory. The

Valley was by no means under Federal control, and the reinforcing of McClellan had stopped. The Confederate Congress voted to the Valley Army their thanks. Men came in to join such a famous army. Ashby's cavalry soon mustered 2,000 men. By April 15th Jackson had more than 6,000 of all arms. There weren't at the moment enough rifles to go round. Jackson ordered 1,000 pikes from Richmond. "Under divine blessing, we must rely upon the bayonet when firearms cannot be furnished."

In the interval Jackson maintained the watchfulness of a hawk; he knew everything that happened. But he found time to write letters to his wife and his friends, to discipline his troops and to pray. He was still an anomalous figure to the rank and file, and even his officers made little of him. They never knew why they were told to do anything; Jackson managed to issue his orders in a form that never revealed their ultimate purpose; he expected his subordinates to obey as machines. He knew how easily information leaked out. A subordinate officer, proud of his knowledge, could seldom hold his tongue. All this fanatical secrecy, this praying, this solemn intimacy with preachers, was, in spite of the general's efficiency, the symptom of a diseased mind. More than one private wrote home that their commander was a madman. Why, he was even trying to bend to his crazy ideas that fine, irregular body of men under Ashby, and Ashby was threatening, justly, to resign. Secretary Benjamin, seeing Ashby's brave deeds, had given him an independent command; he was to co-operate with Jackson but he need not obey him. . . .

"What I desire," Jackson wrote to a Mr. Boteler, a friend in the Confederate Congress, "is to hold the country, as far as practicable, until we are in a condition to advance; and then, with God's blessing, let us make thorough work of it. But let us start right." All this time Jackson had been planning the destruction of his more numerous and victorious enemy. Whether he believed that his tactical defeat at Kernstown had been due to his having attacked on the Sabbath, no one can definitely say; yet the fact disturbed him; and he wrote a long piece of casuistry to his wife justifying his unrighteous act. He hoped, he said, never to do it again. His duty kept him from going to church. He wrote his wife on April 7th: "Yesterday was a lovely Sabbath day. Although I had not the privilege of hearing the word of life, yet it was like a holy Sabbath day, beautiful, serene, and lovely. All it wanted was the church-bell and God's services in the sanctuary to make it complete."

On April 16th the Confederate Conscription Law had been put into effect. A regiment of the Stonewall Brigade, its enlistment for a year having expired, demanded its discharge. Colonel Grigsby, in great excitement, came to Jackson for instructions. Jackson knew the regiment was now subject to the Conscription Law. To the perplexed colonel he sent word by an aide:

"Tell the colonel he need not ask me how to deal with mutineers. Shoot them where they stand!" . . .

Three men had deserted to the enemy. For this crime there could be only one punishment, and the court-martial found them guilty. The men were raw recruits;

they had never felt the bonds of military discipline; they were ignorant of what it really meant. Thus their friends argued their case with Jackson. Their chaplain shortly before the hour of execution burst into Jackson's tent. He cried: "Do you know you are sending these men's souls to hell?" Jackson must have got the point of theology; but to impute to him the responsibility was nonsense. He took the chaplain by the shoulders and threw him out of his tent. His respect for ministers was too rational to permit a confusion of the two orders, the human and the divine. He gave no advice in religious matters; in military, he asked none of his parsons.

After weeks of bad weather the sun broke out on April 17th. The roads began drying, and the snow swelled the creeks. Great patches of white clung to the pine forests on Massanutten. But the Valley Turnpike was a glistening yellow thread that led southwards. General Banks at last decided to move. His sudden activity startled the Confederates. He surprised and captured a whole company of Ashby's cavalry.

The main body of the Confederate army began to fall back from Mount Jackson. This town Banks immediately occupied, and then pushed on to New Market. From New Market, on the 19th, he led a detachment across Massanutten to Luray, where he seized the two bridges over the South Fork of the Shenandoah. Jackson had sent some of his cavalry to burn them, but they arrived too late. Banks drove them back.

To all appearances Jackson was in a pickle. If he fell back towards Staunton, Banks' 20,000 men could easily overcome him in the open country south of Harrisonburg, where the Valley expands to a flat width of twenty-five miles. There were no strong defensive positions in that region. (See map, p. 115.)

Besides this, his communications with General Ewell's 8,000 men, just east of the Blue Ridge on the upper Rappahannock, would be cut if Banks pushed his men down from Luray to Elk Run Valley. Banks had shown unusual energy, and Jackson called on his men for a forced march. On the morning of April 18th his men were at Harrisonburg, twenty-five miles from Mount Jackson. On the 19th they crossed the Shenandoah at Conrad's Store, and that evening went into camp in Elk Run Valley, at the foot of the Blue Ridge. The communications with General Ewell were made safe. In three days the Valley Army had marched fifty miles round the southern end of Massanutten.

What a useless march, said the men.

To all appearances Jackson had got out of one pickle only to get into another. Could not Banks send a force of six or seven thousand men to bottle Jackson up in Elk Run Valley, and then move against Staunton with 13,000 men? Edward Johnson's brigade of 2,500 was already sorely embarrassed by the advance of Fremont's army from the west. It looked as if Jackson had courteously got out of Banks' way, by moving to the east, so that the eminent politician could walk into Staunton at leisure. The handful of men under Edward Johnson could be crushed, as in a vise, between Banks and Frémont. Sixty thousand Federals, from Harper's Ferry to Staunton, could hold the Valley. There would be only one move for Jackson to make: to save his army he would have to join Ewell east of the Blue Ridge. The Valley would be lost.

If Major-General Jackson felt any anxiety he did not show it. He was quite.satisfied. In his "dilemma" he was planning, not to save his small army, but to drive Frémont back into western Virginia. As to Banks, he intended nothing less than the complete destruction of that general's army.

As this situation was beginning to reach its present form, the Confederate Government had a serious mental disturbance—only on this assumption can the action about to be related be understood—and appointed General Robert Edward Lee to the chief command of all military operations. It was an act of considerable wisdom, though at the time it was somewhat criticized. General Lee had failed in his western Virginia campaign, and as soon as he came to Richmond he laid out elaborate fortifications. Mr. Pollard's Richmond newspaper had a just view of these two facts: Lee was little better than a coward. He couldn't fight successfully in the open field; so he intended to hide behind earthworks. The satire of Mr. Pollard and the other newspaper strategists was bitter. General Lee was not popular at this time.

Two days after Jackson had arrived in Elk Run Valley he received from Lee a most remarkable letter:

. . . I have no doubt that an attempt will be made to occupy Fredericksburg and use it as a base of operations against Richmond. Our present force there is very small (2,500 men under General Field), and cannot be reinforced except by weakening other corps. If you can use General

Ewell's division in an attack on Banks, it will prove a great
relief to the pressure on Fredericksburg.

The letter is remarkable because it reveals an idea of the
military situation identical in every respect with Jackson's.   The great fault of President Davis' strategy was
in his failure to see the theatre of war as a whole: he had
not realized that to exert pressure upon one part of the
enemy's line was to relieve his own line from pressure
at some other point.   He believed in manning every
separate point, and in waiting until a more numerous
enemy came up to knock over the isolated detachments.
Every detail of Lee's letter had long ago taken hold
in Jackson's mind.   He had made up his mind to attack
Banks and to use Ewell's division in the operation.
Why Lee and Jackson expected to thwart McClellan
by attacking Banks' army in the Valley could not have
been clear to the intelligent citizen in Richmond.   It was
not clear to so good a soldier as General Joseph E.
Johnston.   His idea of the Valley campaign was to unite
Jackson and Ewell on the Blue Ridge to receive attack
from Banks.   The idea was good, but it ignored the
Federal general's character.   He would never attack.
Besides the character of Banks, the character of Mr.
Lincoln and the political terrors that harassed him day
and night deserved careful study.   Both Jackson and
Lee gave them the study they deserved.   Not once in the
correspondence between the two Southern generals was
this idea made explicit.   There seemed to be from the
first a full understanding of the problem that required
no name but only action on their part.   They knew that

the Shenandoah Valley was never away from Mr. Lincoln's thoughts and probably haunted his sleep.

But it had been a month now since the alarm at Kernstown, and Lincoln was at last persuaded that the Valley was safe. On April 26th Mr. Stanton wrote to General Banks:

> It is not the desire of the President that you should prosecute a further advance towards the south. It is possible that events may make it necessary to transfer the command of General Shields to the department of the Rappahannock [i.e., to McDowell's corps], and you are desired to act accordingly.

Moreover, Banks was told that he was not to look to Fremont for support. Frémont was given the same warning with regard to Banks. There were nearly 80,000 men available for operations in the Valley. But Lincoln and Stanton had split them up into comparatively small armies which acted out of concert because they were ordered to. Jackson did not know that Banks had been ordered to advance no farther than Harrisonburg. He simply acted on the assumption that Banks was too timid to advance.

Jackson, seeing the scattered and uncertain condition of his opponents, wrote to Lee on the 28th that now was the "golden opportunity for striking a blow." He ordered Ewell to march to Elk Run Valley, taking his time, coming a roundabout way to deceive the enemy, and resting his troops on Sunday. He now submitted three plans to Lee. Lee replied that he couldn't judge the situation at a distance—Mr. Benjamin could have done it—and left the choice of a plan to Jackson.

The situation in the whole theatre of war on April 30th was, on the map, decidedly unfavorable to the Confederates. Johnston, on the Yorktown Peninsula, had 50,000 men to meet McClellan's 110,000. At Fredericksburg, General McDowell had 33,000 menacing 12,000 Confederates under J. R. Anderson; he expected momently the arrival of Shields' division from Banks' army, delayed more than a month; it would bring his corps up to 40,000 and permit him to advance overland to McClellan's support. In the Valley, Banks including Shields' division had 20,000 men at Harrisonburg, and across the Alleghenies Frémont's army of 25,000, scattered from the Potomac to the hamlet of McDowell, twenty-seven miles west of Staunton, threatened Edward Johnson's 2,500. There were 60,000 Federals in the Valley in various positions. Jackson and Ewell combined had 14,000 men. Adding Edward Johnson, the whole Valley Army came to 16,500. It was outnumbered more than three to one.

Jackson, moreover, had apparently left the Valley. He was at the foot of the Blue Ridge. The citizens of the Valley were getting anxious. Staunton was about to suffer the fate of Winchester.

On April 30th Jackson put his army in motion. General Ewell with his 8,000 men came over the Blue Ridge of Swift Run Gap and occupied Elk Run Valley. General Ewell was a small man with dark frizzled hair. He looked like a woodcock. When he talked he leaned his head to one side, and his large pop-eyes stared quizzically at the person he was talking to. The general was one of those old-style Virginians who could not express their thoughts without the assistance of profanity. He belonged to the school of General Henry A. Wise, whom the decorous Lee once took to task for his swearing. "General," said Wise, "you and Jackson do all the prayin' for the whole Army of Northern Virginia, but in heaven's name let me do the cussin' for one small brigade." General Ewell had convinced himself that he had a bad stomach; he ate only wheat cereals. Ewell was a fine soldier.

Jackson's men took the road to Port Republic in a driving rain. The rain poured down all of three days. The men were puzzled; there was a better road to Staunton; it seemed to be sheer wilfulness in Jackson to demand useless labor of his men. In the three days they marched only twelve miles, and bivouacked under the Blue Ridge at Brown's Gap. They were off the direct route to Staunton. Jackson seemed determined to stay as far eastward as he could, so that Banks could enter Staunton unopposed. Perhaps Jackson realized that he could not cope with the overwhelming numbers of the Federals. The people in Staunton were wild with excitement. Then news came that Jackson had disappeared. (See map, p. 115.)

The morning of the 4th of May broke clear and the Valley Army turned its back upon the Valley and filed through Brown's Gap into eastern Virginia. The men were discontented; they were leaving their homes to the invader! Still they were ready to go to the defense of Richmond if the time had come. Some took a more melancholy view. They said they were being sacrificed to the designs of a lunatic. "As sure as you and I live," a staff officer wrote in a letter, "Jackson is a cracked man and the sequel will show it."

That night the Valley men camped at Mechum's Station, ready to take the cars next day for Gordonsville and Richmond. There the cars were, long lines of freight cars and cattle cars and coaches.

The 5th of May was Sunday. Jackson wanted to rest his men and let them observe the Sabbath. But early in the morning he received a message. The men were ordered to get on the trains. When all was ready, the engines puffed away from the station, not eastward to Gordonsville but back to the Blue Ridge and through Rockfish Gap on to Staunton. The soldiers were pleased, but only a maniac would have taken them such a roundabout way.

In Staunton the Yankees were expected hourly from the direction of Harrisonburg. The blue cavalry had been seen on the hills north of the town. Suddenly long trains of cars steamed into the station, and even before the rumor could spread the gray marching columns of the Confederates filled the streets. The citizens of Staunton had protection at last.

Then the mad general disappointed them. The Valley Army was expected to march north to drive Banks away. It marched west towards the Alleghenies.

Again Jackson was leaving the way clear to Banks. He had made up his mind to destroy that general. It appeared to sane men that he was retreating. This was his idea of an advance.

XII

MR. LINCOLN TRAPS JACKSON—ON THE MAP

JACKSON had disappeared, had been swallowed up in the earth, and Banks, now taking his enemy's absence from his front to be security, grew ambitious. On April 28th, while Jackson was still in Elk Run Valley, he telegraphed Washington that he was "entirely secure." "The enemy is in no condition for offensive movements. . . . A negro employed in Jackson's tent . . . reports preparations for retreat of Jackson today."

Jackson's "retreat" began, as we have seen, on April 30th, and on that day the redoubtable Banks again wired his superiors: "All quiet. Some alarm excited by movement of enemy's cavalry. . . . Jackson was to be reinforced by Johnson and attack *via* Luray. Another report says Jackson is bound for Richmond. This is the fact, I have no doubt." General Banks then asserted that he had nothing more to do in the Valley and that he was eager for orders to cross the Blue Ridge. Such an order, he said, "will electrify our force." He was not to receive the order, but he was to be shortly electrified.

Rumors spread and every hour they took a new turn. General McDowell at Fredericksburg got news from deserters, "very intelligent men," that Jackson was marching north in eastern Virginia. The alarm threw Lincoln and Stanton, who had suspected that Jackson at Elk Run Valley meant mischief, into great momentary anxiety. Shields was withdrawn at last from Banks, who was now left with a force not larger than 10,000 men. This force was ample because Jackson was no longer in the Valley. A greater force was needed to meet him elsewhere.

Secretary Stanton was alarmed, but not for the right reason. He said on May 8th that a "considerable force has been sent toward the Rappahannock and the Shenandoah to move on Washington. Jackson is reinforced strongly." Jackson might at any moment be expected to appear at the upper fords of the Potomac and descend through Maryland upon the Northern capital.

These fears had almost become a certainty on the 8th of May.

On the 9th, in the morning, General Jackson came upon Captain Imboden on the road west of Staunton. He told the captain, who was going to Staunton, that he wanted him to send a message to Richmond. He wrote out a long message; then he tore it up. He wrote another, much briefer. He tore that up too. At last, he hastily wrote out a single sentence:

> "God blessed our arms with victory at McDowell yesterday."

Jackson, who had retreated, or had gone to Richmond, or was about to assault Washington, had quietly united with Edward Johnson at West View and

marched thirty miles west of Staunton to McDowell.
He had overwhelmed the advance-guard of Frémont's
army. General Milroy had not been routed, and the
Confederate victory on the field had not been decisive;
but his numbers were small, only a single brigade, and
he could not hold his advanced position in face of the
odds that the Confederates could bring against him.
He had to fall back upon the main body of Frémont's
command at Franklin. (See map, p. 115.)

Jackson pressed on in hard pursuit until May the
12th, when he was forced to give it up and return to the
Valley. It had not been his intention to annihilate any
part of Fremont's army, which, united, greatly outnumbered his own; but only to drive back its advance-
guard, and thus to neutralize for the moment Fremont's
movements towards Staunton. He had wisely fallen
upon and crushed first the weaker of his enemies, and
cleared the rear of his operations against Banks, before
actually proceeding to that general himself. Mr. Stanton's strategy could not have been better for Stonewall
Jackson's purposes if Jackson had given the Federal
generals their orders. There was a vast force opposed
to him, but the ingenuity with which it had been scattered was remarkable. And the old adage that the
greatest general is he who makes the fewest mistakes
must be reversed: the greatest general is he who pounces
upon the mistakes of his adversary. Jackson never let
a single one pass unused.

The return to the Valley began on May 12th. By the
17th Jackson's men had reached Mount Solon, a village
a few miles south of Harrisonburg, where communica-

tions with General Ewell at Elk Run Valley were resumed. Jackson's situation was now disagreeable. He had crushed a small force of the enemy, but the victory, at least in the opinion of the Federals, was insignificant, and in the opinion of General Johnston at Richmond Jackson should confine his further movements to observing Banks, now strongly fortified at Strasburg. President Lincoln had been greatly reassured to learn that Jackson had not marched east of the Blue Ridge and, later, no longer menaced Fremont, but had returned to his harmless position in the upper Valley: he consented to the continued march of Shields to the support of McDowell, who had by now pushed his advance-guard below Fredericksburg. The wings of McClellan's great army were about to unite before Richmond, and now that Jackson's threat of attack, caused by his disappearance, had vanished, there remained no doubt that the Confederate capital would fall.

The Confederacy had already seen black days in 1862, but the dark clouds that had come down had been only the long gathering of the storm now about to break with irresistible fury. McClellan's great host of 110,000 men could be seen from the steeples and housetops of Richmond. General Johnston with his 50,000 had fallen back inch by inch, so that his field artillery parked in the suburbs of the city warned the citizens that blood might soon be shed in their very dooryards. But would there be a struggle for the city after all? President Davis had ordered the archives of the government packed for removal; the gold in the treasury was loaded into cars; people were hastily gathering their property for flight. Richmond could not be saved. But the people were making a supreme effort. Bankers, merchants, planters, and slaves worked side by side, day and night, on the fortifications at Drewry's Bluff six miles down the river where the smokestacks of the Union gunboats were in plain view. The public clamor demanded the holding of Richmond to the last man. But could it be held? Davis, one among many, did not think it could.

All through May the crowds in Washington, after Jackson's illusive threat had subsided, filled the streets and talked of little but the fall of Richmond. They packed the theatres, where comedians threw them into laughter with jibes at "Southern chivalry"; they shook hands in the streets over the certain downfall of the slave-empire. By the night of May 22nd the crowds had reached a great height of enthusiasm.

Mr. Lincoln and Mr. Stanton enjoyed untroubled sleep. In four days the President would go to Fredericksburg to review the fine army of McDowell. The ceremony would be most auspicious; it would portend, with due regard to the poetry of events, the already assured success of McClellan's great expedition. The life of the Confederacy could now be numbered in days.

General Banks wrote his superiors that he believed Jackson would advance only as far as New Market, where he could keep in touch with Ewell at Elk Run Valley. He was sure that Jackson was still near Harrisonburg in his front, which was well protected by the Strasburg entrenchments. His force of less than 10,000 was scattered in various detachments, the largest, 7,500, being stationed at Strasburg and the smallest, 1,000, under Colonel Kenly, at Front Royal. Front Royal was an important post because through it ran the Manassas Gap Railroad, and its possession by the Confederates would put his flank in danger, turning his entrenchments at Strasburg and threatening the rear of his position at Winchester. Colonel Kenly's 1,000 men could not adequately defend the town. But, then, it needed little defense. Jackson was miles away in the valley of the North Fork. Not even Ewell was on the South Fork, for had not the famous Louisiana Brigade of his division been seen on the road from Harrisonburg to New Market? Banks felt that at both Strasburg and Front Royal his security was complete. (See map, p. 115.)

On the night of the 22nd of May, when the security of the eminent Massachusetts politician was matched by the optimism of Mr. Lincoln and Mr. Stanton, who slept in Washington upon the consciousness of a just cause about to be vindicated,—on this night an ex-professor of mathematics, at the head of 17,000 men, bivouacked in the pine woods of the Luray Valley, ten miles from Front Royal.

Five days before, Jackson, still at Mount Solon, had received a letter from Lee more remarkable for what it just missed saying than any other he had written. We have seen that Jackson had not much respect for the superior numbers of the enemy. Lee had as little. Throughout the correspondence between Lee and Jackson one idea, never quite made explicit and certainly never carried to speculation upon its ultimate possibilities, controls all their discussion of strategy. Who first conceived it we shall never know. It may be asserted with full confidence that each invented it for himself; else the almost intuitive understanding of the one for the other would not have been so immediate and subtle, nor their coöperation so successful. Both Lee and Jackson knew that the springs of McClellan's power lay less in his heavy cannon and numbers than in the human character, harassed by fear and anxiety, that directed them. This character was the Northern President. On May 16th Lee said:

> Whatever movement you may make against Banks, do it speedily, and if successful drive him back towards the Potomac, and create the impression, as far as possible, that you design threatening on that line.

This is the first time that Lee's and Jackson's long-held intention of playing upon the fears of Lincoln for his capital comes definitely out. Nothing is said of these fears directly, and the city of Washington is not even mentioned.

Jackson was ready to move, but Johnston interfered and he felt that he was not at liberty to move upon Banks without a change of orders. General Johnston believed that the approaching crisis would have to be met man to man, that is, tactically; that there was no way of manoeuvring the Federals into strategic difficulties. He had decided to wait for some obvious mistake and take advantage of it. The idea of playing with Lincoln's political anxiety for the symbol of his power had not occurred to him; if it had it would have appeared to be the sheerest fantasy. Neither Jackson nor Lee had, of course, made plain to him the ultimate design of their plans for the Valley Army, and he could see in them no superiority over the policy of defense that he proposed. He wanted to withdraw Ewell for service east of the Blue Ridge. Lee saw farther than Johnston and sent Jackson new orders which countermanded Johnston's. The Valley Army at once moved north from Mount Solon. The men marched rapidly, and Jackson led the march.

The march had begun on May 18th. Ashby's men skirmished constantly with the Federal pickets to let Banks know beyond all doubt that the whole Valley Army followed him down the Valley Turnpike. General "Dick" Taylor's Louisiana Brigade had come round the southern end of Massanutten from Elk Run Valley to march with Jackson's division. The Louisianans, in their conspicuous, bright gray uniforms and white gaiters, could be looked to to confirm the rumor, carefully circulated, that Ewell's entire division had left the head of the Luray Valley, and no longer even remotely threatened Front Royal.

Taylor's men came up with Jackson's on the Valley Turnpike, and as they marched in perfect step, with ranks closed, 3,000 of them, their bands playing the gay Creole tunes of New Orleans, the pious and ragged Presbyterians of Jackson's division by thousands lined both sides of the road, and gazed solemnly into the careless Latin faces.

General Taylor asked an officer where he might find

Jackson. The officer pointed at a figure sitting on a rail fence overlooking the road.

Taylor rode up and saluted. Jackson paid no attention to the salute but went on sucking a lemon, occasionally moving his tired eyes towards the passing Creoles. General Taylor still waited. He had time to look at his general. Dusty cavalry boots, resting on the lower rail of the fence, covered feet of gigantic size. His coat was faded and stained. A mangy cadet cap, pulled down almost to his nose, shaded his intense, weary eyes.

Taking the lemon from his mouth, Jackson asked in a low gentle voice:

"How far have you marched today? By what road?"

"Keezleton road," said Taylor, "six-and-twenty miles."

"You seem to have no stragglers."

"Never allow straggling."

"You must teach my people; they straggle badly."

A waltz struck up by the Creole band broke off the talk. Jackson looked up and, giving his lemon a reflective suck, said:

"Thoughtless fellows for serious work."

General Taylor spoke the commonplace due the remark. Jackson closed the interview by returning to his lemon.

The sun climbed up the east side of Massanutten, and as it threw long rays into the valley of the North Fork on the morning of the 21st of May, the head of Jackson's column, the merry Creoles, passed through New Market. Suddenly they were turned to the right.

In a few minutes there could be no doubt that they were marching back to the Luray Valley. Was Jackson mad? Everybody knew that Banks was at Strasburg, and here was Jackson marching away from him. The Louisianans felt peculiarly aggrieved. At Elk Run they had been in the Luray Valley, and Jackson had made them perform three forced marches to reach a town that they could have made in one day by the direct route; Luray was only about twenty miles from Conrad's store. Perhaps, after all, the army was not about to fall on Banks. They were going, really, to eastern Virginia.

On the morning of the 22nd the leading brigade stood in Luray at the cross-roads: where were they going—to eastern Virginia or to Front Royal? The men said that Jackson got them into these dilemmas just to torture them.

Leaving Luray behind, the army headed down the valley. Jackson rode before the infantry. On both sides of the valley forests of oak ran to the mountain-tops. Suddenly from the woods at the roadside darted out a bare-headed girl, breathless, and stopped Jackson. When she had got her breath she said the Yankees were at Front Royal and Strasburg, and told their numbers and positions. She was Belle Boyd, the Confederate spy.

On the night of May 22nd, the Valley Army bivouacked in the pine woods of the Luray Valley ten miles from Front Royal.

At Strasburg General Banks felt quite secure.

At Front Royal Colonel Kenly and his 1,000 men, who for weeks had not seen a gray uniform, went to bed as usual. They must have been bored with the monotony of garrison life. They needed a change of scenery.

Morning, on the 23rd, broke in a clear sky. The hot sun seemed to fill the still air with a peaceful lassitude. Only a few birds chirped in the trees in the village. Buzzards sailed aimlessly overhead.

Then out of the woods at the southern edge of the town burst a long line of Confederate infantry. The blast of many bugles shattered the quiet air. A volley of musketry shot down the startled Federal pickets. Those who escaped ran in panic through the town.

After the first Confederate line came four others in quick succession. Colonel Kenly fought bravely for a moment, then hearing that Colonel Flournoy with his cavalry was cutting him off from his retreat, he ordered his men to retire over the bridge in the direction of Winchester. He was about to escape. The impetus of the first Confederate onset had spent itself.

Jackson ordered Colonel Flournoy to the pursuit. The Virginia horsemen plunged into the waters of the Shenandoah. In a few minutes the entire 6th Virginia Cavalry had formed up on the other side of the river, a squadron, four abreast, in the road, the rest of the men deploying in the fields on both sides. Then they charged.

Kenly, down the road, was trying to get his men into line to receive the blow. It was too late. The horsemen came on at a gallop, thundering four abreast in the road. The squadrons at the right and left closed in. The onset was terrific. The Yankees broke and scattered. The brave Colonel Kenly was cut down with a bad wound.

Only 400 of the 1,000 escaped, and they ran off in all directions. The garrison had been practically annihilated. Within an hour the remnant of Colonel Kenly's men who got away were completely cut off from any hope of immediate reinforcements. Jackson cut the wires from Front Royal to Washington. Munford's cavalry guarded Manassas Gap to the east; to the west Ashby held the road to Strasburg.

Jackson's surprise had been successful.

Old Jack had crept up on the flank of his secure enemy, destroyed it, and then was ready to march upon his rear.

Two hours after Kenly's disaster a mounted Federal orderly dashed into Strasburg and brought the sleepy 7,500 Yankees to their feet. But his news was vague. What had he seen or heard? Was it only a cavalry raid? It must be; for Jackson was known to be far up the Valley, between New Market and Harrisonburg. Banks sent a regiment off towards Buckton. It was all he did for a long time.

For General Banks, even after stragglers from Kenly's force drifted in with the tale that Jackson with 5,000 men had driven their command off towards Middletown, could not be moved. He only said: "I must develop the force of the enemy."

He recalled the regiment from Buckton.

Night came on. The sutlers in Strasburg did a good

business, and the strolling players capered and danced to the careless, undisciplined hundreds.

Banks' officers tried to persuade him to give up Strasburg. He made no effort to send to Winchester the vast stores of food and ammunition. He only said: "I must develop the force of the enemy."

Then, at last, pressed hard, he rose and shouted:

"By God, sir, I will not retreat! We have more to fear from the opinions of our friends than from the bayonets of our enemies!"

General Banks was, it will be remembered, a politician.

At seven o'clock next morning he wired Secretary Stanton, by way of Harper's Ferry, that the reports of the enemy's powers were exaggerated, that only Ewell with 6,000 to 10,000 men confronted him, and that Jackson was still in his front far up the Valley Turnpike. At ten o'clock he sent his subordinate, General Gordon, a message; he told him that the Confederates had assumed a passive attitude at Front Royal and that reinforcements were coming from Washington. He meant to remain at Strasburg until further orders.

How it happened no one knows. Banks suddenly made up his mind to retreat. He was "electrified." It was not quite too late. The Confederates at Cedarville were, however, two miles nearer Winchester than Banks was at Strasburg.

The Federal retreat from Strasburg began at ten o'clock in the morning of the 24th. Such is the energy imparted by fear, Banks beat the Confederates to Middletown and led his infantry safely into Winchester.

The rear of his army at Middletown presented the veritable image of havoc and confusion. The wagon trains had moved more slowly than the infantry. Ashby fell upon them. He captured wagons, teams, tents, food, ammunition, nine thousand rifles, and many prisoners. The panic of the Federal rear-guard could have been spread through the main body. Ashby was expected to press on.

His men broke ranks and looted the captured wagons. Some gorged the rich food in the sutlers' wagons. Others took horses; they rode away, some of them to see "the home folks." The main body of the Federals went on to Winchester. Jackson found Ashby indispensable; but he wished his men were better disciplined. A great chance had been thrown away.

The morning of May 25th found the Confederates in line of battle before Winchester. The brilliant spring sun shimmered on 10,000 bayonets. The Confederates yelled and advanced as one man. The Yankees broke and ran through the streets of the town.

Jackson galloped down a hill at the head of his old Stonewall Brigade. The reserved and awkward Presbyterian professor seemed transfigured.

"Press forward to the Potomac! Forward to the Potomac!" he shouted.

The Confederates swarmed through the town. They fell upon the broken enemy at street-corners, in alleys. The citizens rushed out amid the flying bullets to greet their deliverers.

The Federals fled into the open fields. As the Confederates emerged from the ends of the streets, they saw crowds of fugitives running pell-mell down the Martinsburg road. Fear gave the routed Yankees a speed that the victorious Confederates could not match. The distance between the pursuers and the pursued widened. Jackson sent despatches in all directions for his cavalry.

Where was Ashby? In the crisis Ashby had only 50 men, for the rest had again left the ranks to pillage the captured wealth of the Yankees. Even these 50 were far away to the right. G. H. Steuart, who commanded Ewell's cavalry, refused to obey orders that did not come through his immediate superior.

Banks escaped. He should have been destroyed. Jackson was enraged. Again the Richmond authorities had thwarted his purposes. Ashby was an able man, but he had no idea of discipline; and his independent command had kept Jackson from getting the horsemen under military control. Steuart was a military pedant, unfit for command.

By noon of the next day, the 26th, Banks had crossed the Potomac at Williamsport. "There were never more grateful hearts in the same number of men than when at midday on the 26th we stood on the opposite shore." But he said that he "had not suffered an attack or rout, but had accomplished a premeditated march of nearly sixty miles in the face of the enemy, defeating his plans and giving him battle wherever he was found."

Banks could deceive himself, but no one else. The morning edition of the New York *Herald* had carried a leader entitled "The Fall of Richmond." That same evening it announced that the whole Southern army was marching on Washington. On Sunday the Northern people, coming out of the churches, heard newsboys crying in the streets:

DEFEAT OF GENERAL BANKS!   WASHINGTON IN DANGER

"There is no doubt," wrote Stanton, "that the enemy in great force are marching on Washington."

The governors of thirteen Northern States were called upon to send all the "volunteer and militia force" at their disposal.

Jackson, on May 28th, advanced to Harper's Ferry, found the enemy, under General Saxton, demoralized as a result of Banks' defeat, and threatened to cross the river into Maryland. The panic throughout the Northern States was general. Jackson's force was believed by his enemies to be 30,000 to 60,000.

President Lincoln had been so deeply moved that all thought of McClellan's operations against Richmond was put aside. McDowell was again told to remain at Fredericksburg. The grand review of his army was, by general consent, postponed. Lincoln thought only of crushing Jackson. He at once ordered Frémont to close in from the west on Jackson's rear and cut off his retreat from the Potomac. Shields' and Ord's divisions, 21,000 men, of McDowell's corps were put in motion from Fredericksburg; they were to converge with Frémont and block Jackson's path. 35,000 men were about to surround 17,000.

Jackson was in a tight place. But he felt no unusual anxiety. On the 29th he began the return march to

Winchester. He feared not at all the converging columns of the Federals. He knew that coöperation between them was almost impossible. Unless they closed in on him at the same moment he could defeat them in detail. The very fear of this would make them timid. They would be torn between eagerness and timidity, and might make some fatal blunder.

At Winchester Jackson got the news that the Federals under Shields had retaken Front Royal. He smiled but made no reply to the courier. Then he seemed to be looking at some distant object. Suddenly he closed his eyes and fell asleep.

In a little while he woke, and said to his political friend, Mr. Boteler:

"Banks has halted at Williamsport, and is being reinforced from Pennsylvania. Saxton is in my front. . . . I have just received a despatch informing me of the advance of the enemy upon Front Royal, which is captured, and Frémont is advancing from Wardensville. Thus, you see, I am nearly surrounded by a very large force."

The total force available, on the map, against Jackson was about 60,000.

"What is your own force, General? asked Boteler.

"To meet this attack I have only 15,000 effective men."

"What will you do if they cut you off, General?"

Jackson hesitated a moment, then calmly said: "I will fall back upon Maryland for reinforcements."

At that time Jackson might have reasonably expected to get reinforcements in Maryland, but his greatest support would have been the panic of the Northern people. That McClellan might have been hastily withdrawn from Richmond, and Johnston left free to follow Jackson's invasion of the North, is by no means a wild speculation upon the possible course of events.

On May 31st, General Johnston, seeing the opportunity made by McDowell's failure to join McClellan's army, attacked the two Federal corps isolated south of the Chickahominy. The Confederate attack was piecemeal; the battle ended drawn. McClellan lost 5,000 men. He was now certain the Confederates had 200,000 men; his caution would henceforth be even greater than before. Johnston was wounded, and Lee succeeded to his command. The battle at Seven Pines gave the Confederates the advantage of delay.

By June 1st Jackson's army had reached Strasburg. As his wagon trains passed over Fisher's Hill going south, the advance-guard of Frémont's army appeared from the west. At the same time Shields' division, at Front Royal, threatened to close in. But Shields, who had a few days before boasted what he would do to Jackson, feared to attack, and not even the presence of General McDowell roused him to action. Jackson bluffed, with his cavalry and skirmishers, both Frémont and Shields, and as night fell, the Valley Army, unmolested, reached Woodstock.

In the fourteen days from May 19th to June 1st, the Valley Army of 17,000 men had marched one hundred and seventy miles. It had put to flight an enemy of 12,500 and, in the whole theatre of war, had paralyzed the activity of 170,000. It had threatened the North with invasion. It had captured property amounting to three hundred thousand dollars, 3,000 prisoners, and 9,000 rifles. At last, surrounded by 60,000 men, it had brought off a large convoy without the loss of a single horse and wagon. It had achieved all this with the loss of only 600 officers and men.

But Jackson was not satisfied. Like the bird in the fairy tale, whose every persecution of his enemy seemed crushing enough to be the last, he might have said, "I am not through with you yet."

Frémont was "pursuing" Jackson up the Valley Turnpike. Shields was coming up the Luray Valley. They were still acting independently of each other. Jackson knew this.

As Jackson rode into Woodstock, mounted on Little Sorrel, his mangy cap down on his nose, a little boy ran out into the road. He yelled to the general:

"Where are you going, General Jackson?"

"Little boys shouldn't ask questions," said the general, giving his lemon a reflective suck.

XIII

WHERE IS JACKSON?

JACKSON, knowing that Shields would follow him by way of the Luray Valley, sent cavalry to burn all the bridges of the South Fork from below the town of Luray up to Port Republic. The river, flooded by heavy rains, could not be forded. Shields was isolated from Frémont on the east side of Massanutten. The chance of their coöperation was slight.

But Shields was hopeful. He was more than hopeful: he was vainglorious. He reported that he was "thundering down on Jackson's rear," and he told Frémont that between them they would "finish Jackson." He wrote the officer commanding his advance-guard:

> The enemy has flung away everything, and their stragglers fill the mountain. . . . No man has had such a chance since the war commenced. . . . You have only to throw yourself down on Waynesborough before him, and your cavalry will capture them by thousands.

Shields, in his haste, had forgotten General McDowell's warning. He had let his division get strung out along the Luray Valley in a line twenty-five miles long. He was to pay dearly for his haste.

The Confederate cavalry, covering the retreat of the

infantry up the Valley, had skirmished daily with Frémont's advance-guard. On June 6th, near Harrisonburg, in a rear-guard action, Ashby's lines began to
break before the Federal onset. Ashby, riding to the
front, had his horse shot from under him. Getting on
his feet, he shouted:

"Charge, men! For God's sake, charge!"

The men rallied. As they swept forward from the
woods, Ashby fell, shot through the heart.

Jackson had rated his cavalry officer in high terms
for the indiscipline of his men at Middletown and at
Winchester. There had been a coolness between them
since. But it had been made up. Jackson, in a note
to Major John Imboden, said: "Poor Ashby is dead.
He fell gloriously—one of the noblest men and soldiers in the Confederate army."

The Confederate infantry, on June 6th and 7th,
rested near the site of an old inn that had borne the
sign of Cross Keys. Three miles away lay Port Republic. Signalers on the southern end of Massanutten
reported the approach of Frémont from Harrisonburg
and of Shields from the valley of the South Fork.

Unfortunately neither knew exactly where the other
was. Jackson knew precisely where both were.

On June 8th Frémont, feeling his way, collided at
Cross Keys with Ewell's division, and a bloody battle
followed. By evening Frémont had got a severe beating and had withdrawn in the direction of Harrisonburg.
Ewell with 7,000 men had defeated 12,000 Federals.
Frémont had fought his men timidly; he wanted to win
the battle, but he was too much afraid of losing it.

Ewell had directed his men with great energy and skill. He disliked the restraints of command, and once he rushed forward with his skirmishers. Having "refreshed himself," he returned to his staff hoping that "Old Jack would not catch him at it."

Jackson's note to Major Imboden had been written on the night of June 8th. Imboden was at Mount Crawford, and the note, besides mentioning Ashby's death, ordered him to report to Jackson at Port Republic before dawn.

As dawn began breaking Imboden came over the bridge at Port Republic. The village stood on a small peninsula formed by two branches of the South Fork. To the north rose the mighty brow of Massanutten, trembling in the long rays of the summer morning sun. To the north and east ran, range after range, the long purple back of the Blue Ridge. Great forests of pine and oak covered the mountains everywhere, and extended for miles in all directions down into the valleys. Except for the scattered houses on the Port Republic peninsula, the vast landscape was to the eye a virgin wilderness.

Imboden found the house Jackson was in, and was told that his adjutant-general was in the first room upstairs to the right. He got his directions reversed and walked in on Jackson.

Old Jack lay full length across the bed, his boots on, his sword and sash fastened at his side. A low candle guttered on the table. Imboden started to withdraw. Jackson turned over and sat up.

"Who's that?" he said.

Imboden started to apologize for his intrusion.

"That's all right. It's time to be up. I'm glad to see you. Were the men all up as you came through camp?"

"Yes, General, and cooking."

"That's right. We move directly. Sit down. I want to talk to you." Then he spoke of Ashby, whose body lay in a house nearby.

Imboden said: "General, you made a glorious winding-up of your four weeks' work yesterday."

"Yes," said Jackson, "God blessed our army again yesterday, and I hope with His protection and blessing to do still better today."

And he did.

The old Stonewall Brigade, under General "Charlie" Winder, advanced to the attack on the Lewis farm. They met serious resistance from two Federal brigades under Tyler. The Louisiana brigade had been ordered to attack Tyler's left flank, but these men had not arrived on the field.

The Stonewall Brigade gave way a little. Jackson galloped to the front line and called out:

"The Stonewall Brigade never retreats. Follow me!"

He led them back to their first line of battle.

But in the meantime Taylor's Louisianians came up, and the Federal resistance collapsed. It turned into a rout. The Federals retreated down the Luray Valley. Jackson's cavalry followed them eight miles, then returned. Shields, by stringing out his division, had let two brigades fall into Jackson's trap.

While the struggle on the Lewis farm was going on,

Frémont stood timidly in his previous position near
Cross Keys, where he could hear the guns of Shields'
battle. Jackson had contemptuously withdrawn the two
brigades left on the west side of the river to observe
Frémont: he had withdrawn them, and burnt the bridge
behind them. Frémont was helpless—besides being
frightened—and all he could do, after the rout of Tyler,
was to throw shells upon the Confederate ambulances
gathering up the wounded of both armies. The yellow
flags of the medical corps were flying in plain view.

Frémont began retreating to Harrisonburg. Jackson sent his cavalry, now since the death of Ashby under
Colonel Munford, in hot pursuit. General Frémont
supposed his army to be pursued by the main body of
the Confederates. He abandoned Harrisonburg and
large quantities of hospital supplies. By June 14th
he had reached Strasburg. The Confederate cavalry
still harassed him. He could only guess where the Confederate infantry was. Defeated and bewildered, he
would be quite harmless for a long time.

On the 12th Jackson took his army once more westward, as if he were soon going to follow Frémont, and at
the village of Mount Meridian, on the Shenandoah, the
tired veterans in ragged butternut for five days rested
from their hard times, only to plunge into harder times
to come.

In the five days of rest Jackson used every device at
his command to deceive the enemy, his own army, its
officers, and the citizens of the region. No civilian could
pass a picket line. (A few were let through, however,
carefully supplied with false information.) Jackson

ordered Captain Hotchkiss, his engineer, to get ready a large-scale map of the Valley, telling the captain and other officers, who felt proud to share the secret, that he planned elaborate operations against the beaten Federals—that, now having the upper hand, he meant not only to maintain it but to clear the Yankees out of the Valley altogether. He might even invade Maryland.

This plan spread broadcast had upon the Federals the desired effect. Jackson's purpose was twofold. He was bent upon keeping McDowell's corps on tenterhooks as long as possible: Shields and Rickett, now in command of Ord's division, were kept, as a result of Jackson's deception, near Front Royal. His second intention was not to alarm McClellan, so that that officer would not correct a faulty position he had taken up astride the Chickahominy River. If he got wind of any plan of Jackson's to join Lee at Richmond he would withdraw Porter's corps from its isolated position north of the Chickahominy. This position had been selected because the arrival of McDowell's corps from the north would so reinforce Porter as to make it safe. Mr. Lincoln's fear for his capital had communicated a paralysis to McClellan (who was already possessed by caution) by sending McDowell on a wild-goose chase in the Valley.

Jackson and Lee were about to deliver the great counterstroke against the invader. On June 17th a letter came from Lee to Jackson outlining the whole plan, which had been forming in Jackson's mind too. Lee intended to gather a great army, of which Jackson's divisions were to be the most important unit, and to pounce upon Porter's exposed corps with overwhelming numbers. To that end Lee sent the division of General Whiting and the brigade of General Lawton to the Valley to reinforce Jackson for his operations there against the already beaten Federals! As the men boarded the trains in Richmond, their numbers and destination were an open secret; Federal prisoners, casually marched by the railroad station, were allowed to count the regiments; and later in the day, were allowed to escape. But Generals Whiting and Lawton took their orders at their face value. No one but Lee and Jackson, and Colonel Munford upon whom Jackson's stratagems depended, knew the truth.

Where is Jackson? asked the Federal authorities. No one knew exactly. He was expected to appear anywhere. Frémont was certain, as Banks had been three weeks before, that he was in his front above Strasburg.

On the 18th of June, Ewell's division started for Charlottesville, and Whiting and Lawton, who had been marched from Staunton to Mount Meridian, to fool Frémont, were marched back again to take trains for Gordonsville. General Whiting was enraged. Jackson had not explained his purposes. General Whiting told Major Imboden that Jackson was a fool and had no more sense than his horse.

Once in eastern Virginia, the Valley Army expected to be told their destination. They were told. The pastor of the Gordonsville Presbyterian Church, whom Jackson naturally sought out as soon as he had got there, informed many of them, and the news soon spread that they were to march up to Culpeper Court House to intercept some mysterious force of the enemy. The pastor had got this from Jackson himself. On the march the men had been told that they were not to answer questions put by civilians, that they must invariably say, "I don't know." One of General Hood's "Texicans" was climbing up a cherry tree, which had sorely tempted him out of the ranks. Jackson had no patience with any breach of discipline. He saw the man and rode up to him.

"Where are you going?" he asked.

"I don't know," said the soldier.

"What command do you belong to?"

"I don't know."

"Well, what State are you from?"

"I don't know."

Old Jack turned and asked another soldier:

"What's the meaning of all this?"

"Well," the man said, "old Stonewall and Gineral Hood give out orders yestiddy that we warn't to know nothin' till after the next fight."

Jackson, who had no patience with a breach of discipline, laughed and moved on.

On June 21st the leading brigade of Jackson's army had got to Frederickshall in Louisa County, where they were halted for Sunday worship, so wantonly neglected of late amid the uncertainties of war. The rest of the army was still behind. But they were coming. And no one knew it.

General Jackson, at Frederickshall, was the guest of a Mrs. Harris. It was a Sunday, and he went to camp-meeting. Sunday evening, June 22nd, Mrs. Harris asked the general if he would be present for breakfast. He replied by asking her to have it ready at her accustomed time.

In the morning Mrs. Harris sent for the general. Jim, his negro servant, answered: "Sh! you don't spec to find the gineral hyar at this hour, does you? He left hyar 'bout midnight and I spec by this time he's whippin' Gineral Banks in the Valley."

Jim and "Gineral" Banks had much the same view.

At one o'clock in the morning Jackson, accompanied by his chief-of-staff, Major Robert Lewis Dabney, rode quietly through the darkness towards Richmond. No one knew they had gone. Jackson took such precautions that, even should his absence be detected, no one should know where they were going. Dabney had got from the enraged Whiting an order, which only a major-general could issue, permitting Jackson to impress horses. On they rode, taking at intervals fresh horses from irate planters.

Early Monday morning, June 23rd, Jackson and his staff-officer rode through the streets of Richmond. The citizens they passed in the streets gave them no attention whatever. Jackson, the mysterious hero who went into battle praying, was far away in the Shenandoah. What a figure he must be! There must be something incomparably grand in his presence, the very figure of martial spirit!

Shortly after noon an officer in a frayed, dusty uniform, wearing a faded cadet cap grimed with sweat and dust, got off his horse before a farm-house on the Mechanicsville road a few miles northeast of Richmond.

As he dismounted, another officer, neatly dressed, rode up and dismounted. Jackson, raising his tired eyes, looked at the man, and greeted his brother-in-law, General Daniel Hill of North Carolina. Together they walked up to the house. Hill could not get over his surprise at seeing Jackson. Why, everybody knew that he was menacing Frémont miles away. Jackson told Hill he had ridden fifty-two miles since midnight.

The brothers-in-law passed the sentry at the door and went in. They were told to knock at another door leading away from the hall. They knocked. The door was opened by a tall man, plainly but elegantly dressed in spotless Confederate gray; his clear blue eyes, perfectly set in a large, delicately molded face, contained no surprise, and seemed to give all they saw their own unhurried calm. General Lee shook hands with his officers and took them back to the hall, where stood a large table circled by several chairs.

As they approached the table, two other officers appeared. James Longstreet's massive frame towered in the room. His large stone-like face had all the calmness of that of his commander, but it seemed too immobile, less alert, indecisive. Ambrose Hill, the other general, slight in figure, stood aside, his sharp, almost beautiful face instinct with energy; he was a brave, skilful soldier, but he was careless. The five Confederate officers were about to sit down, but General Lee turned to Jackson and asked if he would have something to eat after his long journey. Jackson said no.

"Will you have a glass of milk, General?"

While Jackson sipped his milk a little away from the

group, Lee began talking. The four officers he had
invited to the council of war, he said, were selected to
deliver a counterstroke against that part of McClellan's
army which lay north of the Chickahominy River. Mc-
Clellan had not withdrawn Porter from his dangerous
position; he still hoped, being still led to hope by the
Washington authorities, that McDowell would soon
arrive. Now Lee had at last got the Federals distributed where he wanted them, and while their fears and
uncertainty kept them from protecting themselves, he
had made up his mind to fall upon one of the exposed
fractions of their army.

Jackson understood the plan perfectly. Had it not
been his own policy in the great campaign just ended?
In the whole theatre of war the Federals had outnumbered him about three to one; yet he had so manoeuvred
his army, and so bewildered the enemy, that only in one
battle, Kernstown, had the Federals had superior
numbers on the field. His own skill and the fortunate
coöperation of President Lincoln had permitted him to
defeat the three fractions of his enemy, Banks, Shields,
Frémont, not as an integer, but in detail. Lee planned
to do the same thing to McClellan.

Lee told his four division commanders that their combined power would be about 60,000 men. Jackson, with
18,500, was to come from Gordonsville and Frederickshall to Ashland, twelve miles from Richmond, whence
he was to descend at Beaver Dam Creek upon the right
flank of Porter, who would have to fall back. At the
same moment, Jackson's turning movement having
driven the Yankees from the bridges, Ambrose Hill.

Daniel Hill, and Longstreet were to cross the Chickahominy from the south and attack the front and left of
Porter's position.   Porter had about 30,000 men, and
the Confederates with 60,000 might hope to destroy him
utterly before McClellan could reinforce or withdraw
him.   The destruction of his corps would compel
McClellan to fall back to protect his base of supplies at
the White House, down the peninsula on the Pamunkey
River.   If he could be cut off from this base, he might
be demoralized and his whole army, now 105,000 men,
annihilated.

The manoeuvre was full of peril for the Confederates,
but Lee, the man who hid behind earthworks, balked at
no hazard; all risks were worth running for the great
end.   In every battle from now on Lee is willing to
stake all on a single hard blow.

The earthworks before Richmond would be manned
by Magruder's 28,000 men, and the main body of 60,000
would be liberated for offensive action.   But it would
be a dangerous situation.   If McClellan's nerve could be
got up—Lee thought this unlikely, for he knew his opponent—he could throw 75,000 men against Magruder
and walk into Richmond, making Lee's attack on Porter
a wild-goose chase.   But McClellan, the Young Napoleon, was one of the most efficient wish-thinkers in
America: he still believed that an army of 200,000 would
have permitted an army of 105,000 to push its picket line
within four miles of the city it was defending.   Lee
had studied the character of his opponent: his indecision,
his caution, his boastfulness.

The great risk of the attackers would lie less in the

boldness of the manoeuvre than in their armament. Few
of the infantry carried rifled muskets; many were armed
with flintlocks and shotguns. The smooth-bore cannon
could not match the rifled pieces of the Federals.

When Lee had explained his plans he withdrew to his
office, leaving the details of the attack to be settled by
the division commanders. Longstreet asked Jackson
when he could be at hand. Jackson answered the 25th.
All depended upon Jackson. The other divisions could
not advance until Jackson had got in Porter's rear and
turned his position; otherwise the men of the two Hills
and Longstreet would be committed to a brutal frontal
attack upon Porter's entrenchments. Longstreet, always cautious and rightly so now if never again, advised
Jackson to give himself more time. Jackson, who disliked the giving of time to himself no less than to his
enemy (which was the same thing), hesitated; but at
last gave himself one more day, and named the morning
of the 26th, the hour, three o'clock.

It was settled. As Jackson rode off, to return to
his advance-guard at Beaver Dam Station forty miles
away, the Valley campaign came formally to an end.
He had done great deeds, and now the eccentric professor of mathematics was to walk on a larger stage,
fight in greater battles, and perhaps win greater fame.
Was not distinction the one aim of the soldier? Old
Jack had not even used the word for months. It had
somehow disappeared. The magnitude of affairs had
obscured it. Like an older hero, pious as he but not
Presbyterian, he might have looked at what he had
done, and said, *Quorum pars magna fui*. He did not

even think it. God only bore a great part in the mighty struggle.

On June 25th the Valley Army arrived at Ashland.

Jackson was expected to appear momently at any point on the Federal line from Romney to Fredericksburg. Banks was certain that he was only thirty miles from Winchester. Ewell's division was expected by Frémont to appear at Moorefield: Ewell was at Ashland, one hundred and seventy miles away! Mr. Lincoln was frantic: he was sure the blow would fall anywhere but where it did.

It fell on June 26th. But Jackson did not strike it.

XIV

THE SEVEN DAYS

1

Ellerson's Mill: Gaines' Mill

BY the early morning of the 26th of June, 1862, the
three Confederate divisions of Ambrose Hill, Daniel Hill, and Longstreet had advanced to the Chickahominy bridges. They were ready to cross. Ambrose
Hill was in the lead. The morning passed, but he did
not cross. Jackson, from the north, was expected every
moment to attack the left flank of Porter's position;
the bridges would automatically be released, and a passage would not have to be forced.

Hill's men stood on the Mechanicsville road in column of fours, ready to move. The hours passed. There
was no sign of Jackson. Away to the right shells were
being hurled back and forth across the river. The hot
sun beat down on the impatient infantry. At intervals
a shell dropped into the helpless ranks of the waiting
men.

The country gave out a damp heat that penetrated the
very eyes of a man. Great tangled woods stretched off
far as sight could go. Thick oaks and pines and lux-
urious blossoms grew up to the river's edge on both

sides, forming a green roof over the water. Swamps lay everywhere. The roads were crooked and uncharted. Here and there, far apart and hidden in the jungle, stood the manor houses of the planters. Tidewater Virginia after two hundred fifty years of European culture was a desolate wilderness.

Hill's men still waited. The head of his column looked up. A shrill whine rose in the air and flew to the rear. Suddenly a man, standing in the ranks, became headless; his body quivered the fraction of a second, and collapsed in a heap. The soldiers nearby shuffled their feet; then looked seriously ahead.

Hill's men waited until three o'clock, and Jackson had not appeared. Then General Hill, fearing lest the whole gigantic plan fail if McClellan were given a day's warning of their approach, forced a passage across the Meadow bridge, and drove in the pickets of the enemy towards Beaver Dam Creek.

Ambrose Hill led the advance down the north bank of the river; Longstreet and D. H. Hill followed. Still no news arrived of Jackson. Just as the sun was about to touch the horizon, Hill ordered an assault upon the Federal position at Beaver Dam. (See map, p. 177.)

This position was impregnable. Its front was protected by a swampy, wooded creek. Lining the bank of the creek, earthworks and felled trees covered the riflemen. Artillery backed the infantry, and swept the wide flat area across the creek.

Hill's men rushed headlong over the open space and plunged into the swamp under the very muzzles of the cannon. Rank after rank was shot down; the men fell into the creek or sank in the ooze of the swamp. Fresh lines followed, stepping over the corpses of their comrades. In a half-hour nearly 2,000 Confederates lay in the water and ooze round Ellerson's Mill. Only 360 Yankees had fallen.

The first stroke of the great manoeuvre had ended in a bloody defeat. Jackson, as Hill had at the last expected, had not come to his aid at the sound of the guns.

While Hill's battle was raging, Jackson, at Hundley's Corner, three miles north, listened, but did not move.

Jackson's orders had said that the four attacking divisions were to communicate, but he had received no word from Longstreet or either of the Hills. Ewell's division had run into Daniel Hill's, but Ewell had sent no word to Jackson. Until the four divisions were in touch Jackson was convinced that no attack would be delivered. The sound of the guns at sunset did not necessarily mean that the Federal position at Beaver Dam was being assaulted. It might indicate fighting at the Chickahominy bridges; it might mean a counter-attack against Ambrose Hill by the advance-guard of Porter. The sharp firing had lasted only a half-hour or so, and Jackson could not be certain that it was a battle. He could not foresee that Hill would so liberally interpret his strict orders. Jackson was a literalist.

But Jackson, the literalist, had seriously fallen short of Lee's orders to him. He had been instructed to leave Ashland at three o'clock that morning. He had not left until nearly nine. Even after he had got under way, blunders by his subordinates in a strange region, the lack of rations for his men, the bad maps of the country, made his march unusually slow. Guides were untrustworthy; people who had lived always in Hanover County seemed to know little more of the roads than he. Cavalry pickets of the enemy, the enemy's sharpshooters, retarded his march. There were reasons why he was late. But he need not have been late at all if he had chosen the 27th instead of the 26th.

The bloody and futile slaughter of 2,000 men at Ellerson's Mill would have been avoided. Porter saw dense clouds of dust rising in the north; he knew that Jackson was coming; but the clouds rose so late in the afternoon that he saw no use in retreating till nightfall, when he could do it unmolested.

Under cover of darkness he fell back down the Chickahominy to the line of Powhite Creek, on the bank of which stood an old mill belonging to Doctor Gaines. The east bank of the creek was strongly fortified; to the rear the ground, rising steadily, overlooked the country on the west bank.

Early next morning all the Confederates had crossed the Chickahominy, and were concentrated for the attack upon Porter in his new position. Longstreet moved down the bank of the river; at his left, advancing towards Powhite Creek, marched the decimated brigades of Ambrose Hill. Jackson was at last in touch with the rest of the army, and took up the advance due south from Hundley's Corner in the direction of Walnut Grove Church, where he was to turn due east to Old Cold Harbor. Old Cold Harbor lay to the right and rear of Porter's position, and Porter would supposedly

have to retreat directly across Jackson's path in order
to reach his base at the White House. The Confederate
plan was perfect. The concentration of the army was
achieved. The trap was about to be sprung.

Jackson rode ahead of his column and met General
Lee and his staff near Walnut Grove.

As Jackson and his staff dismounted, silence fell upon
the little group of officers that stood round Lee. They
looked at Old Jack, and as the Valley hero and his chief
walked to one side, they exchanged discreet whispers.
Jackson's staff at last understood the magnitude of
their leader's successes in the Valley. Lee and Jackson
walked some distance away and sat upon a fallen tree.
Lee was giving Jackson his instructions for the morning's work. He was to wait at Old Cold Harbor until
the frontal attack on Porter drove him to Jackson, who
would then fall upon him and destroy him.

While the Confederate preparations progressed on
the north bank, Magruder south of the Chickahominy
in the intrenchments began a warm demonstration
against the main army of McClellan. Magruder, Jackson's old officer in Mexico, was the "prince of bluff."
And McClellan's scouts and skirmishers reported no
decrease in the enemy's strength. Obviously Lee had
the 200,000 men that Pinkerton, the Federal secret service agent, had reported. He could afford to detach
a large force. McClellan judged Lee by himself, for
he would not have dared leave his front exposed. Mc-
Clellan could be depended upon not to reinforce Porter.

At two-thirty Ambrose Hill's men, being opposite
the enemy's center, rushed forward to the attack. Their

lines swept in fine order out of the woods across the open country between them and the creek. They drove in the advanced line of the Yankees. Then, sticking in the mud of the swamp and scrambling through the felled timber in front of the Federal lines, they fell like grass before a scythe. As one line withered and vanished, another took its place. Hill's men were fighting their second battle in twenty-four hours, and again they were fighting it unsupported. They fought for an hour; the other Confederate divisions were silent. Jackson had disappeared again.

When Jackson's men marched down from Hundley's Corner, they found the road obstructed by the enemy, and they took a round-about way. They were late getting to Old Cold Harbor. But even then Jackson was not concerned. He had been ordered to wait till the enemy was driven in his direction. The enemy had not budged. The enemy seemed strangely indifferent to his line of retreat.

Hill was still fighting a desperate battle. He was near defeat. Longstreet was at last thrown in to save him. Evidently Porter was not to be ousted by a mere threat at his communications; manoeuvre was not enough, the Confederates would have to exert their whole fighting strength.

As the minutes passed, Jackson, hearing the increasing roar of the battle fought by Hill and Longstreet, decided that the original plan had gone wrong. He sent in his own and Daniel Hill's division.

All along the line the Confederates burst out of the woods, 50,000 of them, and at the double-quick ran, without firing a shot, up to the intrenchments of the Federals. They swept, under a murderous hail of bullets, over the low hill and delivered a volley into the faces of the enemy. Hood's "Texicans" first broke through the line. The Yankees scattered. They retreated to the Chickahominy. Some cavalry and a few batteries of artillery, as night came on, covered the retreat and let the demoralized Federals escape to the south side of the river. The great battle of Gaines' Mill was over.

It had been won by the Confederates at a terrific cost. They had expected to force Porter out of his position by manoeuvre. They had defeated him only with overwhelming numbers and with a loss of more than 8,000 men. The Federals had lost 7,000, including prisoners.

Night settled down on the battlefield. Confusion made it hard to distinguish friend from straggling and defeated foe. The retreat was not pushed. An enemy cannot be followed without cavalry. Lee had expected Porter to fall back to the White House, and to intercept him had sent Stuart with 2,000 horsemen down the peninsula.

Jackson riding with some officers through the tangled woods pulled up in the midst of the Federal picket. He spurred his horse and, charging, ordered them to surrender. The men threw down their muskets. On the march to the rear the prisoners proudly boasted that they had been captured by Stonewall Jackson. Jackson had barely escaped capture himself.

All night the two armies rested on their arms.

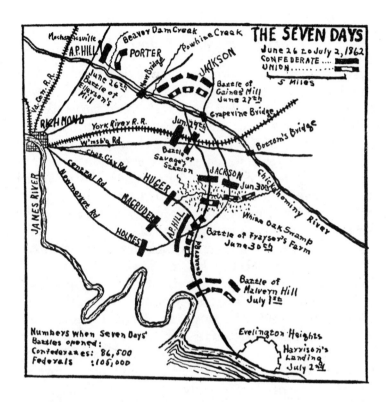

The positions marked here were not occupied simultaneously, but successively, beginning at Ellerson's Mill (June 26th) and ending at Malvern Hill (July 1st). A moment's study of the map will disclose five distinct battlefields on a semicircular line twenty miles long.

2

Frayser's Farm: Malvern Hill

At dawn on June 28th Lee found that the only Federals left on the north bank of the Chickahominy were stragglers and wounded men. Porter's corps though battered had escaped, and Lee was puzzled. He was convinced that McClellan would retreat, but the direction of his retreat, which seemed a certainty twenty-four hours before, could not be guessed. For Magruder, still confronting the Federal main body, reported that the Union army was in its lines and that no movement in any direction was perceptible.

It was still possible that McClellan might attempt to reach the White House by the lower bridges of the Chickahominy; or he might retreat down the peninsula to Yorktown or Fortress Monroe. In either case Lee's army would have to pursue from the north bank of the Chickahominy. He felt that it would be "injudicious" to move from the field of Gaines' Mill until the route of the Federal retreat could be discovered. The whole Confederate army lay idle on the 28th.

Idleness, for any reason, it could ill afford. Porter had been defeated, but unless even greater damage could be inflicted upon the 75,000 Yankees still intact, Lee's own losses at Gaines' Mill would be wasted. If McClellan escaped uninjured he could recuperate at leisure; in a short time he would be formidable as ever. His resources in men were unlimited, but Lee might never again be able to collect an army of nearly 90,000 men for the defense of Richmond. It was now or never.

Magruder, on the 29th, sent word to Lee that the Federal army was beginning to move, and Lee could not longer doubt that McClellan had secretly changed his base and now meant to retreat to some point on the James River.

Had Lee but known it, General J. E. B. Stuart's bold raid with 1,200 horsemen on June 14th (the general dressed in his gold lace and his dark brown plume waving) clear round the whole Federal army, had alarmed the easily scared McClellan; and McClellan had transferred his base of supplies to Westover Landing, fourteen miles south of his position, on the James.

When the news of McClellan's activity got to Lee, he sent orders back to Magruder to strike his flank. The short but bloody battle of Savage's Station followed. Magruder was repulsed. There was nothing more to be done that day. (See map, p. 177.)

Early on the morning of the 30th the Confederates had all crossed the Chickahominy and were trying to catch up with the Yankees. Longstreet collided with a Federal division at Frayser's Farm, and the crisis of the Seven Days had been reached.

For McClellan, struggling in the swamps and jungles, hampered by 5,000 wagons, had succeeded in bringing off his great army, having cleared overnight the tangle of White Oak Swamp, almost impassable in a great thunderstorm; and he was now about to get away. But Longstreet's collision with the Third Army Corps was the signal for the other Confederate divisions to pitch in.

A bloody battle, fought back and forth in the rough, heavily timbered country, ended indecisively with the dark. 20,000 Confederates of Longstreet's and Ambrose Hill's divisions had tried to perform the work scheduled for the day, which was the destruction of the whole Federal army, while more than 50,000 other Confederates, within hearing of the battle, stood by and hardly fired a shot. Jackson, who had been ordered to force the passage of White Oak Swamp, and descend upon the Federal rear, while Longstreet struck the Federals in flank, remained all day north of the swamp and threw shells across the creek at Franklin's corps, the Federal rear-guard. Again the Confederates had failed to combine on the battlefield. And although severe losses were inflicted upon McClellan, and his morale had suffered a still further decline, he was permitted to continue his retreat. A great opportunity had slipped away.

What had been the matter with Jackson? On the morning of the 30th his division, now about 27,000 men —for Lee had entrusted him with the largest command in the army—had crossed the Chickahominy, and arrived before White Oak Bridge about noon. Earlier in the day, as dawn came up, Colonel Munford, from the Valley, rode up to Jackson to make his excuse for being fifteen minutes late; for Munford had been ordered to force back the Federal pickets so that the bridge could be repaired. Jackson would accept no excuse. Munford, looking at his general, found him in a "peculiar mood."

The Federals began shelling the bridge where the

men were at work repairing it, and Jackson gave up
any hope of crossing there. Then he tried Brackett's
Ford, a few miles away; it also was heavily guarded.

Jackson's conduct was "peculiar." In the first place,
he had spent all day of the 29th in camp. General Lee
had ordered him to move; his inactivity had kept one-
third of the Southern army from reaching the swamp
until noon of the 30th. *But the 29th had been Sunday.*
Besides, had his Valley Army not fought a long hard
campaign before it had come to Richmond? Should his
soldiers do all the fighting? They were tired.

After Jackson reconnoitered the position of White
Oak Bridge and had sent a detachment to look at
Brackett's Ford, he did nothing more. The mighty
barrier of White Oak Creek was six inches deep running over a sandy bottom. Besides the regular crossings, there were above the bridge four good passages,
and one below; there were other paths known to the
natives.

Jackson had never behaved in this way before. Could
the long marches, the loss of sleep, the anxiety he felt,
have prostrated him? He had got chills and fever in
the lowland swamps. . . .

General Hampton found several of the crossings.
He came up to Jackson to report them. He found
Jackson sitting on a stump, lost in revery. Hampton
described the passages he had found.

Jackson looked at him absently; then, without making
a reply, or even seeming to hear, he rose and walked
away.

If Jackson had forced the passage of the swamp, or

had even sent his divisions round the swamp to reinforce Longstreet and Hill, there can be little doubt
that the Federal army would have been annihilated.
As it was, Longstreet and Hill broke, for a time, the
Federal line.

But Jackson, who as a professor had not been willing
to change his uniform without explicit orders, was not
the man to change, unlicensed, the position of his troops.
The maxim of war—march to the sound of the guns—
he preferred to ignore because Lee was only forty minutes away, and could have sent orders to him to march
round the swamp to Longstreet's aid. Evidently Lee
had supposed the demoralization of the Army of the
Potomac to be so complete that 20,000 men could undo
them. . . . .

And, next morning, the discarded baggage, the abandoned rifles, coats, haversacks, tents, wagons, blankets,
wounded men, cluttering all the roads towards the south,
whither the Federals had again retreated, bore out Lee's
belief—if such evidence can ever be conclusive. The
advancing columns of the Confederates picked up prisoners everywhere. The whole country was littered with
the refuse of a great army. Havoc and disorder
could be the one meaning of all this. And Lee urged
his subordinates on.

The Army of the Potomac had taken up a formidable
position across the top of Malvern Hill, and it had been
fortified by the able General Porter, whose corps, having suffered most in the campaign, led the retreat. All
the Federal reserve artillery stood, tier upon tier, in a
semicircle, on the crest of the hill. Every thicket, every

ravine, every fence sheltered the hordes of infantry. To the north the face of the hill swept the open, marshy country for miles.

Franklin's corps the night before having left Jackson's front at White Oak Swamp, that general led the Confederate advance. Only three roads, one of them a track through the woods, ran to the Federal stronghold. The Confederates, crowded in the narrow roads, were slow.

General Lee was sick, and Longstreet being sent to look the ground over came back with the advice that the hill should be stormed. Artillery firing from the woods over the heads of the infantry would shatter the Federal guns; and the infantry would follow up the bombardment and drive the enemy over the south side of the hill. Jackson saw the power of the Federals, and talked against the frontal attack. But Lee, now desperate in the face of the imminent escape of his enemy, after a little parley ordered the attack.

It was not until four-thirty that the Confederates were lined up. At last they saw the fearful task before them. The wide open fields leading to the foot of the hill hid marshes and swamps. The artillery floundered and could not move: the Federal guns put the Confederate artillery out of action as it emerged from the woods. Nevertheless the infantry charged.

Daniel Hill's men charged across the swamps. The whole Confederate line was expected to move, but Hill's men charged alone, up to the center of the Union line where they stopped, cut down by canister and grapeshot. The hurricane of lead and iron mowed down the

wheat standing in the fields, or tossed it along with the
bloody fragments of men, high in the foul air.   Before
help could reach Hill he was defeated, and his demoralized soldiers fell back, scattered.   Huger and Magruder
launched another isolated assault upon the Union left.
It received an even bloodier defeat.   Other attacks,
disjointed and unsupported, were defeated.   At the
end of three hours the Confederates had made no impression at all upon the Army of the Potomac, and
withdrew from the field with a loss of 5,000 men.   The
Federals had lost only a third that many.   The Confederates had not a chance of success.

A bold counterstroke must have driven the Confederates from the field.   McClellan was not the man to
deliver it.   He was not even present at the battle.   He
was away in conference with a naval officer on the James,
where he intended to bring·his army victorious or defeated.   McClellan had so lost his reason that he could
not realize that his men had been defeated in only one
battle of the campaign—Gaines' Mill.   But if the army
was not defeated, its general was.   His low morale had
infected his officers.   The officers in command at Malvern Hill lacked the initiative to press the Confederates
after their defeat.   They were thankful, in the panic
of retreat, to get off unharmed.

The private in the Union ranks supposed himself
beaten.   In great battles the individual never knows
what is happening.   The Union private knew only that
he was falling back.   The direction of his marching
greatly determined his morale.

Before the battle of Malvern Hill was fought, Mc-
Clellan had telegraphed to Washington:

> Our losses have been very great, and we have failed to win
> only because overpowered by superior numbers.

Right after Gaines' Mill he had wired that

> if I save this army now I tell you plainly that I owe no
> thanks to you or to any other person in Washington. You
> have done your best to sacrifice this army.

McDowell's corps had been continually promised him
all summer, and there was some truth in what he said.
There would have been also a justification of it had Lee
had the 200,000 McClellan believed him to have.

The morning of July 2nd seemed to the Confederates
long coming. All night Jackson's division commanders
had been sending in reports of disaster. The men were
lost from their commands; they were tired; the rain beat
down upon them; gloom had settled upon their desola-
tion and confusion. Jackson heard the reports in silence.
But at last, being told that the dawn would see the
Yankees attacking them, he said:

"No, they will clear out in the morning."

Few officers in the Confederate army thought so.
But Jackson never forgot the condition of the enemy,
however bad his own condition might be; and when the
mist, shortly after dawn, rose from the crest of Malvern
Hill, not a gun, not a company of infantry manned the
heights. A few cavalrymen rode back and forth on the
hill. The victors, demoralized, had fled in the night.

Jackson had his divisions fed and under arms by eleven
o'clock. They stood in three lines of battle, ready to

take up the pursuit. They did not take it up. But it
was not because they were tired or discouraged. And
Jackson's men, at Malvern Hill, as at Manassas, had
borne the brunt of the fight. There was another reason.
They received no orders.

That afternoon President Davis accompanied by his
nephew dismounted before a large brick mansion called
the Poindexter house. He walked in.

General Lee had been in this house several hours
receiving reports from his officers. Longstreet had been
the first to arrive; his report had been discouraging.
Jackson sat very quiet, and said nothing. He seemed
depressed. General Lee, surrounded by Longstreet
and Jackson, Major McGuire and Major Dabney of
Jackson's staff, and Major Walter Taylor of his own
staff, rose to receive the President.

The President and General Lee began a lively discussion of the prospects of following up McClellan.
There seemed to be some doubt about his retreating.
Had he embarked? Had he already got away? Or was
he about to cross the upper James and assail Richmond
from the south?

As the talk ran on Jackson grew impatient. He knew,
even if General Lee did not, what McClellan was doing.
But the conference broke up, with some words about the
impassable muddy roads, and no pursuit was ordered
that day. Jackson believed that if the Yankees could
use the roads for retreat the Confederates could use
them for pursuit.

Next morning, July 3rd, Longstreet's division took
up the march at the head of the column; it had not been

engaged at Malvern Hill. Jackson's divisions followed. Night fell, and because Longstreet had to counter-march away from an obstructed road, the Confederates made only three miles that day.

In the morning General Stuart at the head of his cavalry rode up on Evelington Heights overlooking the disorganized mass of the Army of the Potomac at West-over Landing. The Federals were there, 90,000 men huddled in the mud on an area of two or three square miles. Now, at the very end of the pursuit, lay the great opportunity: the Federals had taken no defensive pre-cautions whatever. Evelington Heights commanded the entire position. General Stuart assumed that Long-street was already close by (he did not trouble to verify the supposition) and threw shells into the Union camp. Confusion and panic ensued, and spread rapidly. But the attack not growing heavier, McClellan preserved the wit to send some infantry to drive Stuart off.

General Stuart, the bravest of men, could never resist a spectacular situation. Had he resisted the fun of see-ing the Yankees for a moment stampede like cattle, he might later, when Longstreet had come up, have had the satisfaction of seeing them lay down their arms.

That night Jackson, with his staff, stopped at a farm-house near the Willis Church, north of Malvern Hill. His rage, kindling all day, now mounted, and no one could approach him. A guide came in with a stupid tale of roads and directions. Jackson turned on him and fiercely drove him from his presence. Addressing his staff, he said:

"Now, gentlemen, Jim will have breakfast for you punctually at dawn. I expect you to be up, to eat immediately, and be in the saddle without delay. We must burn no more daylight."

At dawn Major Dabney, the only staff-officer out of bed, heard Jackson coming downstairs. Jackson looked round.

"Major, how is it this staff will never be punctual?"

He turned to Jim: "Put back that food into the chest, and have that chest in the wagon, and that wagon moving in two minutes!"

He was too angry to eat, and hurrying out of the house, he mounted his horse and galloped away.

But it was too late to hurry. McClellan had been driven from Richmond; he had lost 16,000 men, 52 cannon, and 35,000 modern rifles, which the Confederates sorely needed. But he had got away.

Jim stared at the figure of his master vanishing down the road.

"Phew!" he said softly to Major Dabney. "My stars, but the gineral is jus' mad this time. Mos' like lightnin' strike him!"

But Stonewall Jackson, who was lightning itself, had not struck. On July 8th General Lee withdrew the Army of Northern Virginia to Richmond. The Seven Days' Battles were over. Others, fiercer and bloodier, were to come.

XV

SECOND MANASSAS

1

The Foot-Cavalry Marches North

THE victory of the Army of Northern Virginia over
the Army of the Potomac brought to an end the
second stage of Lee's strategical idea for the expulsion
of the enemy from Virginia. The first stage had ended
with the Valley campaign. Although up to the present
moment this idea had, on the whole, worked out to success, there remained even more difficult feats to be performed. The future looked dark. So far, it is true,
Providence had not taken the side of the biggest bat-
talions, but had favored the side with the biggest brains:
the intellects of Lee and Jackson had enabled the Confederates to bewilder and defeat, with a total of less than
90,000 available men, a host of some 200,000, 105,000 of
whom had been concentrated in one place. But the price
of victory, in a specie the South could least afford, had
been high. Lee had lost 20,000 men; so that now his
army mustered, to meet the continued threat of Mc-
Clellan from Westover Landing and an even more
energetic threat from a new foe north of Richmond,

barely 65,000 men. McClellan had been driven away, but Lee and Jackson, facing the new menace, could not be idle.

For, while the Seven Days were in progress, Lincoln had finally seen that because he had scattered his forces Jackson had beaten them in detail. Accordingly, on June 26th he had united the corps of McDowell, Frémont, and Banks into the "Army of Virginia," and had called from the West, not Lochinvar, but Major-General John Pope. Pope wore the laurels of success in a minor campaign against Island Number Ten in the Mississippi. He was a good rider, handsome, boastful, energetic, brave, and ill-mannered.

When he took command he found his three corps widely scattered and he was not wholly pleased; but he promised great results. His campaign had been planned for him by the desk strategists in Washington, and the plans had been framed before McClellan had been defeated. Pope was to have advanced on Gordonsville, an important railroad junction, and threatened the rear of Richmond, while McClellan stormed its front. The same general plan was now to be carried out, even though McClellan had been thrown for the moment on the defensive.

The Richmond authorities, preoccupied with their own difficulties, exaggerated the power and energy of their opponents. The Confederate army was held round the city. Jackson, as usual, grew restless, and outlined a plan to his friend Mr. Boteler, who carried it to the President. Jackson urged the immediate formation of an invading army of 60,000 men, which would go north into Maryland and Pennsylvania before Pope could bring his scattered army together. He argued that McClellan, who was still feared, was paralyzed for good, and would stay in his intrenched camp. He alone had visualized the condition of the Army of the Potomac after Malvern Hill; and he was now the true prophet of its future action.

He knew, also, like Lee, that Mr. Lincoln's chief concern was not Richmond, but Washington; that a northern invasion would not only bewilder the unorganized Pope, but would draw McClellan after it like a magnet. President Davis gave Jackson's ideas perfunctory consideration; then put them aside. He trembled so in his own capital that he could not see Lincoln shaking in his. Mr. Davis was not a man of ideas; he was a man whose fears kept his speculation in a weak solution. Lee and Jackson had not merely to fight the enemy; they had to fight Mr. Davis for the privilege. But they would win anyhow. . . .

When General Pope arrived on the scene, he issued a remarkable address to his army. The Federals in the West had been successful; he told the Eastern army how to be. The address, in part, follows:

> I have come to you from the West, where we have always seen the backs of our enemies. . . . I desire you to dismiss from your minds certain phrases, which I am sorry to find in vogue amongst you. I hear constantly of taking strong positions and holding them—of lines of retreat and of bases of supplies. . . . Let us discard such ideas. Let us study the probable lines of retreat of our opponents, *and leave our own to take care of themselves.*

When Pope had thus successfully insulted his subordinate officers, he announced his attitude towards the civilians in the "enemy's" territory. For the first time, the Union army was ordered to live on the country; Shenck's and Blenker's Germans, mild in the face of the enemy, were hell on the region they passed through; houses and granaries were pillaged and burnt; women insulted; old men threatened with their lives. The civilian population Pope held to account for the raids of Southern cavalry; and if the raiders were caught, they were dealt with not as organized soldiers, but conveniently as guerillas, and were shot. Hard as this policy was, Pope's edict of July 23rd put it out of mind. Civilians within the district occupied by a Union force were to have the oath of allegiance to the "United States" administered to them; if they refused to take it, they were to be driven from their homes.

"This new general," some one told Jackson, "claims your attention."

"And, please God, he shall have it," Jackson said.

By July 13th, McClellan being still inert, Lee had returned to his old device of frightening the Northern President. The original Valley Army, reduced to less than 12,000 men, was ordered to Gordonsville. The old rumors, like a malignant Lazarus, came to life, and Jackson was marching to the North with 60,000 men.

Jackson meant to give Pope his full attention, but for a while he would have to be exceedingly cautious. For Pope's army mustered about 47,000 men, and Lee could not afford to send reinforcements from Richmond until McClellan's intentions became clear. Jackson could not

safely advance beyond Gordonsville; but if he could en-
tice Pope farther south, Lee might send enough men to
effect his destruction, and then rush them back to Richmond before McClellan knew what had happened.
Jackson began deceiving Pope. . . .

Had Jackson such a large force after all? If he had,
what was the matter with him? He had never been
known to stay in one place longer than four days, and
by August 6th he had been at Gordonsville nearly a
month. Even the reinforcements that had come to him
had not stirred him up. Ambrose Hill's division, although it was known to have arrived, contained an uncertain power. Pope had been ordered to divert Lee's
army from McClellan, and if Jackson, a part of Lee,
had a small force now it was Pope's intention that he
should have a greater. The arrival of Ambrose Hill
gave Old Jack a total strength of 24,000 men, and he
was luring Pope on.

Lee, on July 27th, had written: "I want Pope sup-
pressed."

On August 6th Pope advanced from Sperryville towards Culpeper. Next day Jackson started his corps
in the same direction, to fall upon Pope's advance-guard
before his whole army could concentrate.

But it was a hot day, and General Hill, who had received only peremptory orders the purpose of which he
was left to guess, failed to coöperate. Jackson's army
made only eight miles.

Next day it made only three or four. Jackson had
offended his subordinate by his passion for secrecy.
There was no need of secrecy in these marches, but Old

Jack seldom altered a rule to fit the case. Jackson's character was, with respect to will, overdeveloped; he was a moral Procrustes. General Lee, before Hill's division left Richmond, had slyly hinted to Jackson that Hill could be trusted. Jackson had refused to take the hint.

But Fortune, that goddess who, in eighteenth-century fiction, neatly controlled the affairs of men, now stepped upon the stage in the familiar shape of General Banks, the eminent Massachusetts politician, who led the foremost corps of Pope's army. Old Jack's "foot-cavalry", for such was the title that fame for their swift marches had awarded them, looked upon his approach with no little satisfaction. And with some affection. They liked General Banks. They looked upon him as an officer in the commissary department of their own army. They called him Commissary Banks. He could always be depended upon, after a battle, to feed them when they were hungriest and to clothe their ragged backs.

When Jackson heard who was in his front, he said: "Banks is in front of me, and he is always ready to fight." Then, looking at Major McGuire, his surgeon, he added: "And he usually gets whipped!"

General Banks, eager to retrieve his broken fame and to be revenged upon Jackson for Winchester, came rushing down through Virginia, and, on August 9th, without asking Pope for reinforcements or telling him what he proposed to do, fell upon Jackson's corps at Cedar Mountain, seven miles south of Culpeper Court House. Banks' men, making up in courage what their general lacked in character and intelligence, attacked the left flank of Old Jack's line, and put it to rout. (See map, p. 115.)

But Fortune had decreed that Banks' haste should bring him to the field with only 8,000 men, and when Hill deployed his division the broken line was restored. Banks could not beat off 20,000 men, and as darkness fell, it being too late to call for help, he fell back, routed, to Cedar Run. His two divisions had been virtually destroyed; Pope pronounced them unfit for service. Mr. Lincoln had united his forces in Virginia to prevent the overwhelming of isolated detachments.

After two days of facing Pope out on the Rapidan, Jackson fell back to Gordonsville. Pope did not know where he had gone. Why had a victorious army retreated? He supposed Jackson had been severely battered at Cedar Mountain. Lincoln, suspicious, knew just a little of Jackson's ways, and forbade pursuit.

Pope's army was a mere collection of corps that lacked confidence in themselves and in their bombastic leader. It was about to be assailed by a powerful and organized unit commanded by the two most competent officers in America.

For, on August 13th, the last soldier of McClellan's great army had marched from Westover Landing to Fortress Monroe, where it embarked for Washington. Lincoln and his new military adviser, General Halleck, despairing of ever getting McClellan to resume the siege of Richmond without heavy reinforcements, had decided to bring him back, depriving him of his command and putting his corps at the disposal of Pope. Reinforcements could not have been sent him overland: Lee's army stood in the way, and Jackson's advanced position at Gordonsville put the fear of God in Mr. Lincoln's heart. Sent round by sea, the reinforcements would have denuded his capital, and Old Jack, who would surely have blushed to do it, would have walked up and taken possession of that lady *en déshabillé*. So reasoned, without the metaphor, the Northern President.

On August 13th Longstreet's corps set out for Gordonsville. The Confederate army had not yet been formally divided into corps, but it consisted of two wings commanded by Longstreet and Jackson.

If Lincoln and Halleck had let Pope "pursue" Jackson, that optimistic general, who took no thought of his line of retreat, would have played directly into Lee's plan of luring him south; he would have run into the whole Confederate army concentrated to receive him.

Now Lincoln believed that if Lee had let McClellan get off so easily, he had done so only because he intended the direst punishment for Pope, before McClellan's army could be brought round to reinforce him. "It is the fear of this operation," said the London *Times* correspondent in New York, "conducted by the redoubtable Stonewall Jackson, that has filled New York with uneasy forebodings. Wall Street does not ardently believe in the present good fortune or the future prospects of the Republic."

By August 17th Lee's army of 55,000 men lay hidden near the Rapidan River behind Clark's Mountain. Before Lee arrived, Jackson's topographical engineer, Captain Hotchkiss, had made a large map of all the country between the Rapidan and Washington. The

campaign that Old Jack had proposed to President
Davis a month earlier was now, after needless delay, to
be executed. But there was little time now; McClellan,
harmless on the Peninsula, would be powerful united
with Pope; and he was coming. (See map, p. 115.)

On the crest of Clark's Mountain Lee and Jackson
could see, twelve miles away, the unsuspecting camps
of the Federal army. Pope had his men disposed at
random; only a few pickets had been thrown out; the
cavalry was idle. The white dots of the tents, the lazy
curls of smoke climbing the sun-drenched air, the long
parks of glistening guns, all were the sign of unsuspecting repose, and invited the swiftest destruction.

Pope had no idea the Confederate army was near.
Jackson had, by his false retreat, lured Pope into a false
position. The great opportunity had come.

Lee ordered Stuart to dash at Rappahannock Station and burn the bridge in rear of Pope. Fitz Lee, who
was to take part in the movement, got his orders wrong.
A staff-officer bearing despatches from Lee fell into the
clutches of the Yankee cavalry. Fitz Lee delayed the
surprise-attack, and Pope learned Lee's plans. Before
the mild huntsman, the Army of Northern Virginia,
could sprinkle the salt on the bluebird's tail, the bird had
flown.

Jackson had urged Lee to attack Pope without the
advantage of Fitz Lee's cavalry, and in spite of the absence of the commissary wagons. Jackson had mentioned the large supply of food to be pillaged at Brandy
Station, which could easily be captured, and the green
apples and corn at every roadside. Lee thought the men

could not subsist on such food.   He decided against the attack.

As he announced his decision, Jackson turned away, and groaned.   Longstreet, who stood near, reported the groan to Lee.   Longstreet never groaned; he argued; he argued even when the best opportunities were slipping away. . . .

Stuart now made up for the blunder of his subordinate by capturing Pope's headquarters under the good man's very nose, and brought off his despatch book.   The information it disclosed was of immense value; but it was disquieting.   It betrayed the positions of Pope's corps. It also heralded the near approach of McClellan's Army of the Potomac.   The Confederates must act quickly. 30,000 of McClellan's army had landed at Alexandria. There were 20,000 men available from the Washington garrison.   These reinforcements increased the number of troops in Pope's district to 100,000 men.   When the rest of the Army of the Potomac landed, in a few days, there would be 150,000.

In Richmond, even after McClellan had sailed, President Davis held back the divisions, 20,000 men, of Daniel Hill and Lafayette McLaws.   Lee wrote that they should be forwarded to him.   He had to write a second time.   At last they were promised.   They lay at the far end of nearly a hundred miles of bad railroad.

Against the presence of 100,000 men, against the threat of 150,000, Lee still had only 55,000 men to carry out the desperate measure he had been reduced to try.

On the afternoon of August 24th he moved his headquarters up to the village called Jefferson, at the south

end of Bull Run Mountain, where Jackson, for several
days, confronting Pope, had been encamped. Pope's
army lay east and northeast of Sulphur Springs in the
direction of Warrenton, and entirely on the east side of
Bull Run Mountain. If anything happened on the west
side of the mountain it was not likely he would find
it out. (See map, p. 115.)

On the afternoon of August 24th General Lee and
General Jackson stood talking in the village called Jefferson. Jackson was moving his hands and jerking his
head; he raised up the left arm, palm turned out, again
and again. He drew maps in the dust with the toe of
his enormous boot. He seemed greatly excited. Lee,
listening intently, nodded his head in occasional assent.
Then, Lee nodding a last time, they separated.

2

The Banquet

Before dawn of the next day Jackson's men had
"fallen in", and the whole corps of about 23,000 moved
towards the ford on the upper Rappahannock at Hin-
son's Mill. In the cool pitch-black before sunrise the
men stumbled, stumped their toes on stones, half-awake.
They were used to this sort of blind marching. They
were used to starting off hungry before daylight. They
asked no questions. In the gray dawn the long column,
dipping into the shallow waters, came out on the north
bank of the narrow river.

At their backs the sound of desultory cannon below the Rappahannock must be Longstreet's artillerymen sparring with the pickets of the Federal army. Boom! Then the echoes faded to a whisper. Boom! Boom, boom! The foot-cavalry marched on. As the sun came over the trees, making Bull Run Mountain towards the east a great torch of gold in the mist, the sound of the cannon grew fainter and fainter; then the men thought they could still hear it; then it died away.

A kind of inquisitive excitement came over the column stretching out for ten miles in the lonely by-paths and valleys; and as the artillery on the rocky road creaked and bumped, as the lean horses whinnied, the men smiled at one another. They were going to Winchester. They were going to Harper's Ferry. They were going to Washington. Where were they going? Not a man in the ranks, not an officer on Old Jack's staff, could have guessed. But not a man questioned whether he should go. The bewildering marches in the Valley, the sudden descent upon McClellan on the Chickahominy, had taught them long ago, even the outraged General Whiting, that Old Jack's inexplicable plans were not the maunderings of a fool. Wherever they were going, it was to some purpose, and the ragged private had learned to expect a square meal and a change of underwear at the end of the march.

The day wore on; the Rappahannock lay far behind; and Bull Run Mountain cut off the world of General Pope's ambitions to the east. On, on, the clump-clump of steady feet told off the miles. The head of the column never knew where it would be turning a mile farther on.

Jackson gave out his marching orders to his division commanders—"March to a cross-road; a staff-officer there will inform you which fork to take; and so to the next fork, where you will find a courier with a sealed direction pointing out the road." Every twenty minutes the whole column halted for two minutes; the men stacked arms; they lay flat on their backs. "A man rests all over when he lies down," Jackson said. The two minutes up, the men marched on, on, on.

In the afternoon, near sunset, Jackson rode to the head of the leading brigade. He complimented the officers on the condition of the men. They had marched more than twenty miles. Then, at the roadside, facing the west, the long sunrays full in his brown face, he paused to review the passing soldiers. Ewell's division was going by, and the general, his head cocked on one side and his eyes popping, gave Old Jack the salute. The men, recognizing the lean ascetic face of Stonewall, started to raise a cheer, but he held up his hand for silence. The men passed the word:

"Don't shout, boys, the Yankees will hear you."

Then came the old Stonewall Brigade, the men he had trained at Harper's Ferry, the men he had led to the charge at Manassas, and in spite of orders, a mighty yell went up. It was a breach of discipline.

But old Jack turned to his staff, and said:

"It's no use, you see I can't stop them."

As if to himself, he added: "Who could help winning battles with men like these?"

At midnight the column halted at Salem, twenty-six miles from Jefferson; and before dawn the Confederates, having breakfasted on green corn, resumed the march.

The morning passed and every soldier knew that he was marching to the rear of Pope's army. The excitement grew, and the stragglers lining the roadside quickened their step to catch up. The line of march soon led the half-famished tatterdemalions over Bull Run Mountain, through Thoroughfare Gap, down to the plains of Manassas.

There was no talking in the ranks. Only the clink of harness, the thump of feet. Only the order, whispered: "Close up, men! Close up!"

Farther and farther they marched. What if Pope had got wind of the march? At any moment an overwhelming horde of the enemy might descend upon them. Lee was forty miles away.

Lee, the soldier who hid behind earthworks, had, in the face of an enemy that outnumbered him more than two to one, divided his army. All the rules of war were against it; all the rules of common sense. Jackson had been for it. He may even have suggested it. He was certainly carrying it out.

All—the army, their reputations, the independence of their country—had been staked on a single throw. Jackson could not have done it without Lee's support. Nor could Lee have made the decision without the presence of Jackson's skill. It took something more than skill, something that was skill and courage, skill and character combined. Jackson, with less than half the army, had marched right into the hornet's nest of the enemy. If he faltered for the least second, if fear drove him on too fast or recklessness, contempt of the enemy, held him back, he would be destroyed.

The blistering noonday sun beat down on the steadily advancing Confederates as they came to Gainesville. They were now thirteen miles in the rear of Pope's headquarters. A concentrated army of about 60,000 lay directly between the 23,000 foot-cavalry and the 30,000 men of Longstreet's corps south of Warrenton. And a roundabout march of fifty miles separated the two Confederate columns. (See map, p. 115.)

The shattering realization of the great odds against him would have been the just excuse for any mistake Jackson might have fallen into coming through Gainesville. He made no mistakes whatever.

Only small parties of the enemy had been encountered, and they had been gathered in by Colonel Munford, so that no news drifted ahead to warn Pope of his coming. At Gainesville, Jackson, to the surprise of his troops, wasted time by marching, not directly to Manassas, where the great Federal supply station lay, but seven miles south of that village to Bristoe Station. Here he threw his main body across Pope's path, and sent Stuart on to Manassas to begin the pillage. He began it with a will.

Stuart, supported by Trimble's brigade, pressed on in the hot moonless night, and took the depot with a rush. He captured the garrison. Pope lay at Warrenton perfectly at ease. The base of his supplies of food, clothing, transportation, arms, ammunition, was in the hands of his enemies.

On the morning of August 27th Jackson rode back to

Manassas. He first gave orders that a warehouse full of whisky be put under guard.

Then he looked round. The streets of the village were lined with large open sheds, storehouses bursting with food and clothing. High pyramids of shells and round-shot stood in long rows. Barrels of pork, flour, biscuit, packing-cases filled with tinned meats, covered acres of the surrounding open fields. It was an Alibaba's cave: Old Jack had spoken "sesamé."

Fitz Lee's cavalry picketed all the roads to the east as far as Fairfax Court House, and destroyed the line of communication with Washington. The ragged and starving Confederates, now all concentrated at Manassas, had a holiday of rest and pillage. In the middle of the dusty streets, tall, gaunt men, barefooted and in rags, gorged pickles and caviare, and washed them down with Rhine wine. The men charged the storehouses, tumbling over one another, scrambling under one another's feet, in a frenzy of covetousness and hunger. Such luxury, such incredible wealth they had never seen piled up in one place before. Here and there, men stood on barrels to auction off goods that had fallen to them but which they were willing to swap for other things they needed. Underwear purchased blankets; a pair of shoes bought a belt or a jacket. One man, the look of triumph in his eyes, stood guard over a toothbrush, a box of tallow candles, and a barrel of coffee. Old Jack had ordered the heads knocked out of the barrels of brandy, whisky, wine. Men fell on their faces, guzzled the liquor trickling down the ditches and wagon ruts. All the while, the men squatted in the streets eating their lobster-salad, caramel candy, potted ham, sardines.

But in the midst of the banquet the officers and some of the men began to feel uneasy. They were now safe, but what would the morning bring? An officer, unable to contain his anxiety, walked up to Jackson. It was a bold thing to do.

"General, all of us are desperately uneasy about Longstreet and the situation. Has Longstreet passed Thoroughfare Gap successfully?"

Jackson smiled. "Go back to your command, and say, 'Longstreet is through, and we are going to whip in the next battle.'"

At nightfall, the whole Confederate corps, after setting fire to all that they couldn't eat or carry off, disappeared in the darkness.

The first step in the desperate plan had been carried out, but it was not enough. Stuart, with his horsemen, could have ridden round to Manassas and set fire to Pope's stores. The infantry had come for another purpose.

For three days, the 25th, the 26th, the 27th, Pope had been quite in the dark. Jackson's column had been seen marching north on the first day, but Pope believed, as some of the foot-cavalry themselves believed, that it was going to Winchester. He dismissed Jackson from immediate consideration, and kept his eye on Longstreet. On the 26th, all at Warrenton was quiet. Longstreet still threw shells at his pickets; this, on a lazy August day, was enough to keep him occupied. On the 27th stragglers from Manassas and Bristoe came to Warrenton with tales of the Confederate raid. But it was only a cavalry raid. Jackson was in the Valley.

However, although Pope had no idea of the power of his enemy, he issued sensible orders. He knew that the raiding party, whoever they were, would have to retreat by Thoroughfare or Aldie Gap, and he immediately sent 40,000 men to Gainesville to cut off the retreat.

Pope could not have realized how good his orders for the day actually were. He did not know that the other wing of Lee's army had taken the road, and was already approaching Thoroughfare Gap. His army, concentrated at Gainesville, would separate the two Confederate corps, and could fall on the converging columns, as Jackson had fallen on Frémont and Shields, defeating them in detail.

After dark, on the 27th, he arrived at Bristoe, and looked east to Manassas.

High in the air, like a volcano, a great steady flame stood in the windless sky, and through it rose sudden jets of more intense fire. Shells exploded. The din gathered and receded, like a great battle. Pope stood amazed.

"Let us," he had said, "study the probable lines of retreat of our opponents, and leave our own to take care of themselves."

He had carried out his idea to the letter.

Then he suddenly learned that it was not a cavalry raid, but Jackson's whole corps of "30,000 men" that had fallen like a thunderbolt upon his rear.

He lost his head.

3

The Railroad Cut

He now issued orders for the interception of Jackson.
At last the terrible Stonewall was to be run down.
Pope, who had come out of the West, would succeed
where the Eastern generals had failed, and Jackson,
who had eluded so many of them, would be the great
prize of the war, Pope's prize, and that good man would
justify his big talk, and make the Northern press, who
had ridiculed him, eat their words. The Northern jour-
nalists, he well knew, had greater respect for his eccentric enemy than they had for him. Jackson was a hero
everywhere. Northern mothers chastened their children
with—"Keep quiet, or Jackson will get you!" Pope
was convinced that he was about to perform the reduc-
tion of a great reputation.

On the night of August 27th he issued his orders. He
said: "We shall bag the whole crowd, if they [his own
corps] are prompt and expeditious."

Bagging Jackson became the *idée fixe* of Pope's
movements.

First, he withdrew his army from Gainesville to
Manassas, where he was sure that Jackson would wait
for him. On the morning of the 28th, entering the
wrecked village, his blue rebels picked up a few stragglers, lying in the roadside bushes bloated with food and
dazed, but not a clue to the Confederate army could they
find.

Then, rumors coming in that Jackson was concentrated between Centreville and Burke's Station, to the north and northeast, he marched his army, at four-thirty in the afternoon, across Bull Run to Centreville. All his corps were ordered to converge on Centreville. King's and Rickett's divisions, McDowell's corps, bringing up the rear and left of his line, were to come by Gainesville and Groveton.

At Centreville Pope saw only a few Confederate cavalrymen retreating towards the west. It was too late now to recover from his bewilderment. Jackson, such easy prey the night before, had flown. Just before sunset, the tired Union soldiers, worn out by marching and countermarching, settled in their bivouac.

Then, six or seven miles away, westward, across Bull Run, Pope could distinctly hear the roar of artillery, the crackling sputter of muskets; and in a few minutes the western sky was black with the smoke of battle.

Jackson, hidden in the woods west of the Warrenton Turnpike, had attacked King's division as it marched, unsuspecting, towards Centreville. How under heaven had Jackson got round to Groveton? But there he was, up to his old tricks: even threatened with capture, he had not been able to resist falling upon an isolated detachment.

As the sun went down on August 28th, Jackson had not only eluded his enemies; he had fiercely attacked one of their divisions.

How all this came about, Pope, standing in Centreville, had just begun to guess. If it had not previously occurred to him, it was because Jackson's marches had been too simple to be plain to any one but an intelligent man.

Right after Pope, the night before, had stood at Bristoe looking at the great bonfire at Manassas, General Stuart came up to Jackson with a captured dispatch which revealed Pope's headlong decision to march to Manassas. It was just what Jackson wanted. He wanted his enemy to blunder. There could have been no greater blunder than to give up Gainesville, where the Federals had Jackson and Longstreet separated. But Pope, having lost his head, forgot that Longstreet existed; he thought only of "bagging Jackson"; and his orders had permitted Jackson to exchange places with him. At Groveton Jackson now stood between Pope and Longstreet, where Longstreet, emerging from Thoroughfare Gap, could easily, after disposing of some Union cavalry, join him; before, Pope had stood between Longstreet and Jackson.

Jackson, clearing out of Manassas, had marched northeast to Centreville. Now his men, the night before, had just finished a march of fifty-six miles. But Jackson, instead of taking them due west towards Groveton and Gainesville, had marched them on one of his inexplicable roundabout ways. Ambrose Hill's division had marched through Centreville. The result has been seen: Pope had taken the bait, and followed. By the time Pope, moving on the arc of Jackson's circle, had reached Centreville, Jackson was safe at Groveton and was attacking King.

Jackson attacked King, but not because he had an overpowering weakness for destroying isolated detach-

ments. It was a definite part of his program. He had
not marched with 23,000 men to Pope's rear to destroy
a supply depot and then to wait round to see what
turned up. He had come to destroy Pope's army. But
if Pope, whose march north of Bull Run had been necessary to Jackson's safety, were permitted to stay there,
behind strong intrenchments, the Confederate army,
united, could not hope to strike him a very hard blow.

Jackson had therefore risked bringing down upon his
isolated corps, reduced by casualties and straggling to
about 20,000, the whole Union army. He had attacked
King in order to draw Pope's main body to his rescue.
It was a great risk. He would be outnumbered three
to one.

Longstreet was at last forcing Thoroughfare Gap.
Jackson hoped, as the sun went down on the indecisive
and bloody fight at Groveton, that he might hold on
the next day, till Longstreet got there.

Pope, at nine-twenty that night, issued an order:

> McDowell [King's division] has intercepted the retreat of
> the enemy, Sigel is immediately in his front, and I see no
> possibility of his escape.

Pope, so far, had done everything Jackson had wanted
him to do. Now he was going to bring his army west of
Bull Run to the field Jackson had chosen to fight him on.

The night of August 28th Jackson and his division
commanders, Starke, Hill, and Lawton, slept in the
corner of a worm-fence. Ewell had had a leg shot off
that afternoon; Taliaferro had been wounded; Starke
and Lawton succeeded them. There were no headquar-

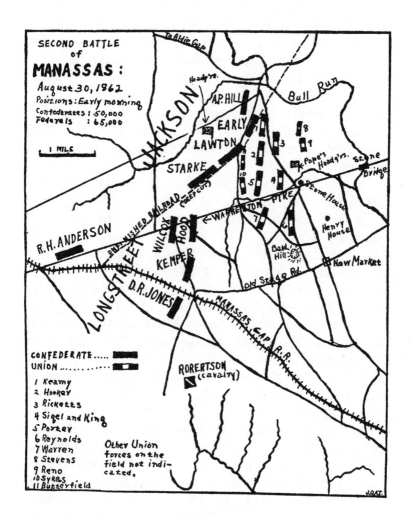

SECOND BATTLE
of
MANASSAS:
August 30, 1862
Positions: Early morning
Confederates: 50,000
Federals : 65,000

1 MILE

CONFEDERATE.....
UNION ....

1 Kearny
2 Hooker
3 Ricketts
4 Sigel and King
5 Porter
6 Reynolds
7 Warren
8 Stevens
9 Reno
10 Sykes
11 Butterfield

Other Union
forces on the
field not indi-
cated.

ROBERTSON
(cavalry)

ters wagons; they had been left below the Rappahannock. They slept with their heads on their saddles, and
to their saddles was tied all the camp-equipment they
had. Long before dawn Jackson was riding round his
lines, getting his division lined up to receive the mighty
attack of nearly 70,000 men.

There were that many near him, but the confusion of
Pope's mind extended to the marching of his corps.
They had marched and countermarched. They were
scattered.

The position Jackson had taken up was the strongest
in the region (see map, p. 211). From the Sudley Ford
at Bull Run an unfinished railroad ran southwest
through a deep cut, or ditch, to the Warrenton Turnpike. On the left, near Sudley, thick woods hid the Confederate lines, occupied by Hill's division, which held a
rocky hill near the creek and guarded the line of retreat
to Aldie Gap. On the center and right, the open fields
ran to the east down into the valley of Young's Branch.
Lawton held the center; Starke, the right. The whole
line extended a mile and three-quarters; and to every
yard there were five riflemen. Jackson stood on a hill
back of the left wing of his line, where he could overlook
the whole field. . . .

The first attack struck Ambrose Hill's line right after
seven o'clock; it was repulsed. Other attacks followed
as other divisions of Pope's scattered army came to the
field. The Federal soldiers fought bravely and several
times broke through Jackson's line, but every time they
were driven back because Pope had not sent in supports;
Jackson's reserves invariably arrived at the right mo-

ment, and restored the line. The battle raged, rising and falling at intervals, until after five o'clock. The Confederates of Starke's brigade, their ammunition running low, fought off their enemies with stones in the deep cut. At last a hard counter-stroke drove off the last attack, and the Yankees retreated for the day. Pope had wrecked, in five assaults, 30,000 infantry. But he had over 30,000 more.

In the meantime, early in the afternoon, Longstreet's men had reached the field, and Lee, seeing that Jackson was holding his own, urged Longstreet to attack at once. Longstreet came down on Jackson's right, not prolonging the line to the southwest; but throwing his men forward, overlapping slightly the Union left, formed an obtuse angle with Jackson. Again and again Lee urged him on to the attack, but Longstreet replied that he preferred to look over the ground. Three times Lee sent the order. But before Longstreet had completed his "reconnaissance in force", it was six-thirty. It was too late to attack. Longstreet had argued while a great chance slipped away.

Night came, and Jackson's men had again been the victors. The enemy had been driven back at all points. In front of Ambrose Hill's division alone lay over 4,000 dead and wounded Federals. Pope's overwhelming desire to make good his fame, breaking since his steady retreat from the Rapidan, had led him to hurl his divisions piecemeal against the most skillful tactician in the two armies. He had better retreated behind Bull Run, and waited till McClellan's corps could reinforce him.

Jackson withdrew his men from the railroad cut.

They fell back a few hundred yards to the woods on the crest of the hill.

Lee, balked by Longstreet's gift for debating, decided now that he could not afford to attack next day. The losses in Jackson's corps had reduced his total power to 45,000 men. Pope might at any moment be further reinforced, and without new men he had a more powerful army than Lee's. The one chance that Lee had left was that Pope might not have had enough from Jackson—he still had 30,000 infantry intact—and would take the offensive himself next morning.

Shortly after midnight even the skirmishing had stopped. Jackson's battered corps rested on their arms. The stink of powder-smoke, of wood-smoke, hung heavy on the air, and the sweet odor of scorched flesh stuck in the men's nostrils as they lay down. To the rear, the doctors were busy operating on the wounded. By the light of tallow candles, aproned from head to foot, they bent over their tables. A few feet away lay piles of arms and legs, climbing higher, till they came up to a man's shoulder. But fast as the doctors worked, the groans and shrieks still rose from the field. Would the night never end. . . .

They had burnt their enemy's food, and he was starving. They had outmarched him, and he was bewildered. They had beaten him on the field, and he was harassed. But, God, what a price they had paid! They had marched till their feet bled, and starved till their bellies stuck to their backbones. As they spread down for the night, the chaplains knelt by them in prayer. They prayed; but whether for their souls, or for victory tomorrow, or that they might die in their sleep, they were too tired to know.

Doctor McGuire came late to Jackson's headquarters. He came near Jackson. He said:

"General, this day has been won by nothing but stark and stern fighting."

"No," said Jackson, "it has been won by nothing but the blessing and protection of Providence."

He folded his cape about him, and slept.

4

Jackson's Retreat

The morning of August 30th dawned hot, bright, and sultry. General Pope, at his headquarters, joked with his staff, and received reports from his couriers. He was, obviously, in a good humor. Five of his assaults the day before had been beaten back, but, as he now realized, the attacks had been scattered. His army had not been sufficiently concentrated. This morning it was all there; 65,000 men stood in their ranks ready to move upon the enemy. Besides, the enemy had retreated.

Early in the morning he had sent out patrols, who came back with the news that the railroad cut was deserted, that only a few pickets at their approach had scampered away. Evidently the enemy was, if a little victorious, at the same time whipped. The last advance made by the enemy on his left had been easily repulsed. This advancing column had, of course, been Jackson's extreme right. It could not have been anybody else. Longstreet had not arrived on the field. There was no definite news of Longstreet, but he was certainly far away.

General Porter, who faced Longstreet, knew whom he faced, but Pope knew better. Other evidence of Longstreet's presence came in: it was not true. A Confederate "prisoner" said that Jackson was retreating: this was true. His patrols had seen with their own eyes the deserted battlefield.

Pope reported to Halleck as follows:

> We fought a terrific battle here yesterday . . . the enemy was driven off the field, which we now occupy. The enemy is still in our front, but badly used up. . . . The news has just reached me from the front that the enemy is retreating towards the mountains.

Pope had decided that since he wanted the enemy to retreat, the enemy was retreating. He had decided to "pursue" him.

All morning the Confederates, having rested and eaten, were beginning to take heart. The lowest private could see that with the arrival of Longstreet a most daring feat had been performed. Two widely separated columns had been united on the field of battle. They sat round in groups, cracking jokes. General Pope was promoted; he now held an equal station with General Banks; he was Commissary Pope. Jackson's men were now ready for anything Pope cared to offer: Longstreet's 30,000 were there.

Shortly after noon General Pope climbed a little hill

near the Stone House on the Warrenton Turnpike and saw his great army ready to attack. A solid mass of 20,000 infantry stood in the first line. Behind them, on the slopes and in the ravines, a host of 40,000 were drawn up in support. 60,000 men, if they could only catch up with the elusive Jackson, could crush his 17,000 in an hour. Longstreet was not there.

The powerful first line stretched from near Bull Run down to the Warrenton Turnpike. It would sweep over the deep cut and on through the woods. The order came to advance. (See map, p. 211.)

As they came to the railroad cut, not having received any disquieting opposition, they stepped jauntily on.

Suddenly out of the woods rang the brassy sound of a Confederate bugle. Other blares sounded, till the bugle calls drowned the rattle of the skirmishers' muskets.

From the crest of the hill behind the railroad cut heavy lines of gray infantry ran out, and plunged down the slope to the embankment. They came down the hill like an avalanche. Jackson had lured Pope on. Lee's chance, slipping away yesterday, had returned.

Jackson had delivered a counter-stroke even before he had been attacked. Longstreet's men, on the right, hid in the woods; their moment was to come.

All afternoon up and down Jackson's front the battle raged. The Yankees rushed to the charge like heroes. Round one Union flag, still held, a hundred corpses lay. Across a wide meadow a mounted blue officer led his regiment into a cyclone of bullets. On he came, miraculously. till he stood within a few feet of the Confederate

riflemen. Suddenly they yelled out—"Don't shoot
him!" It was too late. Horse and rider fell in a heap.
There were never braver men than the Yankees.

But they had been badly led. Again Pope's attacks
had failed in combination. His officers had lost all confidence. Every unit on the field had been thrown
against Jackson's depleted ranks. And every unit was
being battered and defeated.

Longstreet's men had hardly been engaged. At the
critical moment, at about four-thirty, Jackson at last
called for help. Longstreet, one of the most skillful
men in the South, his mind now made up, turned several
batteries on the Federals with a flanking fire, and the
crisis came.

Most of the day General Porter had idly faced Longstreet's men, and although Pope had urged him on to
attack "Jackson", Porter, knowing he confronted 30,000
fresh men, had not advanced. At last Pope had withdrawn him and sent him against the right of Jackson's
real line. Porter's men attacked hard, massed in the
valley between Groveton and the Matthews Hill.

Huddled in the pocket of the valley, where Longstreet's flanking artillery cut them down, they broke
and fled.

The crisis that came quickly on showed the difference
between incompetence and genius. Pope's men, drawn
up before the battle in fine array, had nevertheless attacked by pieces. The Confederate counter-stroke,
from Sudley Ford to the tracks of the Manassas Gap
Railroad, a length of three miles, advanced as one man.
Lee controlled every movement on the field; his army

moved like a machine, steadily, rhythmically, against the defeated enemy.

Longstreet's men poured out of the woods south of the Warrenton Turnpike; they yelled and folded their lines round the weakened right wing of the Federals. Jackson's men, worn out by three days of fighting, rushed across the deep cut after the enemy even before Lee's orders reached them. 45,000 men, a tidal wave, rolled down the slopes into the valley of Young's Branch.

Far as a man could see, the gray lines moved forward. The sun on their backs threw a heavy shadow before them. Their bright bayonets glittered. The sun turned the battle-flags to blood. A wild tumult rose above the smoke and dust. Artillerymen lashed their horses to a frenzy; plunged through the infantry. The massed guns behind the marching men hurled whining streaks through the air, over their heads. Off to the right, on the Henry House Hill, Stuart's horsemen ran down the breathless Yankees. Stuart, yelling at the top of his lungs, his white gauntlets spotless, his brown plume flying, led the charge.

By ten o'clock Pope's great army had been driven across Bull Run. The battle of Second Manassas was over.

Next morning Pope, intrenched at Centreville, wired his superiors in Washington. There were probably never so many lies told in so few words:

The enemy, largely reinforced [*he did not believe this; he still thought Longstreet had not come*], assailed our position

early today [another lie]. We held our ground firmly until
6 o'clock P. M., when the enemy, massing very heavy forces
on our left, forced that wing back about half a mile . . .
the enemy greatly outnumbering us, I thought it best to
move back to this place at dark. The movement has been
made in perfect order. . . . The enemy is badly whipped.
. . . We will hold our own here.

Pope, on September 2nd, held his own by retreating
in disordered haste to the fortifications of Washington.
The day before, Jackson, whom Lee had sent to the
pursuit, with orders to turn Pope's entrenchments at
Centreville, had fought a flank-guard action at Chantilly, an old mansion that the Federals had looted, and
Pope had decided there was nothing more that he could
do. By this time Pope had received 30,000 fresh soldiers from McClellan's army. He was demoralized.

Within the fortifications of Washington, Pope's
Army of Virginia ceased to exist, and merged with the
Army of the Potomac. It was not possible to deliver a
frontal attack upon the Northern capital. Jackson was
withdrawn from his advanced position.

The third and final stage of Lee's great idea had been
successful. The enemy's 200,000 men had three months
ago overrun Virginia. Now they not only were driven
from the Southern capital, but had fallen back into their
own; and the Northern President's usual fears emerged.
Lee, in the late campaign, threatened with 150,000 enemies and confronted at the end by 80,000, had divided
his small army under their very noses, had united it on
the field at the critical moment, and had defeated them.

His own losses had been great. At Manassas 9,000 Confederates had fallen.

But his enemy had suffered more. The Union army was demoralized. 13,000 Federals had been killed and wounded; 7,000 were prisoners. And Pope's army had abandoned 30 guns and 20,000 rifles.

Lee had driven the Federals from the James to the Potomac with a total loss, in his two campaigns, of 31,000 men and 2 guns. The Federals had lost 33,000 men, 82 guns, and 58,000 rifles, besides vast quantities of supplies.

Mr. Davis contemplated the results with some complacency. His policy was to expel the invader, show the virtuous results to Europe, and await intervention. But Lee and Jackson knew that their ordeal was not over. Jackson all along had been chafing at the restraint put upon him. From the Valley he had asked Lee to let him invade the North. Lee had sent back word: "Tell General Jackson he must first help me drive these people away from Richmond." He had helped; and he had succeeded. Now it was time that General Lee kept his promise.

After the indecisive action at Chantilly, Lee rested his army for one day. Then the invasion of Maryland began.

XVI

SHARPSBURG

1

"Special Orders No. 191"

ON the morning of September 2, 1862, General Jackson received orders from General Lee to start for the Potomac. The long-absent divisions of Daniel Hill and Lafayette McLaws, and another small division under General John Walker, with Wade Hampton's cavalry, had at last arrived; and the army, on paper, numbered about 65,000 men. But, a few days later, not more than 50,000 crossed the river. The long marches, the short rations, the nervous exhaustion, made straggling a more terrible enemy than the hostile army. The rear of the army for miles was cluttered with broken-down men. They gathered in groups, and hobbled along as they could, hoping to catch up with the army in time to fight the next battle. But among them were the cowards. And there were the conscripts, neither sick nor cowardly, who did not believe in this war. The roads the army passed over bore another sign of its exhaustion: blood in the dust and on the rocks put there by the bare feet of the men.

Some of the laggards, however, belonged to none of
the classes we have seen. These, after Manassas, had
thrown down their worn-out equipment, and walked
home. They had not been home for months; their farms
needed attention; they wanted to see their folks.
They had already done their duty. They had fought
through two hard campaigns, and they had driven the
enemy back to his own country.

Mr. Jefferson Davis, in Richmond, had exactly the
same view. There was little more to be done in the East.
The war, he began to feel, was nearly over. The only
plan now to be executed was the rout of the enemy from
the West, as he had been routed from the East. Mr.
Davis must have had a bold visual imagination: if the
map was clear, his country was safe. He therefore
turned his attention to the Western armies, and, though
giving Lee consent to go into Maryland, he refused to
support him to the limit.

Some gifted Tiresias, looking at the situation in September, 1862, might have prophesied: there will be a
little success in the East and in the West, but there will
not be overwhelming success anywhere; that is, unless
Jackson's Providence, always on his side, takes a hand.

"The army," wrote Lee to Davis, "is not properly
equipped for an invasion of the enemy's territory. . . .
What concerns me most is the fear of getting out of
ammunition." If an army lacks ammunition, it follows
that it is actually destitute in other material. The men
of Lee's army wore blue jackets and round-top caps.
Even the wagons at Lee's headquarters bore the initials
"U. S. A."

But the invasion of Maryland was worth the effort for three reasons. Maryland, oppressed by the high-handed policy of Lincoln, might be freed, and many recruits added to the army. The Federal army would be drawn north and west, and Richmond relieved. The Shenandoah Valley, the granary of Virginia, would be able to gather its crops, and send them to Lee. Above these three considerations another was contemplated but could not be counted on. Lee might defeat even more disastrously than before the Union army. One victory on Northern soil would count as five in Virginia. Lee hoped for this contingency, and for this alone he had decided to accept the minor benefits of the invasion.

There was an even more pressing reason for the invasion. If he remained in Virginia, the Federal army, free of anxiety, would recover its strength, and later advance with overwhelming power. He would not repeat the events of 1861. Having defeated the enemy, he would keep him on the go.

In 1861 Lee had not been in command of the army; Jackson had been an obscure subordinate. But even now, in 1862, it might not be too late. They could only do what Johnston had not been allowed to do.

By the 6th Jackson's men, who had now given the lead to Daniel Hill's fresh division, came to Leesburg. Through the streets of the town the barefooted legions filed. People lined the walks, and stared at them with pride and pity. An old lady with tears in her eyes, her hands upraised, called out: "God bless your dirty, ragged souls!" The column wound steadily towards the Potomac. The men taking off their shoes and rolling up

their trousers, they crossed four abreast at White's
Ford. Like a great reptile the line slowly crawled up
the farther bank and disappeared in the rolling meadows
and woods of Maryland.

Next day, at Frederick, the Confederate army was
concentrated. In the town, in a wooded lot called Best's
Grove, General Lee had his headquarters. Jackson's
tent, and Longstreet's, stood nearby. For a while General Stuart was there. The ladies flocked to Best's
Grove, bringing presents with them. It was like a
holiday.

Early in the day, outside the town, one of the citizens
gave Jackson a large gray mare. Little Sorrel had been
stolen. The first time he mounted the mare she threw
him. An officer poured him out a drink of brandy, and
Old Jack, shaken by his fall, drank it off. "I've always
liked it," he said. "That's why I let it alone. I fear it
more than the Yankees' bullets."

Jackson stayed in his tent, poring over maps and
nursing his bruises, but once he had to go over to talk to
General Lee. Two young girls stopped him, and
smiled, and asked him questions. Then they suddenly
kissed him. Before the general could suppress his
blushes and speak, they had jumped into a carriage and
driven away.

It was mostly the ladies who came to see the Confederates. The men, who thought politics, were more
timid. Could such an army as Lee's really fight? Their
victories were a myth. They came up a road like a mob.
They looked like highwaymen. They were dirty and
ragged, and their beards were mats full of lice; their hair

had never been combed. Not many men joined the Confederate colors.

Among the women who did not come to see General Jackson and whom General Jackson never saw, was an old woman named Barbara Frietchie.

Jackson, in Frederick, was not a familiar figure to his men. He wore a new light felt hat. It is a great mystery. Captain Hotchkiss claimed the old cap as a souvenir.

September the 8th was Sunday. In the evening Jackson, wearing his new hat, took his staff to church. Through the prayer, through the sermon preached by a minister of the German Reformed Church, Jackson slept soundly. The minister was praised next day by the Unionists for his courage: he had prayed for President Lincoln.

The army's repose was brief. When Lee crossed the river he expected the Federal garrisons at Martinburg, Winchester, and Harper's Ferry to retreat. They held fast, and Lee's advanced position became embarrassing. He had transferred his line of supply from eastern Virginia (it was too near Washington) to Staunton *via* Harper's Ferry. There was only one thing, he supposed, to do. He must capture or scatter the Harper's Ferry garrison. Both Jackson and Longstreet preferred to fight the Yankees before they thought of their communications, but Lee was determined. And he was right. The Federal army was following him, but at a distance. Stuart's cavalrymen held up an impenetrable screen before the Federal commander's eyes. Without information he had to be cautious and he was cautious by nature. Lee thus had plenty of time to send a detachment to clear up his rear.

The orders for the Confederate manoeuvres, describing in detail the part to be played by each division, were sent out. Longstreet memorized the order and chewed it up. Jackson destroyed his copy. It was "Special Orders No. 191."

Again, and this time in country held by the enemy, he had decided to divide his army. Longstreet declined to command the troops for the expedition. Jackson, who did not really believe in it, accepted the responsibility.

"Such an executive officer," said Lee, "the sun never shone on. Straight as the needle to the pole, he advances to the execution of my purpose."

"I would follow General Lee blindfolded," Jackson said.

On the morning of September 10th Jackson was off. Before he left he asked for a map of Chambersburg, Pennsylvania, and the country round it, and asked questions about the roads to the north. Jackson had his own three divisions; Lee reinforced him with the divisions of McLaws, Richard Anderson, and John Walker; the total force was about 23,000 men. As the column marched out of Frederick, Jackson followed by his staff rode to the front and took the lead.

In a small town two pretty girls ran out to the curb and waved little Union flags in Old Jack's face. He smiled at them, and raised his hat. The girls laughed. Jackson turned to his staff, and said: "We evidently have no friends in this town."

On the 12th the Confederate column had reached

Williamsport. The soldiers, ragged as ever and even hungrier, forded the river and stepped once more on Virginia soil. The march had been more gruelling than any other they had made. As they waded across, the bands played "Carry Me Back to Old Virginny." At Martinsburg Jackson learned that the garrison, as he expected, had fled to Harper's Ferry. His plans, as usual, were working out to the letter, and now he had only to march to Harper's Ferry, surround it, and receive the surrender.

At Martinsburg a battalion of ladies charged the general's headquarters in the hotel. He shut the door to write his despatches, but finally he gave in. The ladies crowded through and hugged him; they kissed him; they told him how wonderful he was. He gave one button off his coat to a little girl; the ladies got all the rest. He autographed albums and books, and scraps of paper. The ladies looked threateningly at Old Jack's hair. At this, as his hair was thin, he knew it was time to retreat. He withdrew.

Jackson was now herding the scattered Federal detachments into the corral of Harper's Ferry. On the night of the 13th of September his divisions completely surrounded the town. His troops covered, across the Potomac, Maryland Heights; Loudoun Heights, across the Shenandoah; and Bolivar Heights, in back of the town. 12,500 Yankees were penned up.

Jackson had been away from Lee three days, but so completely had Stuart baffled the Federal general that the hazardous manoeuvres of the Confederates were not, at noon on the 13th, in the least known to him.

This Federal general was the familiar figure of the Young Napoleon, George Brinton McClellan, whose full story cannot be told. When McClellan with the Army of the Potomac had arrived at Alexandria, Pope was "bagging Jackson." He was placed in command of the troops round Washington; but as all the troops there were at the disposal of Pope, he was virtually deprived of his command. Lincoln had not liked his failure in the Peninsula Campaign; he had liked even less McClellan's shifting of the responsibility to him; and least of all he liked the general's politics, which were Democratic, and his persecution-mania, for which there was some basis in fact, that led him to believe that Lincoln had sacrificed his campaign because he was a Democrat. If Pope had not been defeated, McClellan might never have been heard of again. But Lincoln, in spite of the political opposition to McClellan in his cabinet, reappointed him to the command of the army. There was no one else to appoint. McClellan was a great organizer, and the army was broken; he had the confidence of his men; and but for his excessive caution he was a good general.

The Federal army, moving from Washington on the 7th of September, had not got to Frederick until three days after Lee and Jackson had gone westward. McClellan, of course, always marched slowly, but under the circumstances he had done well. He could run no risks; he had been ordered to send Lee back to Virginia, but knowing Lee as he did, he was sure that if he went too fast Lee would pounce upon his mistakes, and he would have failed a second time. His creeping pace, moreover, was somewhat due to the "fears of the authorities at Washington, and the necessity of reorganization."

On the 13th, then, McClellan was at Frederick. Jackson had Harper's Ferry surrounded. Lee had marched westward over Catoctin Mountain and South Mountain, to put these difficult barriers between him and McClellan; and so on the 13th Longstreet was at Hagerstown, and the division of Daniel Hill, 5,000 men, held the pass at Turner's Gap on South Mountain, through which part of McClellan's army would march if it advanced. (See map, p. 115.)

At noon on the 13th McClellan's hesitancy became charged with action. What had come over him? Whatever the reason may be, next morning 70,000 Federals advanced on Turner's Gap. 20,000 more, under General Franklin, marched on the pass below, called Crampton's Gap. This latter pass in their hands, the Federals would be, for the second time in three weeks, directly between the two Confederate corps. All day on the 14th the great host of McClellan deployed in the Valley of Catoctin Creek. The advance guard struck Hill's division in the morning, but Hill, greatly outnumbered, held the pass all day, and although defeated, had gained twenty-four hours in which Lee and Jackson could unite. Franklin, at Crampton's Gap, forced his way, but lay idle on the west side of the mountain. In the night Hill, and some of Longstreet's men who had come to his support, retreated westward across Antietam Creek, and took up a strong position at Sharpsburg. During the march stragglers dropped at every step, and there were signs of demoralization in the Confederate ranks.

The Confederates were in a tight place. Even if they could bring their divided army together, they would have only about 40,000 men to meet an unusually active Mc-Clellan with 90,000.

At Harper's Ferry, on the 14th, Jackson was carefully getting his divisions into position. He had intended to give the Federals a chance to remove the noncombatants, and to storm the town on the 15th. But General Walker, hearing the distant roar of the battle at South Mountain, warned Jackson that McClellan, in his opinion, was approaching, and that because there was no time to lose if they were to get to Lee before he was overwhelmed, the town should be taken without delay. Jackson replied that he was sure the distant firing was only Stuart engaged with the outposts of the enemy.

Walker, unconvinced, made the Federals attack him by exposing two of his regiments to full view. A terrific bombardment followed. It lasted all day. The Yankees, caught like rats in Jackson's trap, could not reply.

Next morning the Federal garrison surrendered. 12,500 men, 13,000 rifles, 73 cannon, and several hundred wagons were the spoils.

Jackson rode into town to receive the surrender. The Yankees, their arms laid down, lined the streets and peered over one another's shoulders to look at the victor. As he passed they gave him the salute; he returned it. "Boys," one of them said, "he's not much for looks, but if we had had him we wouldn't have got caught in this trap."

Jackson immediately assigned Ambrose Hill, with his division, to the duty of receiving the spoils and paroling the prisoners. For he had just got a despatch from General Lee at Sharpsburg. He was ordered to march at once: McClellan was approaching. General Walker had been right.

Jackson and Walker rode together that night towards Sharpsburg. Their divisions, all but Hill's, were following.

Jackson said: "I could not believe the fire you reported indicated the advance of McClellan in force. It seemed more likely to be merely a cavalry affair."

Then he added, as if to himself: "I thought I knew McClellan, but this movement of his puzzles me."

Jackson *did* know McClellan. But he did not know that in Frederick, on the 13th, three days after he had marched away, a man had picked up a piece of paper wrapped round three cigars and had taken it to General McClellan. The quality of the cigars is unknown, but the paper, to McClellan, was invaluable. It was a copy of Lee's "Special orders No. 191." It revealed the whole Confederate plan of action. It told the position of every Confederate division. The Confederate army, if McClellan acted quickly, was doomed.

2

Antietam Creek

On the 15th of September General Lee, at Sharpsburg, stood on a hill just east of the village, and lifting his fieldglass he saw, beyond the rolling hills, checkered with woods and meadows, McClellan's great horde of 90,000 men filing through the passes of South Mountain. On they came and spread out in the fields under the mountains. The green and yellow country to the east changed to a heaving sea of blue.

On the 15th General Lee had at his back about 16,000 men. But he had decided to await McClellan's onset; though part of his troops, at South Mountain, had already been defeated. The rest of his army was far away; but it would get there in time.

McClellan with his speed had surprised him too, and had taken him unawares. But at all costs a battle must be fought before the army returned to Virginia, if indeed it would return, and Sharpsburg was a strong position. The Confederate line ran from the Potomac on the left to a westward loop of the Antietam on the right (see map, p. 237), along a low ridge sheltered by woods and rocky ravines where men on the defense could hide. The place had one disadvantage; if Lee were defeated, he would have to retreat over the Potomac. While his men floundered in the water they would be annihilated. Longstreet urged Lee to return to Virginia.

But Lee was not thinking of defeat. It was possible

even with a small force to hold his ground against McClellan, and perhaps at a critical moment with a counter-stroke to shatter McClellan's army into a thousand fragments. And the risk was not so great as it appeared to be. The Confederate army, man for man, was no better than the enemy's; but as an organization it was vastly superior. In the first place it had never been defeated; then, too, under its two great leaders, it moved with the precision of a machine. It was reduced in number, but the men who remained were not the faint-hearted; they were seasoned veterans.

The defeat of McClellan, if a rout followed it, would permit Lee to stay in the enemy's country, and would put the anti-war party of the North at Lincoln's heels, so that the war might end favorably to the South. If McClellan were annihilated, it would mean instant victory for the South. The North had no other organized army in the East, and would be brought to immediate terms by Lee's advance to Philadelphia, Baltimore, and Washington.

For such great ends great risks could be lightly taken.

Early in the morning of the 16th General Jackson and General Walker crossed the Potomac at Shepherdstown, and rode into Sharpsburg. They dismounted at Lee's headquarters, a brick house on the main street, and went in. General Lee shook hands with them. He congratulated Jackson upon his success at Harper's Ferry. The two officers reported the arrival of their commands. The other divisions, McLaws', Richard Anderson's, and Ambrose Hill's, were still behind. McClellan's Army had begun to cross Antietam Creek, a mile or so above the town, and an attack might be looked for in the afternoon. Lee, now that Jackson had come with his own and Walker's division, had only 25,000 men. McClellan's artillery, across the creek, had already begun throwing shells towards Sharpsburg.

Lee was never more gracious, never more cheerful, than on the morning of September 16th. Jackson could hardly, ever, be called gracious, but he was cheerful. He rode round the lines, and came back approving Lee's decision to stand and fight.

This decision had been made for political reasons, but he could not have dared make it without his knowledge of Jackson. He had depended upon the swiftness of Jackson's marches. He could also depend upon the timidity of McClellan.

All afternoon Lee, Jackson, and Longstreet shut themselves up in the big brick house, and pored over the map of Maryland. Outside, staff-officers and couriers lounged on the curbstone, or talked in groups on the wide stone pavement; their horses drooped lazily in the sun. Little Sorrel slouched on two legs, switching the summer flies; he had been found. Occasionally a shell whizzed over the town. No one stirred. A shell landed, a hundred feet away, in a drove of pigs; they were slaughtered. The lounging officers hardly noticed it.

McClellan's army had reached the east bank of the creek on the night of September 15th. By the morning two whole corps had crossed. The guns thundered. Lee's men lay in the woods and ravines; when they showed themselves they gave the impression of great numbers. McClellan's skirmishers saw a great force in rear of Longstreet and Daniel Hill. The great force was only 10,000 men. Through the afternoon the artillery of the two armies thundered away.

McClellan had the power that day to crush Lee's 25,000 before the absent divisions could march to the field. Before his conqueror in the Peninsula, before the conqueror of the bewildered mob he had gathered up from Pope's retreat, he faltered. "Special Orders No. 191" had brought him to the field, but it could not make him fight. He believed that Lee had on the field 50,000 men.

The hot September afternoon lengthened its shadows and night came down. About sunset the picket firing almost ceased, and the cool air of dusk blew over the parched faces of the soldiers. Another day had been given them before the terrible ordeal, another day to recover their strength, to let the bruises on their bare feet heal up, to restore the wits battered out of them at South Mountain. The arrival of Jackson's two divisions gave them hope. And old Jack himself, who had ridden round the lines, seemed not in the least disturbed.

Near midnight Hood's division on the left came to the rear to cook and eat, and Jackson's men took their place. They lined up north of Sharpsburg across the Hagerstown Pike, the Stonewall Brigade to the left in a meadow between the North and the West Woods, and Lawton's division in a field of tall corn on the east side of the pike, where the men on his right touched the East Woods (see map, p. 237).

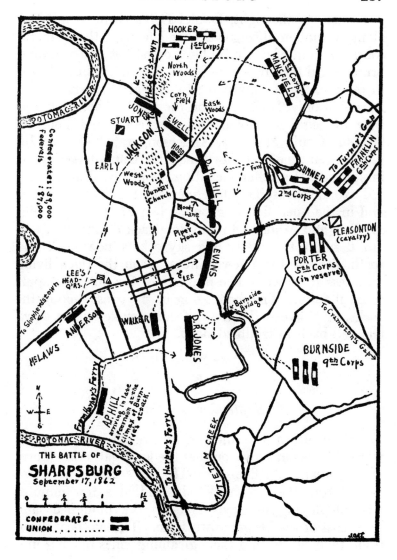

THE BATTLE OF
SHARPSBURG
September 17, 1862

Farther to the right, Daniel Hill's battered men lay along a sunken zigzag road, and beyond them, to the south, in front of the town, lay Longstreet's men, Evans' brigade and the division of D. R. Jones. Behind Jones, in reserve, lay the division of General Walker. There were still only 25,000 men on the field. The battle was sure to begin at dawn, and they could not hold off 90,000. Could McLaws, Anderson, and Ambrose Hill get there in time? If they failed, the Confederate army, in spite of McClellan's caution, would be destroyed.

Beyond Jackson's 5,000 men, in the North Woods and in the open fields beyond, stood 21,000 men under Hooker and Mansfield ready to attack at dawn.

All night the shells like skyrockets flew back and forth, fiercely for a few minutes, then the thick living darkness returned. The muskets of the outposts sputtered fitfully. The men, lying in the grass among the rocks, or between the rows of corn, woke with a start, and fell back in troubled sleep.

3

September 17, 1862

Before dawn the increasing fire of the outposts warned Jackson's division that the long-gathering storm would break. At five-thirty Hooker's 12,500 men emerged from the North Woods, and in a few minutes were deploying in even ranks in the ploughed land northeast of the Hagerstown Pike. The sun beat down upon their heads, and their gleaming rifles moving in a solid mass would break the thin lines of the Confederates. The Confederates hid behind bushes and stone fences, behind ledges of limestone.

Hooker's infantry advanced steadily on both sides of the pike. The battle grew fiercer and fiercer. The lines, hidden in rolling clouds of smoke, surged back and forth, the Yankees gaining here but losing there. In the cornfield, the men stood up at a hundred feet and shot at one another's faces.

Hooker's men, fighting desperately, in close ranks, not piecemeal, were pushing the Confederates back inch by inch. The battle had raged three hours. Now, having gained a slight advantage, they halted; they were fought out. 12,500 to 5,000—all Jackson had used— they had been fought to a standstill. They had been repulsed; and a counter-stroke would drive them back through the North Woods.

But there was no time for a counter-stroke. The lull after Hooker's attack hardly gave the Confederates a good breath before Mansfield's corps, 8,500 men, advanced to Hooker's relief. The battle raged again even more fiercely than before. It was now seven-thirty.

Jackson, sitting his horse behind the Dunkard Church on the Hagerstown Pike, looked calmly round. Shells and bullets dropped thick about him. He seemed to be lost in thought. Seeing Mansfield's men coming on, he quietly sent word to Early's brigade to advance from the far left to his support.

The Federals now drove the Confederates from the East Woods through the open fields into the West

Woods below the Dunkard Church. Hood's "Texicans" had been beaten back, and by nine o'clock a wide gap had been opened in Jackson's line. But Mansfield's corps, too, had been fought to a standstill, and the Federals, having opened the gap, could not press on.

Still, Jackson, to repel the attack of 21,000 men, had used every man available on his wing, and his force of about 10,000 had lost 3,000. He could not be expected to resist another fierce attack. But the attack was coming.

18,000 fresh Northerners were already in sight, crossing the Antietam due east of Daniel Hill's position; part of them under Generals French and Richardson were attacking Hill; the divisions of Sedgwick and Smith, nearly 12,000 men, circled round to the north and west, and moved upon Jackson in the West Wood.

Already riderless horses were plunging into the smoke, squealing and rearing. Batteries rushed to and fro. Columns of marching infantry appeared, disappeared. Down the Hagerstown Pike, back of Jackson's division, poured a stream of men, wounded and panic-struck. Guards, halting the stragglers, demanded to see blood. The men pushed on. Some, the guards shot down. Others took to the fields, and skulked, dazed, in the woods and hollows.

At nine o'clock General Lee, seeing Jackson hard pressed, had ordered General Walker's division to leave Longstreet, who had not been attacked, and to go to the support of Jackson.

General Walker, recalling his skirmishers, hastily put his men on the march. Two miles away the shat-

tering din of Jackson's battle drowned out the roar of
Longstreet's artillery duelling with the enemy at long
range. Along the rear of the Confederate lines Walker
met up with McLaws' and Anderson's divisions, who
had arrived early in the morning and were awaiting
orders. McLaws and Walker together made up a strong
reserve for Jackson—nearly 10,000 men.

As General Walker passed through the village he
saw General Lee standing on the hill east of the town.
Lee had mounted a large limestone rock, and he was
calmly surveying the whole field. He held his field-glass
to his eyes, and his tall gray figure was like a monument
of some hero in the old time.

Jackson, below the Dunkard Church, was still lost
in thought, and, sucking his lemon, seemed perfectly
self-possessed. The Yankees had broken his line, but
they had fallen down, exhausted; they were now contented to hold their positions. The broken line and the
menace of Sedgwick and Smith concerned him not at
all. He was not wondering if he could hold his lines;
he was planning to attack.

It was now nearly ten o'clock. Hooker's and Mansfield's men were out of the fight, but Sedgwick and
Smith were already on the field. Sedgwick was moving
through the cornfield, across the Hagerstown Pike,
into the West Woods. His men marched swiftly
through the West Woods, farther than any other Federal division had gone, without seeing the enemy. So
beaten, he supposed, were the Confederates, that they
could not offer any resistance.

Then suddenly Walker and McLaws, and the remnants of Jackson's brigades, rushed forward in a counter-charge. Sedgwick's men were cut down like wheat; in a few minutes 2,200 of them lay dead or wounded in the West Woods and in the cornfield.

As the Confederates moved forward, 10,000 lungs gave out the Southern yell. Old Jack, riding with General McLaws, said: "God has been very good to us this day."

But support was at hand, and the Confederates, disordered by the charge, were brought to bay. The men of both sides rested where they stood. The firing, except of the artillery, became scattered.

Doctor McGuire had been so appalled at the thousands of wounded, and at the thin line of the Confederates, that he went looking for Jackson. Jackson, for the first time, was going to be defeated. The Federals, though driven back, still had so many men packed together at the edge of the North Woods that they frightened him. Men, in the Conferedate front line, lay several yards apart.

McGuire gave Jackson some peaches, and suggested, for safety, the removal of the hospital. Old Jack took a peach and bit into it. He took another bite. Then, as if suddenly remembering his doctor's question, he turned, and pointing to the cornfield and the meadow beyond, said:

"Doctor McGuire, they have done their worst."

Jackson had re-established his line north of the Dunkard Church, where about 14,000 men, badly shaken but victorious, were ready to meet a new charge should it come. It did not come.

The wreckage of Hooker's and Mansfield's corps, and of Sedgwick's division, cluttered the open ground enclosed by the three woods. Wrecked artillery lay mingled with the thousands of corpses. Men twisted and broken covered the cornfield like leaves. Every separate cornstalk in the thirty-acre field had been neatly cut by a bullet. In the cornfield, in the meadow above it, in the surrounding woods, 7,000 Yankees lay. Nearly 6,000 Confederates had fallen; they were thick everywhere, but near the Dunkard Church in the field of clover they were thickest.

Hooker's and Mansfield's corps, as organized units, had ceased to exist. Hooker was wounded; Mansfield had been killed. In the attack on Jackson the Federals had wrecked about 35,000 infantry; and less than 19,000 men, including Walker and McLaws, had done the wrecking. The battle, on the Confederate left, had ended.

But, at about the time McLaws' men were running through the West Wood, Daniel Hill's division and the division of Richard Anderson, forming the Confederate center, received a fierce attack from French and Richardson. Hill's men, crouching in the sunken zigzag road behind piles of fence-rails, fought against great odds. At last, the Federals, getting at one of the sharp angles, poured a hot fire the whole length of the Confederate line; and Hill retreated to the Hagerstown Pike. Again the Confederate line was broken. French's infantry had almost broken through to the Dunkard Church, where they could take Jackson's men from the rear.

At places the Confederate line was manned by remnants of companies that had lost their regiments. Most of them had not a cartridge. But a hard counter-stroke must be driven against the Federals, or the battle was lost. General Hill, having had three horses shot under him, rallied all the men he could find. They said they would charge the enemy if he would lead. He picked up a musket and led them. The sunken lane could not be retaken, but the line was restored. In the lane, the Confederate corpses had piled up so high that a man might go over the road and never touch the ground.

Hill's battle came to an end about one o'clock, and it had ended for the same reason as Jackson's: the Federals had gained a momentary success, and collapsed. Before the struggle in the Bloody Lane had reached a climax, Jackson, dissatisfied with the results of McLaws' counter-stroke, was planning a decisive attack upon the beaten Union right.

At half-past twelve General Jackson was spinning his schemes, still mounted on the indefatigable Little Sorrel, behind the drawn-up brigade of Barksdale's tall Mississippians. His face black as a nigger's with powder-smoke, one leg thrown over the pommel of his saddle, he was complacently picking apples off the branch of an overhanging tree.

General Walker rode up to report a threatened advance against an unprotected part of his line. Jackson apparently had not heard. He kept on eating an apple. Then, coming to himself, but ignoring Walker's report, he said:

"Can you spare me a regiment and a battery? I want

to make up a command of 5,000 men and give them to Stuart to turn the enemy's right and attack his rear. When you hear Stuart's guns, advance; our whole left wing will advance at the same time."

Then, standing in his stirrups, and compressing his lips to a thin line, he said:

"We'll drive McClellan into the Potomac."

General Walker went back to his division. The hours passed. He listened intently for Stuart's guns. He could not hear them.

After three o'clock he got an order from Longstreet to attack the enemy in his immediate front. Longstreet, who had controlled the defense of the Confederate center with great skill, now planned to cut the enemy's line in two. But Walker was in a dilemma; and he went to Longstreet to explain the orders Jackson had given him. Longstreet withdrew his. And at that moment Jackson himself came up.

"Stuart found the right flank of the Yankees secure on the Potomac. I thought the Potomac was farther away. But Stuart must be right. He has a good eye for ground."

The other officers were silent.

"It's a pity," he said. "We should have driven McClellan into the Potomac."

As the three generals were lamenting the inability of 39,000 men to annihilate 90,000, the last Federal attack of the day came down upon D. R. Jones' division on the extreme right. Burnside, with about 12,000 men, had not been able to force the stone bridge over the creek until the afternoon; Jones had 3,500. But at last he

had crossed, and the heavy masses were forcing Jones
back. Jones' men were fighting desperately on the very
edge of the village, and if Burnside took it, Lee was
certain to be defeated; the Confederate line of retreat
to Shepherdstown would be cut off; and the end of
the Confederacy would follow.

The battle on the left and in the center had long ago
subsided, and Lee could have easily sent help to Jones.
This was not necessary; nor was Lee in danger of defeat.
He knew that Ambrose Hill's men were coming.

Just at the apparent crisis Hill's "Light Division"
poured out of the town and charged the Yankees, driving them down the slope towards the creek.

With the repulse of Burnside, all firing up and down
the battle line died away. The Confederates fell on
their arms. They had been racked with fever and ter-
ror in the Seven Days; they had marched and fought at
Manassas till they could stand no longer; but now they
had to come to the end. They had always been outnumbered, but never before had the odds been so greatly
against them. At Manassas they had been numerous
enough to defeat the piecemeal attacks Pope had sent
against them. McClellan's attacks had been piecemeal
too; but even so, they had not been able to concentrate
enough men at one point to outnumber a single isolated
attack. But, fighting a defensive battle and repelling
the attackers at all points, they had won.

McClellan had not come on the field. The moment
the battle began, he thought of the overwhelming force
of the enemy, and looked to his own safety. In the
presence of battle McClellan was invariably demoral-

ized. Lee, however, from the Sharpsburg hill, had directed every movement; at every moment the battle was in his control. He had used all his men. McClellan, at the end of the day, had nearly 30,000 men who had hardly fired a shot.

Both armies were exhausted. As the men lay down to sleep the moon came up through the trees. Little huddles of men crept through the fields between the lines, bringing back the wounded. A Federal patrol, stealing in the moonlight through the cornfield, came to a halt, surprised. They had run upon a whole Confederate brigade. There the men lay, stretching off in a long line, sleeping on their rifles in almost perfect ranks. One of the Union soldiers crawled near a sleeping Confederate, and touched him. The sleeper was icy cold.

As the men fell in their tracks, gloom settled upon the officers. Upon all but one.

General Lee, mounted on Traveller, stood waiting for his officers on the Shepherdstown road. One by one they came to him. "How is it on your part of the line?" Every one told the same tale—that the men were fagged out, that they must retreat over the Potomac. Even Jackson could not contradict them. General Hood came. Lee asked him how things went with him. He broke down. He said he had no men left.

"Great God!" cried the imperturbable Lee. "Where is the splendid division you had this morning?"

"They are lying on the field where you sent them," Hood said, "for very few have straggled. My division has been almost wiped out."

After all the officers had told their single story, silence

fell, silence that after the roar of the day beat in upon
their ears. Then General Lee rose in his stirrups.

"Gentlemen, we will not cross the Potomac tonight.
You will go to your respective commands, strengthen
your lines; send two officers from each brigade towards
the ford to collect your stragglers and get them up.
Many have come in. I have had the proper steps taken
to collect all the men who are in the rear. If McClellan
wants to fight in the morning, I will give him battle
again. Go!"

4

Old Jack Takes a Ride

The morning sun coming over South Mountain un-
covered the rolling hills round Sharpsburg. Along the
banks of the Antietam and on the ridge running north
and south a mile away, more than a hundred thousand
men lay tense with expectancy. The long rows of cannon, unlimbered for action, stood ready to belch out
their fire. Mile after mile the glistening bayonets of the
Confederates warned the Federals that at any moment
the battle might be renewed. But the silence, as the
morning passed, remained unbroken. The woods rustled
in the hot breeze. Under the warming sun the cornfield steamed.

In the night 6,000 Confederates caught up with the
army, and Lee's power was now almost restored, his
losses of the day before almost made good. On the
front line the skirmishers could see the whites of the
Yankees' eyes, and the Yankees looked back, but not

a shot was fired. McClellan's army had been pummeled and battered, and the bold appearance of the Confederates led him to believe, since in his excitement he could take no evidence, that they were ready to defeat him again. He thought he had been resisted by 97,000 men. His losses had been enormous—13,000 men killed or wounded. He had not been driven off the field, but he had been repelled; and unless an attacking army drives off the enemy it must admit defeat, as the Confederates admitted it after Malvern Hill.

If McClellan had been too badly handled to renew the battle, might he not be attacked? As the hours passed, he did nothing. The officers of Lee's army knew that their fears of the night before had been groundless; that Lee had seen further than they; and that they were now losing less by staying on the field than by leaving it.

Lee had come into Maryland to end the war. Holding to that end, he was not willing to go back without giving McClellan a blow that would shatter him. He knew nothing of the lost order. But he felt that McClellan had not played his part, that there was something wrong. He had planned the campaign with the character of McClellan as a chief factor in it, and McClellan had deceived him. If McClellan had played his part, Lee could have got up his army at leisure; the stragglers that came in on the night of the 17th would have been followed by thousands of others. There were nearly 15,000 still hobbling along the roads of northern Virginia. He had not been able, after McClellan's attacks had collapsed, to strike back; he had lacked the men. But today, the day after the battle, could not something be done?

A courier rode up to Colonel Stephen Lee, an artillery officer, with orders to report to the commanding general. He mounted, and rode off to Lee's headquarters.

"Colonel," said General Lee, "I wish you to go with this courier to General Jackson, and say that I sent you."

Colonel Lee found Jackson dismounted, waiting for him.

Jackson said: "Colonel Lee, I want you to take a ride with me."

Then he got on Little Sorrel, and together they rode down a lane leading northwest from the Dunkard Church till they came to an open ridge on the extreme left of the Confederate line. Here Stuart with his cavalry and artillery had been posted the day before. Now it was deserted. Splintered caissons cluttered the meadow; dead horses and human corpses.

Jackson said: "Colonel, take your glasses and examine the Federal line of battle."

Colonel Lee raised his glasses and saw a formidable line, powerfully supported by artillery. He said: "General, that is a very strong position. There is a large force there."

"Yes," said Jackson, "I want you to take fifty guns and crush that force, which is the Federal right. Can you do it?"

The colonel looked again. He saw more than fifty rifled guns. His own were short-range smooth-bores.

"Yes, General, where will I get the guns?" he said.

"How many have you?"

"About twelve out of the thirty I carried into action yesterday."

"I can furnish you some, and General Lee says he can furnish some."

"Shall I go for the guns?"

"No, not yet." Then he said with emphasis: "Colonel Lee, can you surely crush the Federal right with fifty guns?"

Several times the colonel evaded the question. Every time Jackson came back: "Colonel Lee, can you crush the Federal right with fifty guns?"

Colonel Lee had been asked to settle a great crisis. At last he answered:

"General, it cannot be done with fifty guns and the troops you have near here."

"Let us ride back, Colonel."

Jackson had not been willing to oppose Lee's great desire to fight a decisive battle before he returned to Virginia. But he believed the Confederate army, so reduced, lacked the power for further effort—not for defensive effort, perhaps, but for successful offense. He had left the decision to an expert artillerist. Now there was nothing more to be done.

All day the two armies faced each other. After dark a light rain began falling, and the ground became soft. But the Yankees could hear the heavy rumble of wagons, and the tramp of thousands of feet.

Not till the morning of the 19th did a Federal patrol advance to the Sharpsburg ridge. It was deserted.

Only a few broken caissons had been left behind. There was none of the *débris* of a hurried retreat.

By evening of the 19th the Confederate army had crossed into Virginia. McClellan sent General Porter's corps, which had not fought in the battle, across the river. Jackson, commanding the rear-guard, sent back Ambrose Hill's division. Porter was driven across the Potomac. He stayed on the north side for a long time.

The Confederate army fell back to Winchester.

XVII

FREDERICKSBURG

1

Indian Summer

THE Confederate army, now gathering round Winchester on the banks of Opequon Creek, soon gained in health and strength almost all it had lost in the six months of fighting that had driven the Yankees from the James beyond the Potomac. McClellan, broken too, lay north of Harper's Ferry. Though Mr. Lincoln came down to praise him for his "victory" he went back to his capital feeling that not enough had been done; he prepared orders for an immediate advance into Virginia; but McClellan could not be moved; and the Confederates, fearing nothing from him, enjoyed a holiday. The good October weather, the rich foods of the Valley, put color again into the sallow cheeks of the soldiers and covered their bones. Their elbows were still out, and the seats of their pants were insecure; their feet were still bare; but the bruises were beginning to heal.

On October 11th, the Army of Northern Virginia was reorganized. Since the Seven Days it had fought in two informal corps, commanded by Jackson and Longstreet, and the combination had proved invincible. Jackson had led all the offensive manoeuvres. Longstreet's corps had been nominally the "main body": it waited for the outcome of Jackson's preliminary movements, then acted accordingly. It is significant that Lee always sent Jackson off alone, and remained with Longstreet. Longstreet, next to Jackson and Lee, was undoubtedly the ablest tactician in the Confederate army, East or West; on the field of battle—when he made up his mind that the battle had begun—he was a master; but he was hard to set in motion, and his strategical imagination was limited. Jackson alone, as a soldier, was Lee and Longstreet combined; Longstreet alone was—Longstreet; Lee alone, as a soldier and as a man, was almost God. And that is why, as will soon appear, that Lee, one of the great men of all time, should have left the whole army to Jackson. For Lee, the soldier, was always something more than that. Godlike omniscience, being what it is, puts limits upon its own powers. . . .

"My opinion of General Jackson," wrote Lee to Davis, "has been greatly enhanced during this expedition."

Jackson got his commission of lieutenant-general on the 11th. His half of the army was now designated the Second Corps. On the 13th he wrote his wife that the Christian ministry was the highest of all professions, and he wondered if he had made a mistake in not entering it. The allusion to his promotion was quite bare, and he proceeded at once to the lessons he had learned at divine service the Sunday before. Now that he had attained to next to the highest degree in all military "distinction," he ignored it. In Winchester, his head-quarters for a time were a hundred yards from the Pres-byterian parsonage; he spent his evenings, as he had spent them a year ago, with Doctor Graham. He bounced the children on his knee. He still had on his old coat. It was frayed at the sleeves, and faded; the patches made the general look a little like the Prodigal Son. It was stained with powder-smoke, and the ladies had got all the buttons.

Late one afternoon in October Stuart's adjutant-gen-eral came to Old Jack's tent. The general was alone, and a seedier-looking soldier, said the messenger, he had never seen. Some business was discussed; then Major von Borcke opened a tailor's box and held up a fine gray uniform-coat, decorated with "gilt buttons and sheeny facings and gold lace."

"A present from General Stuart," he said.

Old Jack blushed his confusion and looked awed by the magnificence of the gift. He could hardly bring himself to touch it. At last he folded it up and put it in his portmanteau.

"Give Stuart my best thanks, Major. The coat is much too handsome for me, but I'll take good care of it, and prize it highly as a souvenir. Now let's have some dinner."

But the major insisted that the general at least try the coat on for Stuart would want to know how it fitted. Old Jack, feeling then it was his duty to put it on, has-tily did so, and led Major von Borcke out to the table under the trees. The staff rose, and stood amazed.

Old Jim, toting a huge roast turkey to the table,

nearly dropped the tray. He halted; his jaw dropped; and his eyes bulged.

In a few minutes the news of Old Jack's dandyism startled the camps, and the men came in hundreds to look at their commander. They stood behind trees and peeped.

They always made jokes about him. The ragged veterans followed every movement of the beloved Stonewall. They had cursed him, at first, for his senseless marching; now they said: "We don't know where we're goin', but Old Jack does." Now that they were resting, and their stomachs every day felt tight with "hog and hominy," they looked back on his great deeds. The defeat of the Yankees in the West Woods they counted as their greatest achievement, and Jackson had done it all.

They laughed at his greasy uniform—for after the first wearing he put the new coat away—at his respect for preachers, at his blushes, at his stiff courtesy. But the lowest private found him politer than his second lieutenant; if the private came from the Valley, Old Jack asked after his home folks. When they heard a yell far down the line, they shouted: "Hyar comes ole Jack—or a hare!" "Hyar he comes, let's make him take his hat off." He always blushed to acknowledge a cheer, and Little Sorrel, when the yell went up, broke into a gallop, as if to hurry his master quickly as possible through the painful ordeal. When they were tired of puzzling out his complicated movements, they made up fables of which he was the hero: "Stonewall died, and two angels came down from heaven to take him

back with them. They went to his tent; he was not
there. They went to the hospital; he was not there.
They went to the outposts; he was not there. They went
to the prayer-meeting; he was not there. They had to
return without him. But when they reported he had
disappeared, they found that he had made a flank march
and reached heaven before them." Moses, they said,
took forty years bringing the Israelites through the
wilderness. Old Jack would have double-quicked them
through on half-rations in three days.

On October 9th General Stuart rode a second time
round McClellan's entire army. For fifty-six hours
his horsemen were inside the Federal lines, most of the
time within thirty miles of McClellan's headquarters.
At the end of three days he recrossed the Potomac at
White's Ford, bringing back five hundred captured
horses. The expedition was spectacular, and the results to the Confederacy were for once important. The
Northern people remembered that Stuart was in the
habit of circumventing the Army of the Potomac. Mc-
Clellan's political opponents used it against him. Lincoln repeatedly urged McClellan to advance. It was
not until October 26th that his army forded the Potomac. Lincoln's cabinet, particularly Mr. Stanton,
clamored for his removal. He had delayed too long.

When McClellan's advance became developed, and
it was evident that his movements were to be east of the
Blue Ridge, Lee ordered Longstreet's corps to Culpeper. Jackson stayed in the Valley. Again Lee had
divided his army. The two wings were separated by
sixty miles.

The Army of Northern Virginia in a few weeks reached 78,000 men, about evenly divided between Jackson and Longstreet. But McClellan had 125,000, concentrated. From the Seven Days to the Antietam the Union army had lost more than 45,000 men. It was now larger than ever. Besides McClellan's army, 80,000 protected Washington; garrisons were scattered all along the Potomac; the total force menacing Lee was about 225,000. But Lee knew his Lincoln, and although McClellan's present manoeuvres were directed against the Confederate communications, Jackson's unexpected detention in the Valley put Mr. Lincoln in a fret about his own; the capture of Washington by the mysterious Jackson was feared again.

Something was in the wind, and Jackson knew that he would soon be in the field. Any day he might expect the order.

But now Indian Summer turned the Valley into a sombre but brilliant paradise. The Blue Ridge, rising almost at the door of his tent in the village of Millwood, where he had moved, was red and gold. The Shenandoah at his feet rolled its clear waters towards the Potomac. The soldiers drilled a little every day, did scouting and picket duty; but it was an easy life. Old Jack made them listen to the chaplains a good deal; but not so much as he listened to them himself. Major Dabney, his chief-of-staff, was an eloquent Presbyterian. Every Sunday morning Jackson's staff and his higher subordinates stood under the trees to hear the major's sermon; then Old Jack, at the end, knelt down in his patched coat to pray. The men round their camp-fires told smutty stories, or read the Classics, or played practical jokes. Sometimes they sang:

Come, stack arms, men, pile on the rails;
　Stir up the camp-fires bright;
No matter if the canteen fails
　We'll make a roaring night.
Here Shenandoah brawls along,
There lofty Blue Ridge echoes strong,
To swell the Brigade's roaring song
　Of Stonewall Jackson's way. . . .

Silence! ground arms! kneel all! caps off!
　Old Blue-Light's going to pray;
Strangle the fool that dares to scoff.
　Attention! It's his way!
Appealing from his native sod
In forma pauperis to God,
"Lay bare thine arm—stretch forth thy rod,
　Amen!" That's Stonewall's way.

By November 7th the Union army showed signs of action. Still Jackson did not move from the Valley. He went back to Winchester. But, on November 22nd, General Lee ordered the concentration of his army. The Federals, not under McClellan now, were marching towards Fredericksburg. Longstreet's corps was following, and Jackson was told to move to Orange Court House.

On the 22nd the Second Corps began the march. Up the Valley Turnpike, over the ground so well known, the divisions swiftly moved. A year would not pass before the people of the Valley should see him again. He had seen them for the last time.

An old woman at the roadside stopped Jackson, not knowing who he was. She wanted to know "whar her boy Johnnie was." Jackson asked her her son's command. She said, "Cap'n Jackson's comp'ny." Jackson with grave deference introduced himself as her son's commander, and asked for more precise information. The old woman was surprised that "Cap'n Jackson" didn't know all about her son. She could only repeat with tears that he was in "Cap'n Jackson's comp'ny." Then some of Jackson's young staff-officers, safe behind his back, laughed; but he heard them. Turning in fierce anger, he ordered them to scatter in all directions until "Johnnie" was found.

On November 27th, after a march of eight days round by New Market over Massanutten and through the pass at Fisher's gap, the Second Corps came to Orange Court House. Jackson felt there would be a battle near Fredericksburg. He advised against it, but he was overruled.

2

The Rappahannock

Jefferson Davis has appeared in person in this narrative only twice, but he has been a great figure in it, and he has not been spared. As of most persons it must be said of him that he was a little good and a little bad.

When the Federal movement towards Fredericksburg began, Lee, strongly seconded by Jackson, decided to fall back to the North Anna River. If the

Federal preparations had been quicker, he could have pretended that such a retreat was necessary: if Burnside had crossed the Rappahannock before Lee could concentrate, he would have moved back and exchanged the temporary possession of Virginia territory for an almost certain destruction of Burnside's army. That Burnside would have been destroyed on a fair field, his tactics in the next great battle will prove.

But Mr. Davis' policy did not include the yielding of territory to the enemy for any purpose. He must, as has been said, have looked too much at the map, which he was constantly sending to Europe. The clearer the map was of the enemy, the sooner Europe would recognize the Confederacy. The South was not required to exert its full strength in one mighty blow; it was to fritter it away in trying to keep the enemy out of its territory. Mr. Davis was more interested in proving to Europe that the South could hold its own than in defeating the North.

Thus, in the fall of 1862, Lee was asked to fight the enemy at Fredericksburg. The possession by the enemy of thirty miles of territory between the Rappahannock and the North Anna would embarrass the commissariat, alarm the people of the district, and put a bad face on Mr. Davis' dealings with the European powers.

The Rappahannock at Fredericksburg is about two hundred yards wide. It is a difficult obstacle for a great army to overcome; it is not fordable. The town lies on the south bank, but across the river Stafford Heights, a long high ridge, commands it, and commands the rolling plain behind the town. This plain, varying from a half-mile to a mile in width, is about five miles long, and runs parallel to the river, which is its eastern boundary. The western boundary is a range of low hills, more broken than Stafford Heights, and not so impregnable, but just strong enough to give an army protection and not too strong to keep the enemy from attacking the position.

Lee's army was soon drawn up on this range of hills to receive Burnside's attack. If Lee won, he could drive the Yankees back to the river, but he might not drive them into it. Stafford Heights, commanding the whole plain, would give the Federal artillery too good a chance. The North Anna River gave the enemy no protection of this sort. If he were defeated there, he would probably be annihilated. At Fredericksburg, he would retire to recuperate, and then come back. . . .

The Federal army was last seen crossing the Potomac. On November 7th it was concentrated near Warrenton, twenty miles from Longstreet's corps and even nearer to the road to Jackson at Millwood in the Valley. Longstreet and Jackson were, in the direct line, forty miles apart; sixty, by the route Jackson later took. McClellan had made up his mind to attack Longstreet, and destroy him, or at least to force him back to Gordonsville. It was a good plan and, as a military plan, deserved to succeed.

On November 7th McClellan got orders from Washington to give up his army to the command of General Ambrose Burnside, the head of the Ninth Corps. Burnside, in the opinion of his colleagues, had lost, by his delay in forcing the bridge on the Antietam, the battle

of Sharpsburg. There was, from their partial view-
point, some truth in this. They questioned whether he
had the ability to command a single corps. He was a
political choice for the command of the Army of the
Potomac. McClellan had his faults, but at the time he
was the best general the Union had. Mr. Lincoln had
finally given in to the Radical Republicans, the Abolitionists, and removed him.

For, on the 22nd of September, Mr. Lincoln had
been able to interpret as a victory the first occasion on
which his army had not been driven from the field, and
had issued the Emancipation Proclamation. It was a
daring thing to do. He had waited for a check to Lee's
victorious career before he dared to issue it. The anti-
war party, until Sharpsburg, would not have counten-
anced it. But now, at a time when those people who
were fighting to preserve the Union despaired, and there
was some plausible evidence of success to show to those
people who declared the war a failure, he drew definitely
to the cause another class: those opposed to slavery.
The Abolitionists were saying it was not worth-while to
preserve a slavery-ridden Union. It was a "war-aim,"
a new motive to take the place of the breaking old ones.
After two years of unchecked violation of the Constitution, Mr. Lincoln need not be carped at for this ad-
ditional rape. It had been implicit in his party principles all along; though it is true that Lincoln presumed
to free the slaves largely for political expediency.

McClellan, as a Democrat, could hold his job so long
as Abolitionism had not gained explicit sanction in the
councils of his nation. He could have held it anyhow

if he had been as good a general as Lee or Jackson. But now the hatred of Stanton and Chase, and the jealousy of Halleck, Mr. Lincoln's military adviser, had undone him. They could now openly justify his removal by an appeal to his politics.

Burnside, taking command on November 9th, felt, of course, that he must repudiate McClellan's plan of campaign. He decided to advance by way of Fredericksburg. It was a bad plan. It made Richmond, instead of the powerful Army of Northern Virginia, his objective.

Jackson, on the 29th, having been at Orange Court House two days, moved to Fredericksburg. All idea of fighting on the North Anna had been given up.

On the 30th Lee's army was at or near Fredericksburg. Longstreet held Marye's Hill, and the hills to the north, overlooking the plain in rear of the town. At the foot of Marye's Hill, directly opposite the town, ran a high stone wall, five hundred yards long, hidden from the plain.

Jackson's corps was scattered below Longstreet's along the river for a distance of eighteen miles. Besides guarding the lower crossings—it was not yet certain where Burnside would cross—he would, by his lack of concentration, invite Burnside, should that gentleman's nerve fail him, to attack Longstreet.

Lincoln had told Burnside that his plan might succeed if he was quick. But the days passed. His pontoons had not arrived. Other things failed to come off. The days passed.

Snow fell and covered the ground. The cold nipped

the bare feet of the Confederates. They fortified their lines. They were now practically impregnable.

At last on the 11th of December pontoons were thrown across the river, but Barksdale's tall Mississippians, 1,600 strong, picked off the bridge-builders. Not until four-thirty in the afternoon were the pontoons laid. Another day had been wasted. The point of crossing had been advertised. Jackson's corps quietly came up the river, and massed on Longstreet's right. Once more Lee's army had been divided and then united at the right time on the field.

All of the 12th was spent by the Federals crossing the river. Burnside was not aware that Jackson had come up. Jackson, as at Manassas, hid his men in the woods. Jackson's line was twenty-six hundred yards long. There were twelve men to every yard.

The trap was set.

3

Old Jack Answers a Question

At dawn the heavy rumble of moving artillery, the steady dull thud of thousands of feet on the frozen ground, came to the ears of the Confederates lying on the ridge awaiting the attack. Dense mist, covering the plain, hid the advancing horde from sight. The buzz became a roar, and in the heavy air the sound of excited voices drifted to the Southerners on the hills.

As the sun came up, a handsomely dressed officer, mounted on a big bay horse, rode the length of the front line. Staff-officers followed at a respectful distance. A more martial procession had not been seen by the unmilitary looking Confederates. The staff was brilliant, but not so brilliant as the leader. The artillerymen shifting the long rows of cannon, the infantrymen waiting in line, glanced at him then turned their heads. Some brigadier, they thought, making a show of himself. Not a cheer went up. Where was Old Jack? He was usually about, this time of morning, before a battle, but this man was not he. Look at that gold lace on his coat! And the gold braid on the gray felt hat! And this magnificent horse. Little Sorrel's hindquarters seemed too small for him and his rump sagged. The handsome officer looked at everything with a stern penetrating glance. Then he galloped on.

Old Jack continued along his front line, riding north. The Federal skirmishers, creeping in the tall sedge grass through the mist, fired at the party of officers. Old Jack looked neither to the right nor to the left. At nine o'clock the commander and staff of the Second Army Corps came to General Lee's headquarters on the top of a hill just south of Marye's. The hill looked over the whole battlefield.

General Lee, standing in the midst of his officers, was giving his final instructions for the day. Longstreet was there. Jackson joined the group.

The sun, fast coming up over Stafford Heights, threw a white glare on the mist hiding the Federals. Then the mist rose, and drifted away in the light breeze, revealing the vast blue host.

Never before had the Confederates seen with such

distinctness the huge physical proportion of their enemy. Nearly every man of the attacking force was in sight. Opposite Jackson 55,000 men with 116 guns, under General Franklin, were forming for the assault. Opposite Longstreet, "Fighting Joe" Hooker's 30,000 were deploying for immediate attack. In the town, and across the river, ready to support the attack, stood the dense masses of 35,000 men. The Confederate generals, awed by the spectacle, looked on in silence. Longstreet turned to Jackson.

"General, don't all those multitudes of Federals frighten you?"

"We shall very soon see if I shall not frighten them." Jackson set his lips in a straight line, and put spurs to his horse.

Against Jackson a force of only 4,500 men under General Meade advanced to the attack. Burnside had framed his orders thinking that Jackson was still down the river. Meade's men came on. Jackson's men crouched in the woods. On the right Major John Pelham, "Pelham the gallant," commanding Stuart's horse-artillery, delayed with two guns the advance of 4,500 men for a half-hour.

A tempest of round-shot and shell fell into the woods where the Confederates lay. Meade's men were coming but they were not yet near. Jackson, still in his finery, rode up and down just outside the belt of the woods. Only a single aide rode with him. Two hundred yards away a Federal sharpshooter rose from the tall brown grass. He aimed his rifle.

Crack!

A minié ball whizzed by. Old Jack turned to his aide, and said with good humor:

"Lieutenant Smith, had you better not go to the rear? They may shoot you."

Jackson kept on looking round, and after he had seen all he wanted to see, he rode back to the rear of his lines, to his headquarters on Prospect Hill.

It was after eleven o'clock when the 4,500 Federals came within eight hundred yards of the Confederates. Fifty guns leaped out of the woods, and poured out their grape and canister. The Yankees fell back.

The infantry still waited in the woods. The artillery fire of the Federals now increased, but the shells crashed harmlessly through the leafless branches of the trees. All along the line on both sides the guns thundered. Thick black smoke now took the place of the mist, and rolled in great billows over the plain. The flashing guns were monsters spitting blood.

Then the Yankees moved to the attack again. Meade's Pennsylvanians were rallying, and fresh divisions marched with them. They marched steadily on. They moved against a thick swampy wood that stuck out like a tongue from the center of the Confederate line. The wood stretched for seven hundred yards across the front. Jackson had not put any men in the woods. They stood farther back in the swamp. The swamp, covered with underbrush, was as formidable as a brigade of Jackson's infantry.

But Meade's division marched right through the swamp and surprised Lane's brigade. Lane's men, attacked in flank, fell back. Archer and Gregg could not come up in time to support them. Gregg thought the advancing Federals were Archer's men, and he told his men not to fire. The moment was critical.

The woods were so thick that Jackson had not seen the rout of Lane. An aide-de-camp, galloping furiously, rode up to him on Prospect Hill.

"General, the enemy have broken through Archer's left, and General Gregg says he must have help, or he and General Archer will both lose their positions."

Jackson quietly turned to a staff-officer and said:

"Tell Early and Taliaferro to advance and clear the front with the bayonet."

Then he lifted his field-glass and resumed his scrutiny of the enemy's reserves in the distance.

Early's men ran forward from the third line. The Stonewall Brigade led Taliaferro's division. Meade's soldiers fought bravely, but Franklin had not sent them support. They were mowed down.

The Confederates drove them from the woods. The counter-stroke that followed drove them back to the railroad. The Confederates ran after them pell-mell.

They yelled derisively at the Yankees. Like wolves after a wounded animal they fell upon them.

"Take off them boots, Yank!"

"Come out of them pants! We're goin' to have 'em!"

"Come on, blue bellies, we want them blankets."

"Bring them rations along. You've got to leave 'em."

The Confederates, in between shots, nimbly emptied the haversack of the fallen enemy.

Jackson had ordered the counter-stroke not to go beyond the railroad, behind which the enemy's reserves were drawn up. Some North Carolina regiments, pursuing headlong, could not be stopped. Yelling at the Yankees to take off their clothes, they chased them right up to the massed artillery of the reserves. The officers at last brought them back.

They considered the order to halt a rank injustice. Half-crying with disappointment, they fell back.

"They don't want the North Car'linians to git nothin'," they whined. They accused their generals of favoritism. "They wouldn't uv stopped Hood's Texicans—they would uv let *them* go on."

The battle on Jackson's front now came to an end. The rout of Meade and his supporting divisions had demoralized the enemy, already demoralized by lack of confidence in General Burnside. Lee, not thinking the field gave the opportunity, had not arranged for a counter-stroke on a large scale. No large body of troops for that purpose had been held in reserve. And Jackson, who had not heard the result of the fight on Longstreet's front, did not feel like initiating a great counter-stroke on his own responsibility.

The battle at Marye's Heights, if Jackson had only known it, came to a close at about the same time as his own. The Confederates had everywhere been overwhelmingly successful. Division after division, with a valor that moved the Confederates to admiration and pity, were hurled by the Northern politicians against Longstreet. Every attack failed. The Yankees with desperate courage charged up to within a hundred yards of the stone wall, where the men of Kershaw, Cobb, and Ransom, shot them down. By three o'clock half of the

Union army was broken and demoralized. 8,000 lay on the plain at the foot of Marye's Heights; 5,000, Jackson's men had disposed of. The total loss of the Confederate army was 3,000; only 25,000 had been engaged against 80,000.

Lee's success was so great that he could not, at the moment, grasp it; and he waited for a renewal of the Federal attack. It never came. The Federals were now thinking of defending their lines.

But Jackson, as usual, thought of attack and of attack only. Stuart sent in reports of the demoralized condition of the enemy. Jackson proposed, near sunset, to advance his artillery and follow the "artillery preparation" with every infantryman in his corps. But the confusion of battle had disordered his troops, and the enemy's artillery, which had not been involved in the defeat, still swept his line with a tremendous fire. He had to give up the plan.

But he had not yet given up all hope of destroying his enemies. He sent for Doctor McGuire.

"How many yards of bandaging have you?"

The doctor didn't know exactly. He said: "Enough for another battle."

Jackson looked annoyed at the vagueness of Major McGuire's report.

McGuire asked: "Why do you want to know how much bandaging I have?"

"Because I want to put a yard of it on every soldier's arm in this night attack, so that the men will know each other from the enemy."

It would have taken nearly thirty thousand yards!

McGuire answered that he did not have that much, and that the shirt-tails of the men must be used. But half the men had no shirts!

Jackson intended to drive, at the point of the bayonet —for his men were not to fire a shot—every man of Franklin's 50,000 into the cold waters of the Rappahannock. Again Jackson had inferred the exact moral condition of the enemy. He knew they were beaten. The surprise of the night attack, delivered by a fiercely yelling mass of uncertain thousands, would probably have annihilated the left wing of the Federal army, and opened the way for an attack by Longstreet. But the plan was not carried out.

Lee was against it. Lee, who had the audacity to scatter out his army in the face of a more powerful enemy, balked at the risk. But it could not have been that he did not dare. No one can say what deterred him. Such an attack was more like massacre than war. Lee defeated his enemies by violating the rules of strategy. But could he afford to butcher them? That would be violating something else.

Lee saw intellectually the object of the war more clearly than his statesmen. Like every complex sensibility, he was subject to intuitions that disturbed his vision of this object. Up to certain limits he could pursue it with a single purpose. But his character, unlike his great subordinate's, was not in any respect overdeveloped. He saw everything. He was probably the greatest soldier of all time, but his greatness as a man kept him from being a completely successful soldier. He could not bring himself to seize every means to the proposed end. Jackson, who saw one object only, could use them all.

Late in the night a courier bearing orders from General Burnside to his corps commanders was captured, and the Confederates prepared to renew the battle next day. Burnside, apparently, had not had enough of slaughter. Jackson ordered up fresh supplies of ammunition; the lines were strengthened; and plans for a great counter-stroke were laid.

Jackson wrote despatches till midnight; slept a few hours; then, about three o'clock, rose and began writing again. Writing by the flickering candle, he remembered that General Gregg had been wounded, and he sent to Doctor McGuire to enquire about him. McGuire came in, and said that Gregg—"the gallant Maxcy Gregg" —was dying. Jackson rose. He told McGuire to go look after Gregg in person. In a few minutes he followed.

Gregg had fallen under his displeasure; he could not let him die thinking he had not been forgiven. . . . The last words between the two generals took only a little time. Jackson must have prayed with him. Then he came away. Gregg was a fine man; the South could not afford the loss of many like him. Jackson and McGuire, riding back to headquarters, were silent. The smouldering fires of the soldiers began to light up the gray of the false dawn.

They dismounted. Inside, Doctor McGuire asked Jackson a question:

"How shall we ever cope with the overwhelming numbers of the enemy?"

Jackson, still absorbed in his own thought, for a moment did not answer.   Suddenly he looked up.

"Kill them, sir!   Kill every man."

As the sun lit up the havoc on the Fredericksburg plains, the dull blue of the fallen enemy, lying in rows and heaps near the Confederate lines, was no longer blue.   It was white.   The corpses of the Federals had been stripped.

All day, on the 14th of December, the Confederates waited for the promised attack.   The two armies faced each other.   At intervals the skirmishers fired, and the guns on Stafford Heights threw a few innocent shells across the plain.   But that was all.

After dark a heavy storm came up the Rappahannock, and one hundred thousand men recrossed the stream.   The position of President Davis' choice had permitted the defeated enemy to escape with ease.   The six pontoons gave him more lines of retreat than he would have had in open country.   The Federal army, as in 1861, retired to regain its strength and morale, and to get a new commander.

Mr. Davis assured General Lee, who went to Richmond to suggest a more aggressive policy, that the war would soon be over.   The enemy had been driven back again.   Gold in Wall Street had risen to two hundred premium.   The Northern people would shortly compel Lincoln to stop the war.   The Emancipation Proclamation had not yet done his party any good; nor would it ever; it had only solidified the Southern people against an enemy that had tried to incite a servile insurrection. Not a slave had risen, and John Brown's body lay a-mouldering in the grave. Moreover, France and England would soon recognize the Confederacy. This was the most important point of all.

On December 16th Burnside admitted his defeat by sending out flags of truce. Burial parties from both sides gathered on the desolate field. In the neutral ground a young Confederate private from Alabama picked up a new Enfield rifle. A mounted Federal officer sternly ordered him to put it down, pointing out that he had no right to it, but the Confederate calmly looked it over, testing the sights. Without a word he walked round the Federal, appraising every piece of his clothing and accoutrement. The rifle on his shoulder, he said:

"Tomorrow I'll shoot you and get them boots."

He walked back to the Confederate lines.

XVIII

CHANCELLORSVILLE

1

Winter Quarters

TO Moss Neck, eleven miles south of Fredericksburg, General Jackson, right after the retreat of the Federals, moved his headquarters. His corps resumed the stations it had occupied a few days before the battle. Snow covered the hills; the roads were impassable; and the two armies settled down to a long wait. Suddenly everything was quiet on the Rappahannock.

Jackson, at about this time, could have been seen one afternoon walking from an old mansion across the lawn towards the hunting-lodge near the gate. He had just seen Mrs. Corbin, who invited him to use her home as his headquarters. He politely refused, saying that the hunting-lodge, a one-room house, would do as well, and that it would put her to less trouble. Besides, the general might have said to himself, if he lived and worked in the same room, he could avoid curious people. His admirers were a great nuisance. He had more socks, handkerchiefs, and gloves than he could use.

At the gate a young cavalry orderly stood patiently holding Little Sorrel.

"Do you approve of your accommodation, General?" he asked.

"Yes, sir, I have decided to make my quarters here."

"I am Mr. Corbin, sir, and I am very glad."

The hunting-lodge had a fireplace, one bed, a table, and several chairs. The walls were hung with pictures of race-horses and fighting-cocks, of famous rat-terriers, and with trophies of the hunt. The staff lived in huts and tents in the yard.

Now at last he had time to write up the reports of his campaigns. He had not written a report since the fight at Kernstown; he had been busy getting something worth writing about! More than half his field-officers had been killed, and he could not get complete records; but he worked day and night. He never said "I"; he always said "we". He explained none of his actions, and his account of a campaign was merely scientific, descriptive. He credited nothing to himself. "The men who come after me must act for themselves; and as to the historians who speak of the movements of my command, I do not concern myself greatly as to what they may say." And he said to Lieutenant James Power Smith:

"Can you tell me where the Bible gives models for official reports of battles?"

Smith said, "No," and smiled at the suggestion.

"Nevertheless," Jackson went on, "there are such. Look at the narrative of Joshua's battles with the Amalekites. It has clearness, brevity, modesty; and it traces the victory to the right source—the blessing of God."

The condition of the army was bad. Food was scarce;

the supply depended upon the Richmond railroad, which was always breaking down from overwork; and before long scurvy broke out. Lee ordered the men to gather sassafras buds, wild garlic and wild onions. Jackson did all he could for the comfort of the Second Army Corps. In a brigade of fifteen hundred men four hundred were barefooted. Many had no underwear. Overcoats were curiosities. Whole regiments could not drill for lack of clothes. Thousands could not sleep warm for lack of blankets. Jackson, like many another Virginian, had ordered the carpets in his house cut up to be sent as blankets to the army. On January 23rd, the daily ration was officially a quarter of a pound of beef, and a fifth of a pound of sugar. But there was no sugar!

"The men," said Lee, "are cheerful, and I receive no complaints."

The last demonstration of the Confederates in 1862 was a raid by Stuart inside the Union lines. He led his 1,800 troopers up to Burke's Station, twelve miles from Washington, where he sent a telegram to Quartermaster-General Meigs. He complained of the quality of the mules furnished Burnside's army, saying he was ashamed to take them back, and suggested that a better kind of animal be supplied!

The soldiers built log cabins; they could at least be warm indoors. They amused themselves the best way they could. The more they suffered, the more they joked about it. Their huts dotted the hills and filled the pine woods. Every hut at night was a scene of good times. Hunger and cold could not crush them. They played games, or sang, or told stories. Regular classes in Latin, Greek, and Hebrew were formed; former professors resumed their instruction of their former pupils; those who were not educated had the chance to learn. In the daytime, whole divisions lined up, and fought battles with snowballs. At the front along the river the pickets, huddled over lonely fires, had long ago stopped shooting at each other. All the Yanks together were the enemy; no single one was.

The men, of their own will, built a log church, where the chaplains held regular service and prayer-meeting. The ragged private sat next to the general in gold lace. General Lee, wearing the three simple stars that any colonel could wear, always came; and Stuart, with his jingling spurs and plumed hat, bowed his head as devoutly as Jackson. General Jackson never missed a meeting. This great, simple man seemed transfigured by the service.

A brisk trade sprang up between the Confederates and the Federals. The Confederates swapped tobacco for coffee. A Confederate with a "consignment of tobacco" simply called to his enemy across the stream: "Hey, Yank, I'm comin' over." Sometimes they visited without commerce, for there was very little hatred between the rank and file. The ministers and orators back home supplied that. General Lee could not call the Yankees his enemies; he called them "those people over there."

One day Jackson rode up to a picket, and as usual the soldiers gathered round him to give him a cheer. This time the Yankees heard it.

"What's the matter over there, Johnny?" they shouted.

"General Stonewall Jackson!" was the sentry's reply.

To the astonishment of the Confederates the "blue-bellies" across the river let loose a yell.

"Hurrah for Stonewall Jackson!" they cried.

Christmas day Jackson's staff gave a dinner to the high officers. Roast turkey and oysters, in a land of destitution, graced the table in the hunting-lodge. The officers came one by one, General Lee and General Longstreet. Then General Stuart arrived. Stuart was always in high spirits; he was like a boy. He could never resist teasing his old friend Jackson. He saw the gay decorations on the wall, and pretended to believe that Jackson had put them there, that the dinner-party had surprised one of his secret tastes. He rallied him on the decline of his moral character, and expressed sympathy with the coming disillusionment of the righteous old ladies of his native State. Jackson was not good at repartee, and he could only blush; so Stuart kept on, sparing the simple man not in the least. Then dinner was ready. A female admirer had sent Jackson a pad of fine butter, fine as it was rare in that time. Stuart saw it.

"There, gentlemen," said Stuart, "if that is not the crowning evidence of our host's sporting tastes! He even has his favorite game-cock stamped on his butter!"

Jackson slyly hinted that he might know more about game-cocks and race-horses than Stuart suspected.

But that was all long ago. How many years? Twenty-one years ago he had ridden from Jackson's

Mills with his saddle-bags up to Clarksburg to catch the stage. That was all gone. Uncle Cummins had run off after gold in '49; had died in the West. His relatives were scattered. What were the motives that drove him to such hard work in those days? He was not then responsible to any person or any cause. If he had brought his name to fame, as he had started out to do, what did it matter? The old motives were forgotten. He was the absolute master of 30,000 men, but he felt only responsible to them and to the principles they fought for. Somehow all the past seemed transformed. His early reasons for doing things were vague; he could hardly remember them.

His accidental training had formed him for his task. *All things worked together for his good.* Even his bad eyesight had benefited him; it had driven him to develop his visual, his quantitative imagination into a powerful instrument. The hosts of his enemies he held in the hollow of his hand. Every movement they made he visualized: the whole theatre of war stood immediately present, at every moment of concentration, in his mind. He played against his enemies as if they were pawns in a game of chess. But there was a difference: the pawns of war had will and feeling. From the conduct of a hostile cavalry regiment, thirty miles from the main army, he could infer the Federal general's plan and state of mind.

As winter passed into spring, the Confederate frontier shrank little by little. Something had to be done. Mr. Davis was trying to meet man for man each separate enemy as he crossed the border. The war could not

be won that way. Life at Jackson's headquarters was
dull; it was almost sombre; for Jackson was preoccupied. He said nothing, but he did not like Mr. Davis'
policy with the army. In an unguarded moment he con-
fided to a friend: "We must make this campaign an exceedingly active one. Only thus can a weaker country
cope with a stronger; it must make up in activity what
it lacks in strength. A defensive campaign can only
be made successful by taking the aggressive at the
proper time. Napoleon never waited for his adversary
to become fully prepared, but struck him the first blow."

Davis was trying to defend every foot of a long frontier. Lee wrote to one of his officers: "There is no better
way of defending a long line than by moving into the
enemy's country." Mr. Davis believed that the European powers would be more impressed with the virtue
of successful passive defense. Lee and Jackson gave
little thought to the European powers.

As the winter went on, Jackson kept himself busy
with various schemes. He had Captain Hotchkiss draw
a huge map of all the country from the Rapidan to
Harrisburg. Even the farm houses were shown.

Lee and Jackson had always been of a single mind.
And Jackson, hearing that General Lee planned an
offensive for 1863, took heart. His wife came up from
North Carolina in April and found him in high spirits.

She brought with her their baby, Julia, named for his
mother. "My mother," he wrote when his child was
born in November, "was mindful of me when I was a
helpless, fatherless child; and I wish to commemorate
her now."

The general took his family up to Hamilton's Crossing, nearer Fredericksburg, to the plantation of Mr. Yerby. His wife's visit was not prolonged.

On April 29th, early in the morning, the thunder of cannon shook the windowpanes of the Yerby mansion. The roll of musketry, increasing momently in volume, crackled in the air. The wounded were soon brought to the shelter of Mr. Yerby's outhouses. The Federal army was crossing the Rappahannock.

Jackson hastily sent his wife south. He mounted his horse. God only knew if his time had come. He rode away.

2

Mr. Davis and General Longstreet

In the spring of 1863 President Davis, who had satisfied himself with checking the course of his victorious armies by the negative method of diffusing them, decided positively to direct the grand strategy. It is a long and intricate story; and it need not in its fullness concern us here. Mr. Davis, who had not learned anything in two years of war, now took it upon himself to interfere with his officers in the field.

A Federal garrison of some strength held Norfolk and Suffolk, and stopped the mouth of the James River. The Federal blockade was tightening up; only a few Confederate seaports remained open; and the President and his new Secretary of War, Mr. Seddon, detached Longstreet with two divisions to operate against Suf-

folk. Daniel Hill's division had already been detached
for service south of Petersburg. The Army of Northern Virginia, which at the beginning of April should
have mustered 80,000 men, could show only 60,000.
Longstreet was sent off with the divisions of Hood and
Pickett, to chase the Federal shadow, while the Federal
substance, 130,000 men under General Hooker, might
be expected at any moment, now that the mud was drying up, to cross the Rappahannock and fall upon an
enemy whom it outnumbered more than two to one.

General Longstreet had urged the prosecution of the
Suffolk campaign on the ground that its success would
strike the Federals an "effective blow." The fall of
Suffolk would not embarrass Hooker in the least, and
probably not a single man would be sent from his army
to prevent its fall. Its possession by the Confederates
would relieve the machinery of the commissariat, but
only for a short time. The defeat of Lee, weakened by
the absence of the force that would make its capture possible, would forthwith restore to the Federal possession
not only Suffolk but would give over the whole South.
The greatest possible concentration against Hooker
might ensure his destruction; the Southern ports would
then be automatically released. But Longstreet not
only recommended to Mr. Davis the campaign; he suggested that the main army conform its movements to
those of the detached force, and retreat to the North
Anna! The image of Longstreet is that of a great bull
—powerful when roused by immediate danger on the
battlefield, but, in the intervals between battles, drowsy
and stupid with complacent arrogance.

Longstreet, then, the first week in April, invested the almost impregnable fortifications of Suffolk. He had come to capture the town, but when he got there he informed Mr. Seddon that it could be taken only with a great waste of artillery ammunition or, by assault, with the loss of 3,000 men. He could not decide which method to use; so he used neither. He accomplished only a distance between himself and Lee of one hundred and sixty miles. Lee had consented to the campaign with the understanding that Longstreet should not get himself so involved that he could not return to him at the first threat from Hooker.

If the campaign had to be made, Jackson should have made it. Longstreet never understood the value of time. But the expedition should not have set out. General Lee was never willing to cross the Richmond authorities. He saw intellectually the whole problem of the war. But he would not assert the political, the moral necessities of the problem as he saw it. He was one of those great men in whose failure lies their greatness. He had a kind of sublime humility, a consciousness of the universal moral insufficiency, that kept him from asserting himself. His duty to the South included not only the defeat of the Federal army, but its defeat within the terms of the whole situation; and that situation contained the constituted authority of Mr. Davis.

Only speculation is possible as to Jackson's course in Lee's position. He would have undoubtedly answered Mr. Davis' strategy with a peremptory rejection conveying just a little contempt. Jackson was as able a general as Lee, and he should have commanded the

Army of Northern Virginia, or the armies of the West. Beyond this, speculation, however indirect, must end: though regret, which lies in the province of poetry and has no place here, may proceed without limit.

By the middle of April the situation in the East was simple. Hooker with 130,000 men and 428 guns faced Lee on the Rappahannock. Lee had 60,000 men and 170 guns. His predicament looked hopeless.

After the battle of Fredericksburg the Army of the Potomac had shown symptoms of deterioration. Burnside's régime had broken the confidence of the men, and the army suffered enormously from desertion. But on January 26th, as a result of protests from his corps commanders, he was removed, and "Fighting Joe" Hooker took his place. Hooker was a tall, handsome man, almost as popular with the rank and file as McClellan had been, and almost as good an organizer as that unfortunate officer. Out of the chaos of Burnside's defeat he soon pulled together a wonderfully cohesive body of men, "the finest army on this planet," he called it, and it was true—if an army's quality is the quality of its food, its clothing, its armament. The outlook for the spring campaign was bright. And when Hooker made his plans, the President in Washington had no military advice to offer—he wrote some remarkable political advice—beyond the suggestion that he "put in all his men." Mr. Lincoln had supplied great armies to the Northern cause, but he had not yet found in the East an officer who seemed willing to use them.

Hooker's plan involved the division of his army and the putting of the enemy between the two wings. The left wing was to demonstrate against Lee at Fredericksburg with about 65,000 men; while Hooker, commanding in person the right, was to march round to the upper fords of the Rappahannock, cross the river, and pass through a cross-roads called Chancellorsville. Then, with his right wing of 63,000 men, he would descend upon the rear of Lee's army held fast by the demonstration of the left wing under General Sedgwick. Meanwhile Stoneman, with 10,000 cavalry, would pounce upon the Confederate communications, and Lee would have to fall back. Hooker would then compel the diminutive Confederate army to fight on ground of his own choice, at a great disadvantage.

Hooker was aware of the risk he ran dividing his army. But he knew the Confederate strength to a man, and either wing of his army outnumbered the whole Confederate force.

Forty-nine generals out of fifty, confronted with this vast host, would have fallen back. Lee and Jackson decided to hold their ground. They were not afraid of Hooker's numbers because they knew Hooker. They not only decided to hold their ground; they were going to take the offensive out of Hooker's hands and, if possible, strike his unwieldy masses a crushing blow. On April 27th Lee wrote to Jackson that "if a real attempt is made to cross the river it will be above Fredericksburg." The Confederates knew what was coming. What they could do about it was another matter.

On the 29th, after Jackson had heard the cannon and musketry, he sent his aide, Lieutenant James Power Smith, to General Lee with the news. Smith found

General Lee a mile across the fields. Colonel Venable, Lee's aide, told him to walk into the general's tent.

As he walked in General Lee stirred in his sleep, then awoke. He put one leg out of his cot, and sat up. Smith told the news. General Lee laughed and said:

"Well, I thought I heard firing, and was beginning to think it was time some of you young fellows were coming to tell me what it was all about. Tell your good general that I am sure he knows what to do. I will meet him at the front very soon.'

3

Two Cracker Boxes

Not until six-thirty the same day could any definite information be got of Hooker's movements, although Sedgwick had crossed the river and his men were entrenching the bank. The news came from Stuart that the enemy was fording the Rappahannock and the Rapidan north of Chancellorsville. The division of Richard Anderson marched west over the plank road to test the enemy's strength and to impede his advance.

No further news came that night. Next morning, April 30th, Stuart, who had worried the flanks of Hooker's army, sent a message that he had captured men from three of his corps. Two things were immediately clear: Hooker had divided his army and he meant to turn the Confederate left. The powerful fortifications the Confederates had thrown up at Fredericksburg were now useless.

When the news arrived one of Jackson's officers said that they would have to fight on the defensive, and Jackson overhearing the remark turned sharply:

"Who said that? No, sir, we shall not fall back, we shall attack them!"

It had never entered Jackson's head to do anything else. But how was it to be done? Either half of the enemy was larger than the Confederate whole. Only one thing was certain: the Federal army, however great its size, was divided, and the moral advantage of attacking one of the fractions might be decisive. Jackson urged at first an attack upon Sedgwick, who was directly opposite; but Lee, still mindful of their predicament on December 13, 1862, asked Jackson to reconsider his plan; which he did. The tremendous artillery of the Union army looked down as before from Stafford Heights. Jackson finally agreed with his chief. The only trouble with attacking Hooker at Chancellorsville was the day's march it took to get there. And time was precious. Hooker must be attacked before he had brought his host through the dense tangle of the Spotsylvania Wilderness.

By nightfall of April 30th General Hooker had marched three army corps over the Rappahannock and and the Rapidan; two obstacles between him and Lee had been cleared. Tomorrow he would get through the Wilderness, and, if Lee retreated westward, would attack him in the open country. He had already seized Chancellorsville, the most important cross-roads, and all he had to do in the morning was to march south. The Spotsylvania Wilderness, running twenty miles east and west, and fifteen north and south, gave him little concern. (See map, p. 299.)

Besides the three corps at Chancellorsville two more were rapidly approaching in the night. 72,000 men were massing on Lee's left flank, and he was nearly twenty miles away. So Hooker, surveying the situation, issued congratulations to his army:

> It is with heartfelt satisfaction that the commanding general announces to his army that the operations of the last three days have determined that our enemy must either ingloriously fly or come out from behind his defenses, and give us battle on our own ground, where certain destruction awaits him.

General Hooker did two things: he counted his chickens before they were hatched, and he constructed what the schoolmasters call a dilemma. It did not occur to him that the Confederates would "escape between the horns," and attack.

General Hooker felt dissatisfied with only two things. His cavalry was away: he could get no information. And the Confederate cavalry was at hand observing everything he did. He had expected Stuart to fly off, with his whole force, in pursuit of Stoneman, but Stuart had sent only one regiment to keep watch on Stoneman's raid. These two unexpected turns of fortune, however, lost him little sleep. He had a field telegraph connecting him with Sedgwick; everything Lee did would be reported. He had three balloons from which observers could overlook the whole field of operations.

It might be too much to say that already the North

was exhibiting a fatal confidence in the powers of machinery. As the sun rose on the morning of May 1st a dense fog round Fredericksburg hid the Confederate movements from Sedgwick's aeronauts; the telegraph broke down.

At midnight Jackson had taken the road with McLaws' division and three divisions of his own corps. He left Early's division, reinforced by Barksdale's brigade, in the intrenchments at Marye's Heights—10,000 men to hold off Sedgwick until he could deal with Hooker. Success now depended upon time, for if Sedgwick knew that only a small rear-guard remained before him he would crush it and attack Lee in rear while Hooker attacked in front. But Sergwick, at eleven-thirty, wired Hooker that apparently the Confederate works were strongly manned as ever, and that any movement of the enemy towards Chancellorsville must be a feint. Sedgwick, therefore, remained idle all day, and 10,000 men, boldly displayed, had given Lee and Jackson at least a day in which to dispose of Hooker.

At eight o'clock, May 1st, Jackson arrived at the front. He found that Anderson had entrenched a strong defensive position running northeast from the Catherine Furnace to Mott's Run, north of the Turnpike. This was all very well for an advance-guard of 8,000 men isolated before a powerful enemy. But now about 45,000 Confederates were on the field, and defensive positions could be ignored. Jackson took personal command of all the troops; the intrenching work was stopped; and an advance of the whole line towards Chancellorsville soon began. (See map, p. 299.)

Within three hours all preparations were made, and shortly before eleven o'clock the Confederates pushed rapidly forward, McLaws on the Turnpike, Anderson on the Plank Road (see map, p. 299); the three divisions of the Second Corps stood behind them in support. Lee and Jackson, riding on the Plank Road, were cheered again and again. David plunged into the Wilderness to attack Goliath.

There was brisk skirmishing. The skirmishers of both armies fought so hard that it was soon plain Hooker was advancing too. But the engagement never rose to a battle. By two-thirty the Federals had everywhere withdrawn into the depths of the forest. It was an easy victory, and Jackson was suspicious. Could there be a trap? The Confederates slowed up their advance; the cavalry grew more alert; and the parties of skirmishers crawling through the underbrush looked warily.

Jackson galloped to the front line to see what was the matter, and seeing Stuart he asked him to come with him. The two generals with their staffs, followed by Stuart's horse-artillery, took a bridle-path leading up to a low hill, where they thought the enemy's position might be seen. They rode on for a half-mile, but the thicket was so dense that only one gun could be put in position at a time. A gun was placed, and fired. Then a tempest of shell and canister broke loose from some masked Federal batteries. They were caught in a path upon which they could go neither forward nor backward. Horses kicked and squealed; men fell dead on every hand. The two generals escaped. Jackson never took care of himself. . . . "That is the way all men should

live, and then all men would be equally brave." . . .
His time had not yet come.

By five o'clock enough of Hooker's position had been
observed to reveal the meaning of his mysterious retreat. The Confederate outposts saw powerful earthworks; felled trees blocked access to the trenches; artillery commanded every road and path. For Hooker was
standing on the defensive.

The enemy had not ingloriously flown. He had not
retreated to the open country back of Tabernacle
Church where Hooker, in the morning, believed the
Federal advance-guard would find him. The enemy had
attacked. The Confederate generals were most incon-
siderate. Hooker's ambitious plan to surround the
Army of Northern Virginia had not taken into account
the possibility that it might fight. When a formidable
battle-line met his skirmishers on the Turnpike and the
Plank Road, he became nervous. In spite of the protests of his corps-commanders, "Fighting Joe" withdrew the army to the shelter of the trenches. On this
day, in honor of the occasion and to keep his head clear,
he had not taken his morning nip. One of his officers
said it might have been better if he had.

Next morning, the morning of May 2nd, he rode
round his lines. Everywhere the strength of his position
impressed him. On his extreme right, on the Turnpike
about three miles from Chancellorsville, Howard's
Eleventh Corps, made up mostly of German immigrants, held the flank, facing south. The enemy had
not been seen within five miles of this quarter of the field.
Some earthworks had been thrown up, facing south.

Hooker looked round. He said: "How strong! How strong!"

As twilight gathered on May 1st, Lee and Jackson established headquarters on the Plank Road, a few hundred yards north of a rough track called the Carthapin Road leading southwest. General Fitzhugh Lee soon came in with the report that the Federal right flank was "in the air," which meant that it was not protected by a stream or a hill, and could be taken from the rear. Howard's corps, he said, faced the south, and lay unprotected from attack in the west and northwest.

As darkness fell an immense silence came over the Wilderness. Only the light wind of a spring night murmured in the vast forest of old-field pines and scrub oaks. Jackson lay down to sleep on the pine-needles. A young staff-officer came up to give him his cloak; when midnight came the air would grow chill. Jackson lay with the cloak over him, but did not sleep. The young officer a dozen feet away sank into a deep sleep. Jackson got up, went over and covered the young man with the cloak. Then he lay down again, and slept. . . .

After midnight Lieutenant Smith, Jackson's aide, woke, chilled by the damp night air. He sat up and looked round. A hundred feet away, up a slope among the trees two dim figures were gathering pine twigs and throwing them on a little fire, warming their hands as the blaze rose. They sat down on two cracker boxes left by the retreating Federals the day before. The wind rustled the pines. Their loneliness was absolute; not another man could be seen. One of the figures, holding his face so that the flickering light played over it.

had on a felt hat and wore a short beard, which was gray. The second figure sat humped over the fire, his head drawn down into his coat-collar, his long dark beard on his chest. Down low over his forehead rested the vizor of a forage cap, hiding his eyes; the dim light threw shifting beams on his sharp, aquiline nose. To Lieutenant Smith drifted the murmur of voices; the words were caught up in the breeze and lost in the pines; he fell asleep again.

The men talked on in the night. Before dawn Captain Hotchkiss joined them, and Jackson sent him off to examine the roads to the west of Howard's corps. It was just daylight when he came back, saying he had roused a certain Mr. Welford, who had told him of a secret road west of the Brock Road and parallel to it, running northward. Jackson asked for a fuller description of the route. Hotchkiss pulled up a cracker box between the generals, and got out his map. He traced the direction of the road. Lee and Jackson leaned forward to see.

Lee turned to Jackson and said:

"How shall we get at those people? General Jackson, what do you propose to do?"

"Go round there," he said, running his finger over the map.

"What do you propose to make the movement with?"

"With my whole corps," he said.

"What will you leave me?"

"The divisions of Anderson and McLaws."

Lee thought about it a moment, then he said:

"Well, go on!" He took out a pencil and moving it

up and down gave Jackson his last instructions. Jackson sat smiling and nodding his head. Then getting up from his cracker box he saluted.

"My troops will move at once, sir!"

4

A Rattlesnake Uncoils in the Wilderness

For the fifth time Lee was dividing his army in the presence of a more powerful enemy. From the council of the cracker boxes Jackson went to issue his orders. Stuart's cavalry was to accompany the expedition, throwing out a screen between the Second Corps and the Federal army. The trains were to follow the Carthapin Road, so that the infantry could protect them from Federal raiding parties. The infantry was to march down the Furnace Road, almost due south, until the head of the column struck the Brock Road; there it was to turn west a few hundred yards into the secret road leading up to the Orange Plank Road. On both sides of that road the infantry would deploy for the attack. The march was to be made with great speed; no random shots were to be fired; and stragglers, lest they fall into the hands of the Yankees and give the exploit away, were to be bayoneted. Lee was to hold his own in front with 17,000 men.

Jackson's 23,000 were already pouring down the Furnace Road as their leader came to the roadside to look at them. There he sat, his cap pulled down over his eyes, his heavy jaw stuck out, his lips drawn to a thin line. He joined the march, his staff trotting in the rear.

Some distance farther on General Lee sat his horse, and Jackson, approaching him, drew rein for a few last words. They talked in low tones. Then Lee nodded his head, as if in assent to Jackson's speech. Jackson, his left hand on Little Sorrel's neck, pointed with his right in the direction in which his men were marching; and, his face flushed, he turned away.

The men moved swiftly over the road. They were marching away from the enemy, but by this time they knew Old Jack so well that not one of them believed he was leaving the enemy behind. A kind of excitement, as on the march to Manassas, quickened their step. The warm sun filtered through the trees, drenching the bright bayonets. The pace increased. The sun grew hotter. Here and there men fainted in the ranks. Never slackening, the long rattlesnake, ten miles from head to tail, uncoiled in the wilderness.

Staff-officers, sweating their horses, crowded by the infantry packed in the road. The foot cavalry taunted them.

"Say, hyar's one of Ole Jack's little boys; let him by, boys!"

"Have a good breakfast this mornin', sonny?"

"Better hurry up or you'll catch it for getting behind."

"Tell Old Jack we're all a-comin'."

"Don't let him start the fuss till we get thar."

At Chancellorsville General Hooker, having made the circuit of his lines, enjoyed the amenities of spring fever, and aired himself on the broad porch of the Chancellor

mansion. At about eight o'clock General Birney sent
word to him that a great force was moving across his
front at Hazel Grove. Hooker showed concern, and
despatched orders to Howard that he must look out for
a flank attack and that his position, strong even though
it was, might be strengthened. Howard replied that he
"would send the whole rebel army his compliments and
invite them to attack him." His compliments had not
been sent, but the invitation was already issued.

The Confederate column was so large that Hooker at
first supposed Lee was prolonging his left flank beyond
the Furnace Road. Further news arrived, and the
truth, of course, with it. The Confederate column had
turned south, due south. Lee was thus, after finding
Sedgwick blocking his direct way to Richmond, retreating upon Gordonsville. He was at last playing the
game as he, Hooker, had laid down its rules in his con-
gratulatory message to his troops. A battery at Hazel
Grove shelled Jackson's trains, and forced them to another road. About noon General Sickles advanced with
his corps upon Catherine Furnace, and attacked Jackson's rear. Two brigades returned to repel the attack;
Anderson on the Plank Road delivered Sickles a counter-attack; and although Sickles had advanced so far
that the Confederate army was actually cut in two,
Jackson gave the calamity as much attention as he would
have given the news that a war-canoe full of South Sea
Islanders was setting out to capture Richmond! The
more men, in Jackson's opinion, sent from the center of
the Federal line, the longer it would take them to get
back to Howard's support when he fell upon him.

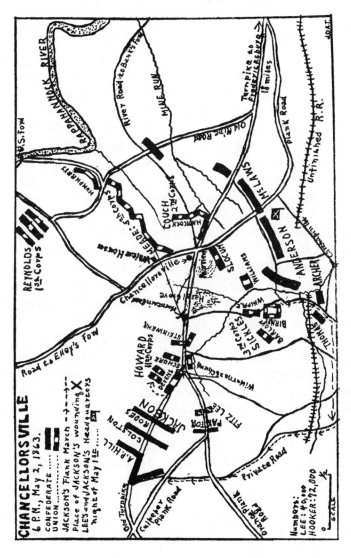

But, as a matter of fact, Hooker was not sure that Lee was retreating: if he had been sure he would have sent a greater force than Sickles' to "capture his artillery." For Hooker was demoralized, drowning in his vast uncertainty, and he clutched at straws. As the hours passed and Jackson's column disappeared, Hooker performed one of those feats of oblivion that only persons under great strain can achieve: because the marching column was no longer visible he was able to put it out of mind.

At two o'clock the two brigades that had turned back to stave off Sickles took up their march: Sickles was quiet. At the same time Old Jack was pushing ahead on the Brock Road. His leading brigade, Rodes' division, reached the Orange Plank Road, by which the Second Corps, turning eastward, would surprise Howard. But at the Plank Road General Jackson met General Fitzhugh Lee.

"General," said Lee, "if you will ride with me, halting your columns here out of sight, I will show you the great advantage of attacking down the old Turnpike road. . . . Bring only one courier, as you will be in view from the top of the hill."

The three mounted officers rode a mile to the hill. Just a few hundred yards away, to the east, the Federal right wing lay in plain view. Jackson bent forward on his horse. The color rose in his face. His eyes seemed fixed.

A line of intrenchments, facing south, lay before him. Stack after stack of muskets covered the rear. Two cannon were drawn up on the pike. But not a man stood in the trenches, and the cannon were deserted. Farther away groups of men sat round on the grass, smoking, cooking, sleeping. Some were playing cards. Others were drawing their rations. To one side beeves were being slaughtered.

By the Orange Plank Road Howard would be taken in flank; by the Turnpike he would be crushed from the rear.

Fully five minutes Jackson looked at the spectacle. His figure remained motionless and he said nothing; but his lips moved. He suddenly wheeled his horse towards the courier. He said:

"Tell General Rodes to move across the Plank Road, and halt when he gets to the old Turnpike. I will join him there."

By four o'clock Rodes' division had come to the Turnpike and the leading brigades had advanced a mile eastward towards Howard's innocents. Colston's division was close up in the rear of Rodes'. Ambrose Hill brought up the rear. Rodes was already deploying his men for the attack. The main column had not seen a single Federal soldier. The cavalry had picked up only a few patrols. Not a shot had been fired.

Jackson, down on the Brock Road, was impatiently waiting for his men to get up into line. Lieutenant Smith rode up and found him sitting on a stump, letterbook and pencil in hand. He was writing this note:

Near 3 P. M., May 2, 1863.

General,

The enemy has made a stand at Chancellor's which is about two miles from Chancellorsville. I hope as soon as

practicable to attack. I trust that an ever kind Providence
will bless us with great success.

Respectfully,

T. J. Jackson, Lt.-Genl.

Genl. R. E. Lee

The leading division is up, and the next two appear to be
well closed.

The men on the Turnpike were now forbidden to
speak. Rapidly and silently they spread out. Long
parallel lines of battle were forming at right angles to
the Turnpike: Rodes in front; Colston in second line
two hundred yards back; Ambrose Hill in third line.
Skirmishers, crawling through the brush, covered the
whole front, and awaited the signal to advance. The
sun's rays were already lengthening over the tops of the
trees, and in the depths of the woods the air grew cool.

The murmuring roar of the battle east of the Furnace
had died away. As the men stood motionless in line, the
low whine of insects filled the air. All round them
stretched away the impenetrable woods. Stunted oaks,
twisted alders enmeshed the earth with a net. Gray
willows trailed their branches on the ground. The huck-
leberry bushes, the dogwood and swamp honeysuckle,
blooming, struggled in the tangle. The men waited.

The thump of artillery wheels suddenly stirred the
men. The guns came to the front.

Jackson, astride Little Sorrel on the Turnpike, held
his watch in his hand; his lips compressed. At his right
stood General Rodes, and at the right of General Rodes
was Major Blackford, commanding the skirmishers.

"Are you ready, General Rodes?" said Jackson.

"Yes, sir!"
"You can go forward, sir."

4

The Mountain Road

At five-thirty the men of General Howard's corps were still lolling in the open fields of Talley's farm. Suddenly a deer ran from the woods towards the breastworks; then a rabbit; in a few seconds, rabbits, deer, foxes scampered through the meadow.

In the quiet a brassy screech came out of the woods, lengthening into the cadences of a bugle call. Other bugles took up the noise. Before the men of the Eleventh Corps could get to their feet, a horde of yelling demons, rising out of the earth, were upon them. Far to the north and south the long, ragged gray lines moved forward like a machine. The forest rang with the wild Confederate yell. The lazy pickets of the Federals fired a few scattered shots, and fled.

Within ten minutes the first brigade of the Eleventh Corps was routed. Pell-mell it rushed back on the other troops, carrying them along in the rout. Here and there regiments tried to change front and stay the enemy. The Confederates came steadily on like a giant harvester, cutting down the men trying to stand before them.

At Talley's farm scattered regiments lined up behind breastworks to meet the onset. In the reeling smoke the defenders looked out and saw the vast mass of the Con-

federates; they saw the flash of the rifles, the oncoming
battle flags, the tanned faces, the blazing eyes of their
mysterious, terrible foes. All their mounted officers
tumbled like bags of meal to the ground. The defenders
fell back in panic.

The first stronghold of the enemy had been carried,
and Jackson riding to the front near Talley's farm
shouted to his men to go on. As never before his reserve
had left him. His eyes burned like coals. He met officers and cried out orders. He raised his left hand to
the level of his eyes, the palm turned out. . . .

To the east of the farm he saw, in the rolling meadows,
a crowd of fear-crazed men. Men fought one another,
kicked their comrades out of the way. Riderless
horses ran down the fugitives; wounded horses, still in
the traces, squealed and plunged. Knapsacks, muskets, blankets; overturned wagons; wrecked cannon;
wounded men fighting the corpses that fell on them at
every step; all in a whirling mass. Through the green
cornfields squads of prisoners, under guard, marched
to the Confederate rear.

Jackson saw within his reach the destruction of the
Federal army. The panic would spread. His men must
press on. They must go up the old Mountain Road to
the northeast towards the United States Ford, and cut
Hooker off from his retreat.

At Dowdall's Tavern the Confederates met a momentary check. But only for a moment. As the Confederate first line dropped men at every step before the
rifles of the four or five thousand rallied Yankees, the
second line, Colstons' division, pushed on, carrying the

position. The Federal infantry disappeared, swallowed by the forest.

A mile and a half away General Hooker sat on the porch of the Chancellor house. The firing in the east had died away. To the south the faint spatter of musketry told Hooker that Sickles was still pursuing the retreating Confederates. Suddenly artillery boomed from the west. One of the general's aides got up and walked out into the road. He raised his glass. He turned and ran back to the porch.

"My God," he said, pointing up the road, "here they come!"

General Hooker mounted his horse and rode to meet the panic-stricken men flying towards him from the woods. They said their right wing had been annihilated. They ran on. Then, from the southwest, from Hazel Grove, another mass of confusion emerged. The trains of the Third Corps were fired on by the Confederate skirmishers; they joined the rout. The artillery held fast. Fifty guns still confronted the advancing Confederates.

It was not these guns, however, that saved Hooker from immediate disaster. For it was now past seven o'clock, and though the sky was still light overhead, the thickets, full of shadows, threw Rodes' men into confusion. The men were mixed, and many wandered in the woods looking for their officers; officers looked for their regiments.

Where the Mountain Road joins the Turnpike the men were ordered to halt. They began to reform. The firing died away. (See map, p. 299.)

General Rodes sent back a courier saying that there were no troops between his line and the Fairview Heights, an open space just northeast of Hazel Grove. Colonel Cobb reported that the entrenchments, less than a mile from Hooker's headquarters, had been occupied by his skirmishers.

But there was a lull in the battle. The mighty attack for the moment had spent itself. Lee, in front, was powerless to take the offensive. Longstreet's absence had crippled him.

The lull was to last only long enough for Jackson to get Hill's division, not yet engaged, into the front line. When the reports of confusion reached Jackson he was at Dowdall's Tavern. Sending a courier to Hill to come forward prepared for a night attack, he rode forward on the Turnpike. He rallied the men. He turned to Colonel Cobb.

"I need your help for a time. This disorder must be corrected. As you go along the right, tell the troops from me to get into line and preserve their order."

It was now eight-thirty. Hill was coming on. Colonel Crutchfield, Jackson's chief of artillery, pushed his guns forward beyond the infantry and opened them on Chancellorsville. The fifty guns at Hazel Grove returned a terrific fire. The reforming of the lines was delayed. But Hill still came on.

Hill's leading brigade, under General Lane, advanced a little beyond the junction of the Turnpike and the Mountain Road, and threw out his skirmishers. He was far in the advance, and at the moment unsupported. The 7th North Carolina he stationed on the right of the Turnpike; the 18th, on the left astride the Mountain Road. He told his men to be on the lookout every moment, and if they heard firing to fire back. Then he returned to the cross-roads.

There Jackson stood alone. Hill had not arrived; his staff-officers were away. Lane came up and asked for further orders. Jackson raised his arm in the direction of the enemy.

"Push right ahead, Lane, right ahead."

In a few minutes Hill arrived with a group of staff-officers. Jackson said:

"Press them, cut them off from United States Ford, Hill. Press them!"

Hill said he was ignorant of the country. Jackson told Captain Boswell, of the Signal Corps, to show Hill the way. General Hill and his guide rode off on the Mountain road, and Jackson turned to follow, but a courier from Stuart stopped him. He read the report, and followed Hill at a distance up the road.

A hundred yards ahead he passed through the ranks of the 18th North Carolina, and riding on for another hundred yards or so, he halted. So quietly had Jackson's party moved that Major Barry, on the extreme left of the regiment, had not heard or even seen them pass.

Jackson and his staff were now between the battle-line of Lane's brigade and his line of skirmishers. There was no firing, but chopping and hacking towards the front indicated that the Federals were fortifying themselves. He listened intently. Then he turned his horse back towards the Turnpike, riding in advance of the party. He stopped again. He turned his head towards the Federal lines. The chopping continued.

General Hill rejoined Jackson's party, and the whole group of horsemen gathered in the rear of Jackson without a word. There was no talk; only the steady chopping in the distance.

Suddenly, some distance away south of the Turnpike, a single rifle shot rang out. The musketry, like seasoned planks clattering down from a great height, rolled along the line. The men of 18th North Carolina crouched in the woods. Major Barry saw through the trees eighty yards away a shadowy group of horsemen. They were surely Federal cavalry, and the firing south of the Turnpike meant that other squadrons lurked in the woods.

He ordered his men to fire, then he ordered them to fire a second time.

Every rider in the group fell to the ground or escaped but Jackson. He was still mounted. But he was hit. Little Sorrel, terrified, plunged towards the Federal lines, nearly brushing his master off among the thick trees. But he grabbed the bridle with his wounded hand. He tried to pull the horse back towards the road.

A few yards from the Turnpike one of his staff-officers seized the reins. At that instant Jackson reeled from the saddle and fell into Captain Wilbourn's arms. His time had come.

XIX

HIS TIME

1

The Turnpike

THEY laid him on the ground. General Hill rode up and leaped from his horse.

"General, are you much hurt?"

"I think I am," he said. "All my wounds are from my own men."

General Hill pulled off his gauntlets, which were full of blood, and bandaged his arm with a handkerchief. The left arm was shattered at the elbow; a bullet had pierced the left wrist and hand; another had lodged in the palm of his right hand. He still lay in front of his own lines, and two Federal skirmishers appeared; but Hill quietly told his staff to "take charge of those men;" they were seized.

Litter-bearers could not be found. Jackson was still lying in the woods near the Turnpike. He lay with his eyes closed, and seemed to hear nothing. Hill ordered the staff not to say who Jackson was. He had not been lifted up, but, his head resting on Hill's breast, he opened his eyes.

"Tell them," he said, "simply that you have a wounded Confederate officer."

The officers got him up on his feet and leaning in their arms he came on to the road. As he gained the road shells and canister crashed through the trees, and the young men, laying him down, crouched round him in a semicircle, their backs to the enemy, to shield him. The shells went high.

Jackson tried to rise. Smith said:

"You must be still, General, it will cost you your life."

The shells flew still higher, and Jackson was got on his feet again. The Confederate infantry poured down the road towards the front line. He turned off the road into the brush to keep them from recognizing him. As he turned, General Pender, whose men crowded the road, saw the stumbling group, and came towards them. He asked who the wounded man was.

"A Confederate officer."

He came nearer, and recognized the officer. He said a few hurried words of regret; then he added that his men might have to fall back.

Shells screamed overhead. Bullets nipped the leaves off the scrub trees. The shouts of men to be led on rose over the tumult, and men, terrified by the confusion, left the ranks and hid in the woods. Riderless horses milled at the roadside, the dead and dying trampled under their feet.

In the wild panic of the moment, Jackson, bleeding fast, raised himself to his full height. He pushed the aides aside.

"You must hold your ground, General Pender, you must hold your ground to the last."

Growing suddenly weak he sank to the earth. The

young officers caught him, and started to lead him away.
Captain Leigh came up with a litter. They lay Old
Jack upon it. The slow march began again.

Still in the woods, one of the bearers, shot in the arm,
let go; and Jackson fell on his left side to the ground.
He groaned.

Canister and shells from the enemy's fifty guns fell
thicker than before. Limbs dropped off trees. Shells
ploughed furrows in the road. The canister, sprinkling
the road, threw sparks off the stones.

Smith stooped over him and said:

"Are you much hurt, General?"

"No, Mr. Smith, don't trouble yourself about me.
Win the battle first and attend to the wounded after-
wards."

His voice was perfectly self-possessed. A moonbeam
streaked through the trees full upon his face. It was
pale. His lips were tightly drawn. There was a smear
of blood on his face.

The young men resumed the march. In a few minutes they came to Doctor McGuire who was waiting
with an ambulance. Doctor McGuire knelt down.

"I hope you are not much hurt, General."

"I am badly injured, Doctor, I fear I am dying."

He lay silent.

"I am glad you have come, Doctor, I think the wound
in my shoulder is still bleeding."

The doctor looked to the bandages. They put him
into the ambulance. He lay by Colonel Crutchfield, who
was badly wounded. They gave him whisky and mor-
phine. Then the ambulance started. It bumped and

jolted. Crutchfield moaned; he was suffering. Jackson
lay still; he said nothing; he lay with his lips tight and
his forehead pinched.

"Doctor," he said, "can you stop the ambulance?
Can't you do something for Colonel Crutchfield?"

The ambulance bumped and jolted on.

At the field hospital they put him in bed. He slept
for nearly three hours, and when he was awake Doctor
McGuire asked him if the amputation should be done
at once.

"Yes, certainly, Doctor McGuire, do whatever you
think best for me."

About half past three Jackson came out of the chloro-
form, and a messenger from Stuart was there. Doctor
McGuire tried to keep him out, but he said the safety
of the Confederate army hung in the balance. Jackson
had been reticent and only General Hill knew his plans;
but General Hill, the messenger said, had been wounded,
and had sent for Stuart.

He walked into the tent.

"Well, Major," said Jackson, "I am glad to see you.
I thought you were killed."

Major Pendleton told him the uncertain affairs at
the front. Jackson knitted his forehead, and set his lips.
Then his nostrils dilated and his eyes flashed. It was
only for a moment.

"I don't know—I—I don't know—I can't tell. Say
to General Stuart that he must go on and do what he
thinks best."

So Pendleton left Jackson. And as Jackson's concentration failed him, the Federal army, though it was

to be battered and sorely defeated, had virtually escaped.

Next morning, as the Confederates drove Hooker's army away from the Chancellorsville entrenchments and reunited their two wings, General Lee heard the news of Jackson's fall.

He wrote this note:

General:—I have just received your note, informing me that you were wounded. I cannot express my regret at the occurrence. Could I have directed events, I should have chosen for the good of the country to be disabled in your stead.

I congratulate you upon the victory, which is due to your skill and energy.

Very respectfully, your obedient servant,

R. E. Lee, General.

2

Guiney Station

Jackson was still in the field hospital when Lee's aide brought him the note.

"General Lee," he said, "is very kind, but he should give the praise to God."

His pain had now nearly ceased, and he talked with all his old animation. He could hear the battle raging, and soon the reports came in. When the Stonewall Brigade happened to be mentioned for good service, he said, "Good! Good!"

"Some day the men of that brigade will be proud to

say to their children, 'I was one of the Stonewall Brigade.' The name belongs to them, not to me."

He talked at intervals all day, and that night the simple-hearted man slept free of pain. Next morning he was getting better. General Lee sent him a message: "Give him my affectionate regards, and tell him to make haste and get well, and come back to me as soon as he can. He has lost his left arm, but I have lost my right."

Jackson discussed his plan, which was not carried out. He said he intended to cut the enemy off from the United States Ford, forcing him to hack his way through. "My men," he said, "sometimes fail to drive the enemy from a position, but they always fail to drive us away." "Our movement," he said, "was a great success, the most successful military movement of my life. But I expect to receive far more credit for it than I deserve. . . . I feel His hand led me—let us give Him the glory."

By eight o'clock on the 6th of May General Hooker had escaped across the Rapidan. There was no pursuit. The Richmond authorities had held back the army supplies and reinforcements. The war, they said in a few days, would soon be over.

On the 6th General Jackson was taken in an ambulance to Guiney Station, south of Fredericksburg, where he lay in bed in a house surrounded by trees. He seemed to be better, and on Thursday, which was the 7th, his wife and little girl came from Richmond. Suddenly he grew weak, and he could hardly talk to them.

Pneumonia had set in. His wounds were healing, but he had exposed himself and he was very ill. Where had he got pneumonia? He did not say; could not remember. On the night of May 1st he had slept without cover on pine-needles; he had forgotten it.

Sunday morning he was almost too weak to talk. He told his wife he was ready to die if it was God's will. He told her he thought he had more work to do. At eleven o'clock Mrs. Jackson came in and sat by him on the bed. She said he could not live beyond the evening. "You are frightened, my child. Death is not so near. I may get well."

She fell upon the bed and cried, and told him again. Then he asked for Doctor McGuire.

"Doctor, Anna tells me I am to die today. Is it so?"

"Yes," the doctor said.

Jackson turned his head; he seemed to be thinking, thinking intensely.

"Very good, very good," he said in a low voice. "It is all right."

At noon Major Pendleton came to see him, and he asked:

"Who is preaching at headquarters today, Major?"

The major answered Doctor Lacy, and said the whole army was praying for him.

"Thank God, they are very kind to me."

His little girl was brought in, and he brightened; then he fell into delirium. He talked, talked. He was on the battlefield. Now he was in Lexington. Now he was praying in camp. For a long time he lay still. Then he cried:

"Order A. P. Hill to prepare for action! Pass the infantry to the front! Tell Major Hawks——"

He lay still again.   After a while he said in a clear voice:

"Let's cross over the river and rest in the shade of the trees."

1. To preserve the continuity of Jackson's story the events immediately following his wounding have been excluded from the text. The battle of Chancellorsville lasted five days. Jackson fell at the close of the second. Colonel Henderson calls the defeat of 130,000 men by 60,000 the tactical masterpiece of the nineteenth century. I quote from Mr. Walter Geer's brief and excellent summary * of the events of May 3rd, 4th, and 5th:

"At dawn on Sunday, the 3rd, Stuart renewed the attack. Hooker had made the mistake of withdrawing Sickles from the heights of Hazel Grove, which were seized by the enemy. Here, Stuart placed thirty guns, which enfiladed a part of the Union line, and reached the space around the mansion. . . .

"After several hours of hard fighting, Stuart forced the Federals back, and occupied Fairview. . . . At the same time McLaws and Anderson were assaulting the left and center of the Union line, which were also compelled to fall back. Finally the flanks of Stuart's and Anderson's forces came together at Fairview. At ten o'clock Lee had possession of the mansion, now only a smoking ruin.

"Just before this Hooker had been knocked down and

disabled by a brick torn by a shell from one of the columns of the front porch of the house. Couch succeeded temporarily to the command, and directed the withdrawal of the Union forces to a new line in the rear. . . .

"Lee was preparing to assault the new position when he was forced to turn his attention to the Federal movement on his rear.

"At nine o'clock on the evening of the 2nd, Hooker had sent Sedgwick an order to carry the works at Fredericksburg; then move on Chancellorsville, and attack Lee from the rear. . . . Sedgwick now had only his own corps, of about 22,000 men. The works were held by Early's division, of some 10,000 men. . . .

"Sedgwick reached Fredericksburg about three o'clock on the morning of the 3rd ,and attacked at daybreak. . . . But a fourth attack carried the strong position in the sunken road, and the Federals soon reached the crest of the hill. Early's troops retreated by the Telegraph Road [i.e., southwards], leaving the roads to Chancellorsville protected only by Wilcox's single brigade.

"This was the news which reached Lee just as he was preparing for a final attack. He at once sent four brigades under McLaws to meet Sedgwick. . . . When Sedgwick came up, about an hour later [four o'clock], a desperate combat ensued, which lasted until dark. Sedgwick could make no further progress; since morning he had lost nearly a fourth of his total force.

"Finding that Hooker did not attack the next morning, the 4th, Lee sent Anderson's division to join McLaws, leaving only what remained of Jackson's old corps in front of Hooker. Meantime Early had retaken Marye's Hill, and then advanced on the rear of Sedgwick, who found himself surrounded on three sides, with only the retreat to Banks' Ford open. Fortunately for the Federals, it was six o'clock before the Confederates were ready to make a vigorous attack, and Sedgwick was able to reach the river at Banks' Ford, where he crossed during the night. . . .

"Tuesday morning, the 5th, Lee concentrated all his forces in front of Hooker, and prepared to assault the Union lines at daybreak on the 6th. When morning came, however, it was found that, during the night, the Army of the Potomac had retreated across the river, leaving behind the killed and wounded; fourteen guns and twenty thousand stands of arms.

"The losses on both sides during the few days of the campaign were:

	Federals	*Confederates*
Killed	1,606	1,649
Wounded	9,762	9,106
Missing	5,919	1,708
	17,287	12,463"

Only a few words need be added to Mr. Geer's summary. Jackson's flank attack had made the victory possible, but his wound had kept the victory from being decisive; Jackson's absence on the succeeding days tended to restore to the Union army the efficacy of its overwhelming numbers, which his presence had neutralized. Lee, alone, could defeat the enemy in detail, but he lacked the reserve power to turn victory into destruction.

2. The battle of Chancellorsville was the most brilliant Confederate achievement of the war, yet for two reasons, the fall of Jackson and the absence of Longstreet, the Union army escaped, and it had better not been fought. Had Longstreet not been away, Lee might have beaten Hooker to the initiative. The Confederate losses at Chancellorsville could not be immediately replaced, and Lee's invasion of Pennsylvania was by this useless victory postponed two months, and by it Jackson was removed from the Pennsylvania campaign. At Gettysburg the tactical situation eminently required Jackson's peculiar genius for swift and overwhelming attack. In the first two days the Confederates defeated four Federal corps, but the attack of the third day (Pickett's charge) went in, unsupported, six or seven hours late. Longstreet had argued and delayed. Although General Stuart and General Ewell must bear much blame for the Confederate failure, it cannot be doubted that Longstreet's complacency in the face of Lee's repeated orders to attack lost the battle. No supposition after the event can be conclusive. Yet Lee himself, who never committed a rash judgment, said: "If I had had Jackson at Gettysburg, I should have won the battle, and a complete victory there would have resulted in the establishment of Southern independence."

The map Lee used in the Gettysburg campaign was the one prepared by Hotchkiss for Jackson at Moss Neck.

Appendix B

Bibliography

In the foregoing narrative quotations from other works have been almost invariably paraphrased, and allusions to previous writers omitted. The wish of the author has been to present, so far as a certain amount of necessary abstract discussion permitted, a continuous narrative, which quotations and references to authorities would disrupt.

Works pertaining to Stonewall Jackson are almost innumerable. The most important bibliography is the work of Mr. Roy Bird Cook, in his *Family and Early Life of Stonewall Jackson* (Richmond: 1925). The results of Mr. Cook's researches into Jackson's boyhood are most interesting; his book brings to light new facts and it breaks many of the legends that cluster round this period of the great Confederate's life. The present volume could not have been written without the aid of the late Lieut.-Col. G. F. R. Henderson's *Stonewall Jackson and the American Civil War* (2 vols., London and New York: 1898). Colonel Henderson, a most able military critic, the author has closely followed in his judgment of military events. In the case, however, of Jackson's failure in the Seven Days the present writer has not been able to accept Colonel Henderson's vindication; he has taken the evidence, which Colonel Henderson ignores, of the late General Wade Hampton; but he offers his conclusions without argumentation. Nor is General Hampton's testimony given in full.

The general reader who wishes to know more of Jackson in detail will find that the following works, besides the two cited above, are most interesting: *Stonewall Jackson*, by John Esten Cooke (1866) ; *Life and Campaigns of Lieut.-General Thomas J. Jackson*, by Robert Lewis Dabney (1866) ; *Destruction and Reconstruction*, by Richard Taylor (1879) ; *Memoirs of Stonewall Jackson*, by Mary Anna Jackson, his wife (1891) ; *Stonewall Jackson and Chancellorsville*, by James Power Smith (1904) ; *One of Jackson's Foot Cavalry*, by John H. Worsham (1913) ; *The Battle of Chancellorsville*, by Augustus Choate Hamlin (1896). This last volume, by a Federal officer, contains the most accurate account of the time and place, and of the complete circumstances, of Jackson's wounding, in all the literature of the subject. One more valuable and intensely interesting work remains to be cited: *Battles and Leaders of the Civil War* (4 vols.), published by the Century Company (1884), is a mine of information, technical and anecdotal. The story of each campaign is told by the leading participants of both sides.

The best one-volume military histories of the Civil War are: *A History of the Civil War in the United States*, by W. Birkbeck Wood and Major J. E. Edmonds (London: 1905), and *Campaigns of the Civil War*, by Walter Geer (New York: 1926).